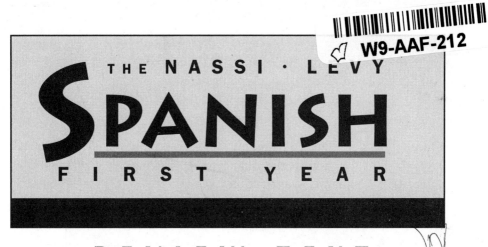

THE NASSI · LEVY
SPANISH
FIRST YEAR

REVIEW TEXT
(New Edition)

Stephen L. Levy
Head, Foreign Language Department
Roslyn (New York) Public Schools

Robert J. Nassi
Former Teacher of Spanish
Los Angeles Valley Junior College
Los Angeles, California

When ordering this book, please specify *either* **R 510 P** *or*
NASSI/LEVY SPANISH FIRST YEAR, Review Text Edition

AMSCO

AMSCO SCHOOL PUBLICATIONS, INC.
315 Hudson Street / New York, N.Y. 10013

To Sergio,
You are the wind beneath my wings!
Q.E.P.D.

S.L.L.

Please visit our Web site at:

www.amscopub.com

Cover photograph of Casares, Spain by Super Stock, Inc.
Illustrations by Felipe Galindo

ISBN 0-87720-142-0

Printed in the United States of America

9 10 11 12 13 14 15   07 06 05 04 03

Preface

The NASSI/LEVY SPANISH FIRST YEAR is designed to give students a comprehensive review and thorough understanding of the elements of the Spanish language that are normally covered in the first year of study. Highlights of Spanish and Spanish-American cultures are provided to familiarize students with the background of native speakers of the language. Abundant and varied exercises help students master each phase of the work.

ORGANIZATION

For ease of study and reference, the book is divided into six Parts. Parts One to Three are organized around related grammatical topics. Part Four provides a comprehensive review of vocabulary, presented thematically. There are also chapters on cognates, synonyms and antonyms. Part Five covers Spanish and Spanish-American Civilizations. It includes the geography, history, lifestyle, science, literature, music, art and architecture of both Spain and Spanish America. Part Six provides materials for comprehensive practice and testing of the speaking, listening, reading, and writing skills.

Each grammatical chapter deals fully with one major grammatical topic or several closely related ones. Explanations of structures are brief and clear. All points of grammar are illustrated by many examples, in which the key elements are typographically highlighted.

Care has been taken in this text that reviews the first stage of a basic sequence to avoid the use of complex structural elements. To enable students to concentrate on the structural practice, the vocabulary has been carefully controlled and is systematically "recycled" throughout the grammatical chapters.

EXERCISES

For maximum efficiency in learning, the exercises directly follow the points of grammar to which they apply. Carefully graded, the exercises proceed from simple assimilation to more challenging manipulation of elements and communication. To provide meaningful practice to the students of a grammatical topic, the exercises are set in contexts that are both functional and realistic. Many are also personalized to stimulate student response and internalization of the concepts under study.

While the contents of the exercises afford extensive audiolingual practice, the book's format also encourages reinforcement through written student responses, including English to Spanish exercises intended to sharpen composition skills, The grammatical chapters conclude with Mastery Exercises, in which all grammatical aspects in the chapter are again practiced in recombination of previously covered elements. All directions to exercises at this level are in English.

FLEXIBILITY

The topical organization and the integrated completeness of each chapter permit the teacher to follow any sequence suitable to the objectives of the course and the needs of the students. This flexibility is facilitated by the detailed table of contents at the front of the book and the comprehensive grammatical index at the back. Both teachers and students will also find the book a useful reference source.

CULTURE

The cultural chapters in Part Five are presented in English. Students gain a wealth of knowledge and insight from the information provided as they proceed from Spanish influence in the United States, to Spain, to Spanish America. Each cultural chapter includes exercises designed to facilitate and check learning.

OTHER FEATURES

The Appendix features complete model verb tables and the principal parts of common irregular verbs, along with basic rules of Spanish punctuation, syllabication, and stress. Spanish–English and English–Spanish vocabularies and a comprehensive Index complete the book.

The NASSI / LEVY SPANISH FIRST YEAR is a thoroughly revised and updated edition. Its comprehensive coverage of the elements of Spanish, clear and concise explanations, extensive contextualized practice materials, and functional vocabulary, will help students strengthen their skills in the Spanish language. As they pursue proficiency, they will also gain valuable insights into the cultures of the Spanish-speaking world.

Thanks are due to our consultants, who reviewed substantial parts of the manuscript and made valuable suggestions.

Contents

Part One
Verb Structures

Part Two
Noun and Pronoun Structures

Part Three
Adjective / Adverb and Related Structures

Part Four
Word Study

Part Five
Spanish and Spanish-American Civilizations

Part Six
Comprehensive Testing
Speaking, Listening, Reading, Writing *361*

Part one

Verbal Structures

Chapter 1

Present Tense of -*ar* Verbs

[1] REGULAR -*AR* VERBS

a. The present tense of regular -*ar* verbs is formed by dropping the infinitive ending -*ar* and adding the personal endings -*o, -as, -a, -amos, -áis, -an.*

b. The present tense has the following meanings in English:

usted canta *you sing, you're singing, you do sing*

él canta *he sings, he's singing, he does sing*

cantar *to sing*			
(I sing, I'm singing, I do sing)			
yo	cant*o*	nosotros, -as	cant*amos*
tú	cant*as*	vosotros, -as	cant*áis*
usted		ustedes	
él	cant*a*	ellos	cant*an*
ella		ellas	

NOTE:

1. The subject pronouns *usted (Ud.)* and *ustedes (Uds.)* are usually expressed in Spanish. The other subject pronouns *(yo, tú, él, ella, nosotros, vosotros, ellos, ellas)* are usually omitted, unless they are required for clarity or emphasis.

   Canto bien. *I sing well.*

   Cantan bien. *They sing well.*

   BUT

   Ud. canta bien. *You sing well.*

   Ella canta bien pero **él canta** mal. *She sings well but he sings badly.*

   Ella y yo cantamos bien. *She and I sing well.*

2. The feminine forms of *nosotros* and *vosotros* are *nosotras* and *vosotras.*

3. *Tú* and *vosotros* (the familiar forms) are used when addressing close relatives, intimate friends, or small children. In many Spanish-American countries, the *ustedes* form is used instead of the *vosotros* form.

3

[2] COMMON -AR VERBS

admirar   *to admire*

arreglar   *to arrange, fix*

ayudar   *to help*

bailar   *to dance*

bajar   *to go down, descend; to lower*

borrar   *to erase*

buscar   *to look for*

cambiar   *to change*

caminar   *to walk*

cantar   *to sing*

celebrar   *to celebrate*

cocinar   *to cook* comprar   *to buy*

contestar   *to answer*

comprar   *to buy*

cortar   *to cut*

dar   *to give*

decorar   *to decorate*

descansar   *to rest*

desear   *to wish, want*

dibujar   *to draw*

enseñar   *to teach*

entrar (en)   *to enter (into)*

escuchar   *to listen (to)*

esperar   *to wait; to hope*

estudiar   *to study*

explicar   *to explain*

ganar   *to win* gritar   *to shout*

gritar   *to shout*

hablar   *to speak*

invitar   *to invite*

lavar   *to wash*

llamar   *to call*

llegar   *to arrive*

llevar   *to carry, take, to wear*

mirar   *to look at*

montar   *to ride* (a horse, bicycle)

nadar   *to swim*

necesitar   *to need*

pagar   *to pay (for)*

pasar   *to pass; to spend* (time)

patinar   *to skate*

practicar   *to practice*

preguntar   *to ask*

preparar   *to prepare*

regresar   *to return*

sacar   *to take out; to take* (photo)

terminar   *to finish, end*

tocar   *to touch; to play* (a musical instrument)

tomar   *to take; to drink*

trabajar   *to work*

usar   *to use; to wear*

viajar   *to travel*

visitar   *to visit*

EXERCISE A

Enrique is telling his cousin what they and their friends are going to do after school. Express in complete sentences what he says.

EXAMPLE: Alfredo / montar en bicicleta
Alfredo **monta** en bicicleta.

1. Sarita / tocar la guitarra
2. Lewis / trabajar en el supermercado
3. Carol y Gloria / bailar el flamenco
4. tú / practicar el piano
5. Uds. / mirar la televisión
6. yo / visitar a mis amigos
7. Roberto y yo / escuchar discos
8. nosotros / pasar un buen rato en la biblioteca

EXERCISE B

Saturday is a day of chores at the Ortegas. Gloria is explaining what each family member does. Tell what she says.

EXAMPLE: Carlos / lavar el carro
            Carlos **lava** el carro.

1. mi mamá / comprar la comida
2. yo / usar la aspiradora
3. mi papá / trabajar en el jardín
4. Eduardo y Clara / arreglar la casa
5. mis hermanitos / sacar al perro
6. mi abuela / cocinar la cena

EXERCISE C

You and some friends are planning a party. Mario wants to know who's doing what. Tell him.

EXAMPLE: comprar el pastel *(Iggy)*
            Iggy **compra** el pastel.

1. decorar el salón *(Gunther y Paco)*
2. comprar los refrescos *(tú)*
3. buscar los discos *(yo)*
4. tocar la guitarra *(Marta)*
5. preparar la comida *(Estela y yo)*
6. ayudar con los preparativos *(todos)*
7. cortar las flores *(Silvia e Inés)*

Pg 6

EXERCISE D

You received a note from a friend who's taking a cruise in the Caribbean. Complete the note with the present tense of the verbs in parentheses.

Querida Lucy:

¡Saludos de la República Dominicana! Nosotros _____ ratos agradables
1. (pasar)

aquí: yo_____ en el mar Caribe; mis hermanos y yo _____ en
2. (nadar)   3. (montar)

motocicleta todas las tardes; mis padres _____ las tiendas y mi mamá
4. (visitar)

_____ muchos recuerdos. Por la noche, toda la familia _____ un
5. (comprar)   6. (dar)

paseo por la playa. Mis hermanos no _____ regresar a casa, pero nosotros
7. (desear)

_____ el próximo sábado. Las vacaciones _____ y tú y yo
8. (regresar)   9. (terminar)

_____ en la escuela el lunes. Es todo por ahora.
10. (entrar)

Hasta la vista,

Rick

[3] -*AR* VERBS IN NEGATIVE CONSTRUCTIONS

A verb is made negative by placing *no* before it.

María **no habla** español.   *María doesn't speak Spanish.*
Yo **no bailo** bien.   *I don't dance well.*

EXERCISE E

Ana and her sister often disagree with each other. Tell what Ana says and what her sister responds.

EXAMPLE: dar un paseo
              ANA: Nosotros **damos** un paseo.
              VIOLETA: **No damos** un paseo.

1. montar en bicicleta

    ANA: Rafael _____.

    VIOLETA:

2. visitar el museo

ANA: Nosotros _____.

VIOLETA:

3. mirar la televisión

ANA: Mis amigas _____.

VIOLETA:

4. comprar un helado

ANA: Yo _____.

VIOLETA:

5. descansar un poco

ANA: Tú _____.

VIOLETA:

EXERCISE F

Look at the people in the following pictures. Say that they are *not* doing what they're doing.

EXAMPLE:

Pedro *(tocar)* _____ .
Pedro **no toca la guitarra.**

1.

Las amigas *(mirar)* _____ .

2.

Yo *(nadar)* _____ .

3.

Carolina *(patinar)* _____ .

4.

La familia *(viajar)* _____ .

5.

Ellos *(arreglar)* _____ .

[4] -*AR* VERBS IN INTERROGATIVE CONSTRUCTIONS

In a statement, the subject usually comes before the verb. In a question (an interrogative sentence), the subject usually comes after the verb.

Ud. **contesta** correctamente.	*You answer correctly.*
¿**Contesta Ud.** correctamente?	*Do you answer correctly?*
Juan **habla** inglés.	*Juan speaks English.*
¿**Habla Juan** inglés?	*Does Juan speak English?*

EXERCISE G

Raúl's little brother always questions everything Raúl says. Tell what his little brother says in response to the statements below.

EXAMPLE: Gloria viaja mucho.
                    ¿**Viaja Gloria** mucho?

1. David baila bien.
2. Mis amigos patinan en el parque.
3. Tú visitas el museo.
4. Nosotros miramos el cielo.
5. Uds. caminan por la ciudad.
6. Yo canto mal.
7. Wong desea comprar un suéter.

EXERCISE H

Luis never remembers what his friends ask. Write Luis's questions based on the answers given.

EXAMPLE: Yo arreglo bicicletas.
                    ¿**Arreglas tú** bicicletas?

1. Esteban visita la biblioteca todos los días.
2. Los hermanos lavan el carro los sábados.
3. Yo nado en la piscina cada tarde.
4. Nosotros practicamos el béisbol.
5. Luz desea ir al cine.
6. Mi amigo y yo miramos un programa a las ocho.
7. Yo viajo por avión cada verano.

MASTERY EXERCISES

EXERCISE I

While visiting Madrid with a group, you took many pictures. Upon your return, you show the slides to some friends. Describe what's going on in each slide.

EXAMPLE:

Alice *(bajar)* _____ .
Alice **baja del autobús.**

1.

Nosotros *(visitar)* _____ .

2.

Javier, Arthur y Cristina *(entrar)* ____ .

3.

Javier *(pagar)* _____ .

4.

Tú *(mirar)* _____ .

5. Nosotros *(tomar)* _____ .

6. Gregorio *(escuchar)* _____ .

7. Kyoko *(comprar)* _____ .

8. Este señor *(trabajar)* _____ .

9. Nosotros *(llegar)* _____ .

10. Yo *(sacar)* _____ .

EXERCISE J

A new classmate is asking you about yourself and your friends. Answer the questions as indicated.

EXAMPLE: ¿Deseas tú mirar la televisión? *(sí)*
Sí, deseo mirar la televisión.

1. ¿Trabajas tú después de las clases? *(no)*

2. ¿Visitas tú a tus parientes a menudo? *(sí)*

3. ¿Sacan Uds. fotografías? *(sí)*

4. ¿Baila bien Alfredo? *(no)*

5. ¿Toman Uds. el autobús al centro? *(sí)*

6. ¿Dan Elena y Joe un paseo por el parque? *(sí)*

7. ¿Escuchas tú discos de rock? *(no)*

EXERCISE K

While watching a Spanish-language TV show with some friends, José makes the following comments. Express them in Spanish.

1. I'm watching an interesting program.

2. This group sings well.

3. They don't dance well.

4. She's wearing a horrible dress.

5. This group is returning to Venezuela tomorrow.

6. They travel a lot.

7. He doesn't play the guitar well.

8. I admire their talent.

9. I listen to their music a lot.

10. At what time does this program end?

Chapter 2

Present Tense of -er and -ir Verbs

[1] REGULAR -ER VERBS

a. The present tense of regular -er verbs is formed by dropping the infinitive ending -er and adding the personal endings -o, -es, -e, -emos, -éis, -en.

b. The present tense has the following meanings in English:

usted come	*you eat, you're eating, you do eat*
ella come	*she eats, she's eating, she does eat*

comer *to eat*		
(I eat, I'm eating, I do eat)		
yo	com**o**	nosotros, -as com**emos**
tú	com**es**	vosotros, -as com**éis**
usted		ustedes
él	come	ellos com**en**
ella		ellas

[2] COMMON -ER VERBS

aprender *to learn*	esconder *to hide* (something)
beber *to drink*	leer *to read*
comer *to eat*	prometer *to promise*
correr *to run*	responder *to answer*
creer *to believe*	vender *to sell*

EXERCISE A

Mike and a friend describe their first day at school. What do they say?

EXAMPLE: el señor Bilbao / vender libros
            El señor Bilbao **vende** libros.

1. los alumnos / comer en la cafetería

2. David / beber jugo

3. tú / aprender el español

4. Angel y yo / correr en el patio

5. la maestra / leer una novela

6. yo / responder en la clase

7. ustedes / comprender la lección

8. nosotros / prometer estudiar mucho

EXERCISE B

Tell what each person is doing in the pictures below.

EXAMPLE:

Guillermo **esconde la tiza.**

1.

Phil _____ .

2.

Shakeela y Víctor _____ .

3.

Yo _____ .

4.

Cristina _____ .

5.

El hombre _____ .

6.

Enrique y yo _____ .

EXERCISE C

Alfredo is baby-sitting his younger brother, who asks a lot of questions. Answer his questions according to the cues provided.

EXAMPLE: ¿Quién vende helados? *(el señor Rossi)*
            El señor Rossi **vende** helados.

1. ¿Quién aprende a nadar? *(Rafael)*

2. ¿Quién comprende el japonés? *(los señores Uchida)*

3. ¿Quién bebe una leche batida? *(tú)*

4. ¿Quién debe comprar unos dulces? *(mamá)*

5. ¿Quiénes comen en el restaurante? *(Grace y Rocío)*

6. ¿Quién responde a todas mis preguntas? *(yo)*

[3] -ER VERBS IN NEGATIVE AND INTERROGATIVE CONSTRUCTIONS

a. A verb is made negative by placing *no* before it.

Felipe **no bebe** leche.   *Felipe doesn't drink milk.*
Yo **no leo** novelas.   *I don't read novels.*

EXERCISE D

Pedro's sister often disagrees with him. Tell what Pedro says and what his sister responds.

EXAMPLE: aprender a jugar al tenis
            PEDRO: Luis **aprende** a jugar al tenis.
            GLORIA: Luis **no aprende** a jugar al tenis.

1. leer el periódico todos los días

PEDRO: Tony _____ .

GLORIA:

2. vender tortillas

PEDRO: El señor Galán _____ .

GLORIA:

3. comer en un restaurante elegante

PEDRO: Nosotros _____ .

GLORIA:

4. correr en el parque

PEDRO: Gabriel y Yuri _____ .

GLORIA:

5. esconder el dinero

PEDRO: Mi hermano _____ .

GLORIA:

6. prometer ayudar en casa

PEDRO: Yo _____ .

GLORIA:

b. In a question (an interrogative sentence), the subject usually comes after the verb.

Felipe **corre** todos los días.	*Felipe runs every day.*
¿**Corre Felipe** todos los días?	*Does Felipe run every day?*

EXERCISE E

Jorge's grandfather is hard of hearing and often repeats what Jorge says in the form of a question. Tell what his grandfather asks after Jorge makes each of the statements below.

EXAMPLE: Mis amigos aprenden el japonés.
  ¿**Aprenden** el japonés **tus amigos**?

1. Mi papá promete llegar a casa temprano.

2. Yo como demasiado.

3. Tú comprendes mis preguntas.

4. Uds. leen todos los días.

5. El señor Robles vende árboles.

6. Graciela no responde a mis cartas.

7. Los niños beben mucha leche.

8. José corre en el parque todos los días.

[4] REGULAR -*IR* VERBS

a. The present tense of regular -*ir* verbs is formed by dropping the infinitive ending -*ir* and adding the personal endings -*o,* -*es,* -*e,* -*imos,* -*ís,* -*en.*

b. The present tense has the following meanings in English:

usted vive	*you live, you're living, you do live*
ella vive	*she lives, she's living, she does live*

vivir *to live*			
(I live, I'm living, I do live)			
yo	viv**o**	nosotros, -as	viv**imos**
tú	viv**es**	vosotros, -as	viv**ís**
usted		ustedes	
él	} viv**e**	ellos	} viv**en**
ella		ellas	

NOTE: The endings of *-er* and *-ir* verbs are the same in the present tense except for the *nosotros* and *vosotros* forms.

[5] COMMON *-IR* VERBS

asistir (a)	*to attend*	insistir (en)	*to insist on*
cubrir	*to cover*	partir	*to leave, depart*
decidir	*to decide*	permitir	*to permit, allow*
describir	*to describe*	recibir	*to receive*
descubrir	*to discover*	subir	*to go up, climb; to raise*
dividir	*to divide*	sufrir	*to suffer*
escribir	*to write*	vivir	*to live*

EXERCISE F

Rosita and a friend are visiting some cousins in Mexico. Tell what goes on during their visit.

EXAMPLE: sus primos / vivir en la capital
Sus primos **viven** en la capital.

1. ellas / decidir visitar Tenochtitlán

2. el autobús / partir a las nueve y media

3. Rosita / insistir en visitar las pirámides

4. Amelia y yo / subir a las pirámides

5. el guardia / permitir cámaras en las pirámides

6. yo / descubrir muchas cosas interesantes

7. tú / escribir muchas tarjetas postales

8. Uds. / describir la experiencia a los primos

EXERCISE G

Yusef tells a sick classmate about the day at school. Write what he says.

1. la maestra / dividir la clase en grupos

2. yo / escribir en la pizarra

3. nosotros / asistir a una asamblea

4. Rogelio / decidir ser cómico en la clase

5. todos los alumnos / subir al laboratorio

6. tú y yo / recibir buenas notas en el examen

7. El equipo de béisbol / partir para México mañana

[6] *-IR* VERBS IN NEGATIVE AND INTERROGATIVE CONSTRUCTIONS

a. A verb is made negative by placing *no* before it.

Luz **no escribe** cartas.	*Luz doesn't write letters.*
Nosotros **no cubrimos** la mesa.	*We don't cover the table.*

EXERCISE H

Gabriel meets a friend he hasn't seen since he moved away. He asks about people in his old neighborhood. Answer his questions negatively.

EXAMPLE: ¿Todavía vives en la calle Londres?
No, ya **no vivo** en la calle Londres.

1. ¿Asiste Peter a la escuela contigo?

2. ¿Escriben Pola y Anita muchas poesías?

3. ¿Insistes tú en jugar al béisbol los sábados?

4. ¿Viven tus abuelos en Guadalajara?

5. ¿Permiten tus maestros radios en la escuela?

6. ¿Reciben Uds. tarjetas de Larry?

b. In a statement, the subject usually comes before the verb. In a question (an interrogative sentence), the subject usually comes after the verb.

La madre divide el pastel.	*The mother divides the cake.*
¿Divide la madre el pastel?	*Does the mother divide the cake?*
Tú sufres mucho.	*You suffer a lot.*
¿Sufres tú mucho?	*Do you suffer a lot?*

EXERCISE I

Kim never remembers the questions her friends ask. Write the question asked based on the answer given.

EXAMPLE: Clara y yo asistimos a la misma universidad.
¿Asisten Clara y tú a la misma universidad?

1. Nosotros vivimos en un apartamento.

2. Sanjeetah insiste en alquilar un apartamento.

3. Yo divido los gastos con ella.

4. Nuestras amigas no suben al apartamento por la escalera.

5. Yo parto en autobús el sábado por la mañana.

MASTERY EXERCISES

EXERCISE J

While waiting in line with a friend to buy tickets for a concert, Marisol's conversation jumps from one topic to another. Complete her statements with the appropriate form of the verbs given.

1. *(vivir)* Mi amigo Tomás _____ en el campo. Nosotras _____ en una ciudad grande. ¿Dónde _____ tus primos?

2. *(comprender)* Este señor no _____ el español. Tú y yo _____ el español y el italiano. ¿Qué lengua _____ ellas?

3. *(responder)* ¿ _____ tú bien? Sí, yo siempre _____ bien. Alberto no _____ en voz alta.

4. *(asistir)* Carlos no _____ a los conciertos. Tú _____ a los conciertos. ¿ _____ tus hermanas también?

5. *(leer)* Mi madre _____ el periódico en casa. Yo no _____ el periódico en la escuela. ¿ _____ tú el periódico los domingos?

6. *(recibir)* ¿ _____ tú muchos regalos? Pedro y Alfredo no _____ regalos. Yo _____ regalos en mi cumpleaños.

EXERCISE K

A new exchange student at your school is asking you questions about yourself, your friends, and the school. Answer the questions as indicated.

EXAMPLE: ¿Comen Uds. en la cafetería? *(sí)*
        Sí, **nosotros comemos** en la cafetería.

1. ¿Aprendes tú mucho en tus clases? *(sí)*
2. ¿Sufren de alergias Uds.? *(sí)*
3. ¿Recibes tú buenas notas? *(sí)*
4. ¿Venden comida española en la cafetería? *(no)*
5. ¿Beben tus amigos café con leche? *(no)*
6. ¿Permite el maestro dulces en la clase? *(no)*
7. ¿Corren Uds. en el parque después de las clases? *(sí)*
8. ¿Parte el autobús a las cuatro? *(no)*

EXERCISE L

You are describing a new friend to your parents. Express the following sentences in Spanish.

1. Pedro lives on Fourth Street.
2. He attends my school.
3. He's learning English while I'm learning Spanish.
4. In school, Pedro writes everything in Spanish first.
5. His parents insist on speaking Spanish at home.
6. He responds in English.
7. They don't understand English well.
8. Pedro and I read the Spanish newspaper together.
9. Pedro decides to do gymnastics.
10. I'm discovering many new things.

Chapter 3

Present Tense of Stem-Changing Verbs (*o* to *ue*)

[1] REGULAR STEM-CHANGING VERBS (*O* TO *UE*)

a. Many verbs that contain *o* in the stem change the *o* to *ue* in the present tense, except in the forms for *nosotros* and *vosotros*.

b. This change occurs in the syllable directly before the verb ending.

c. These verbs have regular endings in the present tense.

	mostrar *to show*	volver *to return*	dormir *to sleep*
yo	m**ue**stro	v**ue**lvo	d**ue**rmo
tú	m**ue**stras	v**ue**lves	d**ue**rmes
Ud., él, ella	m**ue**stra	v**ue**lve	d**ue**rme
nosotros, -as	mostramos	volvemos	dormimos
vosotros, -as	mostráis	volvéis	dormís
Uds., ellos, ellas	m**ue**stran	v**ue**lven	d**ue**rmen

NOTE:

1. All stem-changing verbs that change *o* to *ue* are identified in the end vocabulary by (*ue*) after the verb.

2. The verb jugar (to play) follows the same pattern in that the stem vowel changes in all present-tense forms except those for *nosotros* and *vosotros*: *juego, juegas, juega, jugamos, jugáis, juegan.*

[2] COMMON STEM-CHANGING VERBS (*O* TO *UE*)

almorzar   *to eat lunch*

contar   *to count*

costar   *to cost*

devolver   *to return, give back*

dormir   *to sleep*

encontrar   *to find; to meet*

morir   *to die*

mostrar   *to show*

poder   *to be able; can, may*

recordar   *to remember*

resolver   *to solve; to resolve*

sonar   *to sound; to ring*

volar   *to fly*

volver   *to return, come (go) back*

EXERCISE A

You're working at the returns desk of a department store. Tell what items various people return. Use the verb *devolver* in each statement.

EXAMPLE: yo / los libros de mis amigos
Yo **devuelvo** los libros de mis amigos.

1. mi madre / el vestido nuevo
2. Dolores / el regalo
3. los niños / los juguetes
4. tú / una cámara
5. Ana y José / los discos de María
6. Uds. / la cinta

EXERCISE B

Tell what each of these people counts.

EXAMPLE: el profesor / los exámenes
El profesor **cuenta** los exámenes.

1. los alumnos / los minutos
2. Sarita / sus blusas
3. el niño / de uno a cinco
4. yo / los días
5. el señor Chomsky / su dinero
6. tú / hasta mil
7. Luigi y yo / los libros

EXERCISE C

Tell what each of these people does.

EXAMPLE: el niño / contar de uno a diez
El niño **cuenta** de uno a diez.

1. los alumnos / almorzar en la cafetería
2. el matemático / resolver el problema
3. yo / encontrar a mis amigos en el parque
4. nosotros / volver a la tienda

5. Elsa / jugar en el parque

6. tú / devolver los libros a la biblioteca

7. mi hermano / dormir doce horas

8. mi mamá / poder hablar dos lenguas

9. el despertador / sonar a las siete de la mañana

10. los turistas / volar en avión a Madrid

EXERCISE D

Some of your friends are excited about going on a youth trip to Spain. Write what each one says.

EXAMPLE: yo / no poder esperar más
            Yo **no puedo** esperar más.

1. Gloria y Lourdes / contar los días

2. nosotros / volar el sábado

3. Clara / resolver hablar solamente en español

4. yo / encontrar al guía en el aeropuerto

5. tú / mostrar el boleto a todo el mundo

6. el viaje / costar mil dólares

7. nosotros / dormir en ocho hoteles

8. yo / no recordar cuando nosotros / volver

EXERCISE E Homework ~ 6/30/2006

You call the telephone operator to locate a number for your sister. Complete your dialogue with the operator, using the appropriate form of the following verbs.

costar   encontra   poder   recordar   volver

TELEFONISTA: ¿En qué _____ ayudarle?

TÚ: ¿ _____ Ud. darme un número de teléfono, por favor? Mi

              hermana no _____ el número de teléfono de Aerolíneas

              Españolas y nosotros no lo _____ en la guía telefónica.

              Nuestros padres _____ de Madrid esta noche.

TELEFONISTA: Un momento, por favor. Es el 555-3333.

TÚ: Muchas gracias.

TELEFONISTA: De nada. Este servicio _____ un dólar.

EXERCISE F

Answer the questions a Spanish-speaking student is asking about you and your friends.

1. ¿Dónde juegas tú con tus amigos?
2. ¿Qué deporte juegan Uds.?
3. ¿A qué hora vuelves tú a casa por la tarde?
4. ¿Dónde almuerzan los alumnos?
5. ¿Muestran Uds. películas en tu casa?
6. ¿Puedes tú ver televisión cada noche?
7. ¿Cuántas horas duermes tú por lo general?

MASTERY EXERCISES

EXERCISE G

Using the cues provided, tell how these people react.

EXAMPLE: Gregorio tiene hambre. *(almorzar)*
Gregorio **almuerza**.

1. Jorge está muy cansado. *(dormir toda la noche)*
2. Yo necesito diez dólares para comprar un regalo. *(contar mi dinero)*
3. A mi mamá no le gusta el regalo. *(devolver el regalo)*
4. A mis amigos les gustan los deportes. *(jugar al béisbol y al voleibol)*
5. Mi papá debe llegar a Chicago rápido. *(volar en avión)*
6. Tú encuentras la tienda de discos cerrada. *(volver mañana)*
7. Nosotros buscamos un restaurante bueno. *(encontrar uno cerca del cine)*

EXERCISE H

Your little cousin likes to ask questions about everything and anything. Answer his questions.

1. ¿Puedes tú vivir sin aire?
2. ¿Duermes tú en la cocina?
3. ¿Mueren las plantas en la primavera?
4. ¿Almuerzan Uds. a medianoche?

5. ¿Vuelan tus amigos como los pájaros?

6. ¿Suenan las campanas mientras Uds. duermen?

7. ¿Resuelven tus amigos tus problemas?

8. ¿Recuerdas tú las fechas importantes de tu familia?

9. ¿Juegan Uds. al tenis en la piscina?

10. ¿Cuentas tú el dinero de tus amigos?

EXERCISE I

Rogelio describes how he spends a typical Saturday with his friends. Express what he says in Spanish.

1. I meet my friends downtown at noon.

2. We play electronic games.

3. Each game costs twenty-five cents.

4. I can win many games.

5. Pedro counts the points.

6. Sofía remembers the name of a Mexican restaurant.

7. We eat lunch there.

8. We're able to take the bus at five o'clock.

9. I sleep on the bus.

10. We return home at six o'clock.

Chapter 4
Present Tense of Stem-Changing Verbs (*e* to *ie*)

[1] REGULAR STEM-CHANGING VERBS (*E* TO *IE*)

a. Many verbs that contain *e* in the stem change the *e* to *ie* in all present-tense forms except those for *nosotros* and *vosotros*.

b. This change occurs in the syllable directly before the verb ending.

c. The verbs *cerrar, perder,* and *sentir* have regular endings in the present tense.

	cerrar *to close*	perder *to lose*	sentir *to regret*
yo	c*ie*rro	p*ie*rdo	s*ie*nto
tú	c*ie*rras	p*ie*rdes	s*ie*ntes
Ud., él, ella	c*ie*rra	p*ie*rde	s*ie*nte
nosotros, -as	cerramos	perdemos	sentimos
vosotros, -as	cerráis	perdéis	sentís
Uds., ellos, ellas	c*ie*rran	p*ie*rden	s*ie*nten

NOTE: All stem-changing verbs that change *e* to *ie* are identified in the end vocabulary by *(ie)* after the verb.

[2] COMMON STEM-CHANGING VERBS (*E* TO *IE*)

cerrar   *to close*

comenzar   *to begin*

confesar   *to confess*

defender   *to defend*

empezar   *to begin*

entender   *to understand*

pensar   *to think; to intend*

perder   *to lose; to waste; to miss (train, bus ...)*

preferir   *to prefer*

querer   *to want; to wish; to love*

referir   *to tell; to narrate*

sentir   *to regret, be sorry; to feel*

EXERCISE A

Write the favorite pastime of these people.

EXAMPLE: Eduardo / coleccionar monedas
Eduardo **prefiere** coleccionar monedas.

1. Federico / el dominó
2. tú / la natación
3. yo / jugar a las damas
4. Isabel y Luis / el tenis

5. Javier / el béisbol
6. Ricardo y yo / el voleibol
7. mi hermano / la lectura
8. mis hermanas / la escritura

EXERCISE B

Tell what each of these people loses.

EXAMPLE: yo / la cartera
            Yo **pierdo** la cartera.

1. Elsa / el dinero
2. tú / los libros
3. Rafael y Carlos / las llaves
4. mi mamá / las recetas

5. yo / el tiempo
6. Jorge y yo / el partido
7. mi abuelo / la memoria
8. mi padre / la paciencia

EXERCISE C

Tell what these people do.

EXAMPLE: la señora / cerrar la puerta
            La señora **cierra** la puerta.

1. el niño / confesar la verdad a su madre
2. Carlos y Enrique / no entender el francés
3. yo / defender a mi hermano menor
4. los señores Galván / pensar visitar un museo
5. tú / preferir ver una telenovela
6. Roberto y yo / perder el autobús todos los días
7. la profesora / comenzar la clase a las ocho
8. Ud. / empezar a leer una novela
9. Francisco / querer ir al cine
10. yo / sentir mucho el accidente

EXERCISE D

Mrs. Madrigal talks about the things her family does and doesn't do. Write what she says.

EXAMPLE: Arturito / perder sus juguetes
Arturito **pierde** sus juguetes.

1. Alfonso / no cerrar el refrigerador

2. la abuela / referir cuentos antiguos

3. mi esposo / preferir jugar al golf

4. yo / siempre defender a mis hijos

5. los gemelos / no entender la palabra «no»

6. toda la familia / querer ser buena

7. mi papá / pensar viajar en abril

8. tú / empezar a estudiar más

EXERCISE E

You're living with a Costa Rican family during the summer. Answer their questions about yourself and your life at home.

1. ¿Comienzan las clases en septiembre?

2. ¿Empiezas tú a estudiar después de la cena?

3. ¿Prefieres tú el verano o el invierno?

4. ¿Piensas tú asistir a la universidad?

5. ¿Qué quieres tú estudiar allí?

6. ¿Cuántas lenguas entiendes tú?

7. ¿Qué pierdes tú a menudo?

8. ¿Quieres tú volver a tu casa pronto?

MASTERY EXERCISES

EXERCISE F

Fill in the missing verbs in this entry in Arturo's diary.

El partido _____ a mediodía pero yo no _____ a jugar hasta la una.
      1. (comenzar)   *2.* (empezar)

Carlos no _____ las reglas y el árbitro _____ a explicar las reglas
      3. (entender)   *4.* (empezar)

otra vez. Yo _____ ser deportista profesional. Todos los jugadores
      5. (pensar)

_____ ganar este partido. El entrenador del equipo _____ mucho
6. (querer)   7. (perder)

tiempo porque él nos _____ muchas jugadas antiguas. Yo _____
8. (referir)   9. (confesar)

algo. Nosotros _____ jugar un buen partido a escuchar sus cuentos.
10. (preferir)

¡Nosotros _____ ganar este partido!
11. (pensar)

EXERCISE G

Tell who does the following things.

defender la patria	perder el autobús
empezar una carrera nueva	perder las llaves de la casa
entender varias lenguas	preferir jugar
no cerrar la puerta de la casa	querer visitar otro país
pensar graduarse en junio	referir cuentos de su juventud

1. Tú _____ .

2. Mi papá _____ .

3. Los niños _____ .

4. Mi hermano _____ .

5. El ejército _____ .

6. Los abuelos _____ .

7. Yo _____ .

8. El profesor _____ .

9. La niña _____ .

10. Mis hermanos _____ .

EXERCISE H

Marisol is talking about her parents to a friend. Express what she says in Spanish.

1. My parents always defend their family.

2. My father begins the day very early.

3. They understand our problems.

4. I confess my problems to my mother.

5. She closes the door.

6. We prefer to be alone.

7. She tells me about her childhood.

8. My sister thinks that I'm silly.

9. I don't lose my patience.

10. I love my parents very much.

Chapter 5
Present Tense of Stem-Changing Verbs (*e* to *i*)

[1] REGULAR STEM-CHANGING VERBS (*E* TO *I*)

a. A few *-ir* verbs that contain an *e* in the stem change the *e* to *i* in all present-tense forms except those for *nosotros* and *vosotros*.

b. The change occurs in the syllable directly before the verb ending.

c. The verb *servir* has regular endings in the present tense.

servir *to serve*			
yo	s*i*rvo	nosotros, -as	servimos
tú	s*i*rves	vosotros, -as	servís
usted		ustedes	
él	s*i*rve	ellos	s*i*rven
ella		ellas	

NOTE: All stem-changing verbs that change *e* to *i* are identified in the end vocabulary by *(i)* after the verb.

[2] COMMON STEM-CHANGING VERBS (*E* TO *I*)

medir   *to measure*

pedir   *to ask for, request; to order* (food)

reñir   *to quarrel; to scold*

repetir   *to repeat*

servir   *to serve*

EXERCISE A   *Homework 7/3/06*

Tell what each person orders in the restaurant.

EXAMPLE: mi padre / pescado
            Mi padre **pide** pescado.

1. yo / chuletas de cerdo

2. mi hermana / arroz con pollo

3. mis abuelos / paella

4. tú / una hamburguesa

5. todo el mundo / una ensalada

6. nosotros / helado de chocolate

EXERCISE B

Your shop class is planning a model house. Tell which part of the house each student is measuring.

EXAMPLE: Gabriel / el jardín
Gabriel **mide** el jardín.

1. Rosa / las ventanas

2. Javier y Enrique / el piso

3. yo / la sala

4. tú / las puertas

5. Petra y yo / las paredes

6. Alfonso / la cocina

7. Silvia y Néstor / el comedor

EXERCISE C

Say what the students in the Spanish class repeat.

EXAMPLE: Jaime / la pregunta
Jaime **repite** la pregunta.

1. yo / la palabra

2. todo el mundo / la fecha de hoy

3. tú / la regla de gramática

4. Rosa / el trabalenguas

5. Antonio y yo / la respuesta

6. David y Luis / la frase

EXERCISE D

Complete this entry in Raquel's diary by filling in the missing verbs.

Cada miércoles yo voy a un restaurante con mi abuela. Dos meseros siempre

_____ nuestra mesa. Mi abuela siempre _____ lo mismo: pollo, papas
1. (servir)   2. (pedir)

fritas y una ensalada. Yo _____ una hamburguesa, papas fritas y una
3. (pedir)

ensalada. El primer mesero _____ las ensaladas. Mi abuela y yo _____
4. (servir)   5. (pedir)

salsa de tomate. En otra mesa, una madre _____ a su hijo porque habla en
                                            6. (reñir)

voz muy alta. A veces mi abuela me dice: «Tú _____ la cuenta hoy».
                                              7. (pedir)

MASTERY EXERCISES

EXERCISE E

Using the cues provided, answer the questions posed by a new friend.

1. ¿Quién sirve la comida en tu casa? *(mi madre)*
2. ¿A qué hora sirven Uds. la comida en tu casa? *(6:30)*
3. ¿Qué plato pides tú a menudo? *(papas fritas)*
4. ¿Qué piden Uds. de postre? *(pastel de coco)*
5. ¿Qué bebida pide tu papá? *(café con leche)*
6. ¿Pides tú té con limón a veces? *(no)*
7. ¿Qué sirves tú a tus amigos en tu casa? *(helado)*

EXERCISE F

Gloria describes a meal at her home. Express what she says in Spanish.

1. We serve the meal at two o'clock.
2. My sister and my mother serve the soup first.
3. My father always asks for the soup.
4. I ask for chicken and a little rice.
5. My brother and I ask for soda.
6. My mother serves the soda.
7. My mother scolds my father because he eats too much.

Chapter 6

Verbs Irregular in the Present Tense

[1] VERBS WITH IRREGULAR *YO* FORMS

a. In the present tense, the following verbs are irregular only in the first-person singular *(yo)*:

hacer	*to make, do*	*hago,* **haces, hace, hacemos, hacéis hacen**
poner	*to put, place*	*pongo,* **pones, pone, ponemos, ponéis, ponen**
saber	*to know*	*sé,* **sabes, sabe, sabemos, sabéis, saben**
salir	*to go out*	*salgo,* **sales, sale, salimos, salís, salen**
ver	*to see; to watch*	*veo,* **ves, ve, vemos, veis, ven**

b. The verbs *caer* (to fall) and *traer* (to bring) have an *i* between the stem and the first-person singular ending *(-go)*. Their other present-tense forms are regular.

caer	*to fall*	*caigo,* **caes, cae, caemos, caéis, caen**
traer	*to bring*	*traigo,* **traes, trae, traemos, traéis, traen**

EXERCISE A

Sarita's younger sister is very proud of herself and what she does. Write what she says.

EXAMPLE: saber montar en bicicleta
Yo **sé** montar en bicicleta.

1. ver a mis amigos todos los días

2. saber jugar al voleibol

3. hacer la ensalada todos los días

4. salir con mis amigas

5. poner la mesa cada día

EXERCISE B

Omar is being punished. His parents are making him write a statement about his responsibilities. What is the missing verb in each sentence?

Yo _____ que debo estudiar más. Yo no _____ programas de televisión
   1. (saber)   2. (ver)

durante la semana. Cuando llego de la escuela, yo _____ mis libros en el
                                             3. (poner)

escritorio y _____ la tarea. Yo no _____ con mis amigos por las tardes.
        4. (hacer)   5. (salir)

EXERCISE C

María is having a terrible day. Everything around her is falling. Describe what's happening.

EXAMPLE: la botella de leche / al suelo
                La botella de leche **cae** al suelo.

1. las monedas / detrás del escritorio
2. el niño / en el jardín
3. yo / en el sillón
4. la cuchara / al suelo
5. Carmen y yo / en el patio
6. tú / en la calle

EXERCISE D

Jorge is organizing a picnic at the beach. What do his friends bring to the picnic?

EXAMPLE: Mario / los refrescos
                Mario **trae** los refrescos.

1. Gilberto / los platos
2. Susan y yo / los sándwiches
3. Virginia / los vasos
4. tú / el pastel
5. Vicente y Gerardo / el estéreo
6. yo / las palomitas

[2] IRREGULAR PRESENT-TENSE FORMS

The verbs *oír, decir, tener,* and *venir* are irregular in the present tense.

oír *to listen*	**oigo, oyes, oye, oímos, oís, oyen**
decir *to say*	**digo, dices, dice, decimos, decís, dicen**
tener *to have*	**tengo, tienes, tiene, tenemos, tenéis, tienen**
venir *to come*	**vengo, vienes, viene, venimos, venís, vienen**

EXERCISE E

Several friends are discussing the types of music they listen to. Tell what they say.

EXAMPLE: Roberto / la música clásica
Roberto **oye** la música clásica.

1. Yusef y Luis / la música rock

2. yo / la música de jazz

3. mi padre / la música clásica

4. tú / la música de guitarra

5. Alicia y yo / las sinfonías

6. Josefina / la música romántica

EXERCISE F

Tomás is helping his younger sister master the rules of etiquette. Tell what she says in each situation Tomás presents to her.

EXAMPLE: Tú quieres otro pedazo de pastel. *(por favor)*
Yo **digo** «por favor».

1. Juan recibe muchos regalos. *(gracias)*

Él _____ .

2. Nosotros saludamos al maestro. *(buenos días)*

Nosotros _____ .

3. Tú conoces a un amigo de tus padres. *(mucho gusto)*

Yo _____ .

4. Elena sale de su casa. *(adiós)*

Ella _____ .

5. Los niños pasan delante de una persona. *(con permiso)*

Ellos _____ .

6. Tú entras en la casa. *(hola)*

Yo _____ .

EXERCISE G

Some young people are talking about what they and their friends have to do on Saturday. Using the expression tener que (to have to), write what they say.

EXAMPLE: Isabel / ir al supermercado
Isabel **tiene que** ir al supermercado.

Homework
6/29/06

1. yo / arreglar mi cuarto
2. Pablo / trabajar
3. Ramona y yo / devolver los libros a la biblioteca
4. tú / ayudar en casa
5. Lorenzo y Esteban / ir a un partido de fútbol

EXERCISE H

Tell at what time these people come home.

EXAMPLE: Rosa / 4:00
Rosa **viene a casa** a las cuatro.

1. yo / 5:30
2. mis padres / 6:00
3. tú / 12:00

4. Laura y yo / 9:15
5. Antonio / 11:00

EXERCISE I

Answer the following personal questions.

1. ¿Qué oyes tú en la radio por la mañana? *(las noticias)*
2. ¿Qué dices cuando tus amigos vuelven a sus casas? *(hasta luego)*
3. ¿Qué tienes que hacer después de las clases? *(estudiar)*
4. ¿A qué hora vienes a casa todos los días? *(4:30)*
5. ¿Quién tiene que preparar la comida en tu casa? *(mi mamá)*
6. ¿Quién tiene que lavar los platos cada noche? *(mi hermana y yo)*
7. ¿Quién oye el pronóstico del tiempo en tu casa? *(mi papá)*

[3] IRREGULAR VERBS *DAR* AND *IR*

	dar *to give*	**ir** *to go*
yo	**doy**	**voy**
tú	**das**	**vas**
Ud., él, ella	**da**	**va**
nosotros, -as	**damos**	**vamos**
vosotros, -as	**dais**	**vais**
Uds., ellos, ellas	**dan**	**van**

NOTE: A conjugated form of the verb *ir* followed by the preposition *a* and an infinitive is used to express a future action.

Voy a estudiar.   *I am going to study.*

¿Qué vas a hacer?   *What are you going to do?*

[4] IRREGULAR VERBS *SER* AND *ESTAR*

	ser *to be*	estar *to be*
yo	soy	estoy
tú	eres	estás
Ud., él, ella	es	está
nosotros, -as	somos	estamos
vosotros, -as	sois	estáis
Uds., ellos, ellas	son	están

EXERCISE J

Tell where each member of your family goes every day.

EXAMPLE: mi padre / a la oficina
            Mi padre **va** a la oficina.

1. mis hermanos / a la universidad

2. mi hermana / a la escuela de enseñanza secundaria

3. mamá / al supermercado

4. yo / a la biblioteca

5. el abuelo y yo / al parque

EXERCISE K

What do each of these people give?

EXAMPLE: Carlos / dinero a los pobres
            Carlos **da** dinero a los pobres.

1. yo / regalos a mis amigos

2. Phil y Juan / problemas a sus padres

3. tú / flores a tu mamá

4. el señor Díaz / dulces a su esposa

5. Carmen y yo / pan a los pájaros

6. el profesor / mucha tarea

EXERCISE L

Gloria and her friends are discussing the nationality of people they know. Write what they say about each person.

EXAMPLE:　Lourdes / España
　　　　　Lourdes **es** de España.

1. el profesor de español / Colombia

2. mis primas / Venezuela

3. Raquel / Costa Rica

4. Gladys / Honduras

5. Murray y yo / los Estados Unidos

6. tú / Puerto Rico

7. yo / Perú

8. ustedes / Panamá

EXERCISE M

When Mr. Lara calls home, only Tomás is there. Tell where everyone else is.

EXAMPLE:

Mamá **está en el supermercado.**

1.

Gilberto _____.

2.

Bernardo y Felipe _____.

3.

Yolanda _____.

4.

Tú _____.

5.

Los abuelos _____.

6.

El perro _____.

EXERCISE N

Complete this note that Ramón left for his parents by filling in the missing verbs. Use an appropriate form of *dar, ir, ser,* or *estar.*

Queridos padres:

Yo _____ a casa de mi amigo Marcos. Él _____ de México. Nosotros
     1.   *2.*

_____ a jugar al tenis. Yo _____ a estar en el parque que_____ cerca
 3.   *4.*   *5.*

de la escuela. Yo _____ de comer a Fido después. Marcos _____ a cenar
               6.   *7.*

con nosotros porque sus padres _____ en el centro. Hasta luego.
                                      8.

                               Ramón

EXERCISE O

Answer the questions that your inquisitive grandmother asks you when some friends come to visit. Use in your responses the cues in parentheses.

1. ¿Quiénes son estos jóvenes? *(mis amigos)*

2. ¿Qué das a tus amigos? *(palomitas)*

3. ¿Dónde está tu hermana? *(en su dormitorio)*

4. ¿Qué van a hacer Uds. ahora? *(jugar a las damas)*

5. ¿De dónde es ese chico? *(Argentina)*

6. ¿Adónde vas tú esta noche? *(al cine)*

MASTERY EXERCISES

EXERCISE P

Ricardo describes his neighbors to a friend. What is the appropriate form of the missing verbs?

Todos los días yo _____ a mi vecino, el señor Robles, cuando mi hermana
      1. (ver)

y yo _____ a la escuela. Él _____ en la calle con su perro Campeón.
    2. (ir)   3. (estar)

Campeón _____ muy fuerte y el señor Robles _____ al suelo a menudo.
      4. (ser)   5. (caer)

Nosotros _____ «Buenos días». Cuando yo _____ de la escuela yo _____
        6. (decir)   7. (venir)   8. (oír)

los ladridos de Campeón que _____ en el jardín. Campeón y yo _____
                         9. (estar)   10. (ser)

buenos amigos y a veces yo _____ que cuidarlo cuando los señores
                        11. (tener)

Robles no _____ en casa. Los Robles _____ buenos vecinos y muchas
        12. (estar)   13. (ser)

veces Campeón _____ regalos a nuestra casa. Cuando mi mamá _____
             14. (traer)   15. (ver)

esto, mi hermana y yo _____ que devolver los regalos de Campeón.
                    16. (tener)

EXERCISE Q

A classmate is conducting a survey to find out if people think alike. For each situation select the appropriate reaction from those given.

caer en la misma fecha	ir a la fiesta
dar la cuenta al cliente	oír las noticias en la radio
dar un regalo a mi hermana	traer mi estéreo
decir «Buenos días»	ver el programa

1. Tú trabajas de mesero en un restaurante.

   Yo _____ .

2. Hay una fiesta en casa de tu amigo Ricardo.

   Yo _____ .

3. Tú y tu hermano encuentran a un vecino en la calle.

   Nosotros _____ .

4. El tocadiscos de Ricardo no funciona.

Yo _____ .

5. Tú y un amigo celebran sus cumpleaños el 2 de enero.

Nuestros cumpleaños _____ .

6. Hay un programa bueno en la televisión.

Yo _____ .

7. Es el cumpleaños de tu hermana.

Yo _____ .

8. Estás en el auto y quieres saber qué pasa actualmente.

Yo _____ .

EXERCISE R

Answer these questions that a cousin asks you about school.

1. ¿A quién ves en la escuela todos los días?

2. ¿Oyes las respuestas de los otros alumnos?

3. ¿Traes tus libros a casa cada día?

4. ¿Tienes mucha tarea por lo general?

5. ¿De dónde es tu profesor de español?

6. ¿Vienen Uds. a casa después de las clases?

7. ¿Qué dice el maestro cuando contestas bien?

8. ¿Caen muchos exámenes en el mismo día?

9. ¿Vas al estadio para ver los partidos?

10. ¿Estás en tus clases a tiempo?

11. ¿Dan tus maestros notas altas?

EXERCISE S

Express in Spanish what the teacher tells the students on the first day of classes.

1. I'm never absent.

2. You *(pl.)* come to class on time.

3. I see everything, and I hear everything.

4. You *(pl.)* bring your books to class every day.

5. The books don't fall to the floor.

6. We're going to work a lot in this class.

7. Every student is important.

8. You *(pl.)* always tell the truth when you don't have the assignment.

9. I give many tests.

10. You *(pl.)* are going to learn a great deal in this class.

Chapter 7
Verbs with Spelling Changes in the Present Tense

[1] VERBS ENDING IN -CER AND -CIR

a. Most verbs whose infinitives end in *-cer* or *-cir* have the ending *-zco* in the first-person singular of the present tense. This pattern occurs only if a vowel precedes the *c* in the infinitive.

	ofrecer *to offer*	**conducir** *to drive*
yo	ofre**zco**	condu**zco**
tú	ofreces	conduces
Ud., él, ella	ofrece	conduce
nosotros, -as	ofrecemos	conducimos
vosotros, -as	ofrecéis	conducís
Uds., ellos, ellas	ofrecen	conducen

b. Common *-cer* verbs

aparecer *to appear*   ofrecer *to offer*

conocer *to know; to meet*   parecer *to seem*

desaparecer *to disappear*   reconocer *to recognize*

obedecer *to obey*

c. Common *-cir* verbs

conducir *to drive; to lead*   traducir *to translate*

producir *to produce*

NOTE: The verbs *hacer* and *decir* are exceptions. (See Chapter 6.)

EXERCISE A

In an orientation session on community service, the students in your global studies class offer to perform service in various settings.

EXAMPLE: Gerardo / en el hospital
Gerardo **ofrece servicio** en el hospital.

1. Rosita / en la escuela de párvulos

2. yo / en la oficina de un veterinario

3. Clara y Luz / en la biblioteca

4. tú / en la corte

5. Rogelio y yo / en la jefatura de la policía

6. Elena / en la enfermería

EXERCISE B

Gloria found.in the attic an old box with a variety of documents written in English. You and other friends offer to help her translate them. Tell what each one translates.

EXAMPLE: Victoria / las cartas
Victoria **traduce** las cartas.

1. Ana y yo / los poemas

2. Mariah / la canción

3. yo / el artículo del periódico

4. Kim y Adriana / las tarjetas

5. tú / este párrafo corto

EXERCISE C

Hugo is spending the summer on a farm. He quotes some of the farmer's comments in a letter to you. What are the missing verbs?

El sol _____ con el gallo pero _____ cuando hace mal tiempo.
　　　　1. (aparecer)　　　　　　　*2.* (desaparecer)

Yo no _____ otra vida que la vida del campo. ¿ _____ tú esos
　　　　3. (conocer)　　　　　　　　　　　　*4.* (reconocer)

animales? Los caballos siempre _____ a los campesinos. ¿Y esas flores?
　　　　　　　　　　　　　　5. (obedecer)

_____ muy bonitas, ¿verdad? Nosotros _____ toda la comida
6. (parecer)　　　　　　　　　　　　　*7.* (producir)

que comemos en esta granja. Además, los viernes yo _____ mi camión
　　　　　　　　　　　　　　　　　　　　　8. (conducir)

a un mercado en el pueblo. Muchos turistas visitan ese pueblo y _____
　　　　　　　　　　　　　　　　　　　　　　　　　9. (parecer)

que vienen solamente para comprar las legumbres. Dicen que nosotros

_____ legumbres a precios bajos. ¿ _____ tú una vida mejor?
10. (ofrecer)　　　　　　　　　　*11.* (conocer)

EXERCISE D

Answer the questions your younger brother asks you as you walk on the beach at night. In your answers, use the cues in parentheses.

1. ¿Dónde aparece el sol? *(en el este)*

2. ¿Cuándo desaparece la luna esta semana? *(por la mañana)*

3. ¿Cómo parecen las estrellas? *(muy pequeñas)*

4. ¿Reconoces esa estrella? *(no)*

5. ¿Dónde ofrecen cursos sobre las estrellas? *(en la escuela)*

6. ¿Conoces tú mucho del universo? *(un poco)*

[2] *SABER* AND *CONOCER*

a. The verbs *saber* and *conocer* both mean "to know." All of the present-tense forms of these two verbs are regular except the *yo* form.

saber   *sé, sabes, sabe, sabemos, sabéis, saben*

conocer   *conozco, conoces, conoce, conocemos, conocéis, conocen*

b. *Saber* means "to know a fact, to have information about something, to know how to do something." *Saber* can be followed by a noun, a clause, or an infinitive.

Yo sé tu nombre.	*I know your name.*
María sabe dónde vivo.	*María knows where I live.*
Ellos no saben esquiar.	*They don't know how to ski.*

c. *Conocer* means "to know personally, to be acquainted with, to be familiar with." *Conocer* can be followed by names of people, places, or things.

Conozco a Juan y María.	*I know Juan and María.*
Ella conoce Bogotá.	*She knows Bogotá.*
Él conoce un restaurante bueno.	*He's familiar with a good restaurant.*

d. Note the difference in meaning between the following sentences:

Él sabe el nombre del alcalde.	*He knows the mayor's name.*
Él conoce al alcalde.	*He knows the mayor.*

EXERCISE E

Mr. Moreno is proud of his family's many talents. Based on the drawings below, tell what he says they know how to do.

EXAMPLE:

Alberto **sabe tocar el violín.**

1.

Mi esposa y yo _____.

2.

Xavier _____.

3.

Mónica y Beatriz _____.

4.

Mis padres _____.

5.

Yo _____.

EXERCISE F

Margarita has just moved to your city. She tells you the things with which she and her family are already acquainted.

EXAMPLE: mi mamá / el supermercado
             Mi mamá **ya conoce** el supermercado.

1. yo / el parque

2. mis hermanos / el cine

3. mi papá / a tu papá

4. mi hermana y yo / todas las tiendas

5. el perro / a nuestros vecinos

6. mi familia / a toda tu familia

EXERCISE G

As a party game, Dolores has prepared slips of paper with cues and the names of party guests. Whoever picks the slip must ask a question using *conocer* **or** *saber,* **and the person(s) called upon must respond.**

EXAMPLE: Rafael / jugar al boliche
Rafael, ¿**sabes tú** jugar al boliche?
Sí, **sé** jugar al boliche pero no muy bien.

1. Silvia y César / bailar el tango

2. Estela / el Parque Nacional

3. Isaac y Pedro / cocinar

4. Erika y Elena / la música del grupo «Los Amigos»

5. Ching / el presidente del país

6. Mirta / el número de teléfono de César

EXERCISE H

Pilar and her friend Rocío plan a shopping trip. Complete the dialogue below with the appropriate forms of *saber* **or** *conocer.*

ROCÍO: Yo ya _____ lo que quieres hacer hoy. Ir de compras, ¿verdad?
1.

PILAR: Sí, tienes razón. Tú me _____ muy bien. ¿Vienes conmigo?
2.

ROCÍO: ¡Cómo no!

PILAR: Yo _____ una tienda que acaba de abrir en el centro.
3.

Tienen ropa bonita.

ROCÍO: ¿ _____ si es cara? No tengo mucho dinero.
4.

PILAR: Yo no _____ pero vamos. Mi mamá _____ la dirección
5.   6.

de la tienda. También ella _____ a una señora que trabaja ahí.
7.

Si la tienda es cara, solamente vamos a ver los diseños. Mi mamá y

yo _____ coser.
     8.

ROCÍO: Bueno, vamos. Quiero _____ la tienda.
               9.

EXERCISE I

You're visiting a school while you are in Madrid. Answer the questions the students ask you.

1. ¿Conoces la ciudad de Madrid?

2. ¿Sabes conducir?

3. ¿Conoces a otros chicos españoles?

4. ¿Sabes tocar la guitarra?

5. ¿Conoces la música española?

6. ¿Sabes el nombre de un cantante español?

7. ¿Conoces la comida española?

8. ¿Sabes preparar un plato español?

9. ¿Sabes cómo se llama el Rey de España?

10. ¿Conoces la historia de España?

MASTERY EXERCISES

EXERCISE J

Raúl and Jaime talk about a concert. Fill in the missing verbs to complete the dialogue.

RAÚL: ¿ _____ tú que hay un concierto en el parque esta noche?
     1. (saber)

JAIME: Sí, lo _____ . _____ que todo el mundo va a asistir.
        2. (saber)   3. (parecer)

RAÚL: ¿Qué grupos van a cantar y tocar?

JAIME: Yo _____ el nombre de uno de los grupos que anuncian,
      4. (reconocer)

«The Zeros». ¿ _____ tú su música?
          5. (conocer)

RAÚL: Sí, yo _____ su música y me gusta mucho, pero cantan
6. (conocer)

en inglés. Ellos _____ muchos discos.
7. (producir)

JAIME: ¿En inglés? Yo no _____ inglés. Si vamos al concierto,
8. (saber)

¿ _____ tú las canciones al español?
9. (traducir)

RAÚL: Claro, pero hay un problema. Tengo que estar en casa a las once.

Si yo no _____ a mis padres, no voy a poder salir por
10. (obedecer)

un mes. Tú ya _____ a mis padres.
11. (conocer)

JAIME: ¿De veras? ¿Dices que si tú no les _____ , tú _____
12. (obedecer)   13. (desaparecer)

de nuestra vida social?

RAÚL: Bueno. Yo pido permiso a mis padres, y si yo no _____ ,
14. (aparecer)

vas solo.

JAIME: Está bien.

EXERCISE K

As an exchange student in Caracas, you're being interviewed for the school newspaper. Answer the reporter's questions.

1. ¿Ya conoces bien la ciudad de Caracas?

2. ¿Qué lugares conoces?

3. ¿Qué deportes sabes jugar?

4. ¿Qué clase de auto conduces?

5. ¿Obedeces a los maestros venezolanos?

6. ¿Sabes cuándo aparece esta entrevista en el periódico?

7. ¿Qué comentario ofreces a los estudiantes venezolanos?

8. ¿Qué proyecto produces durante este año?

EXERCISE L

Your friend is writing to her Spanish pen pal about the summer camp you're both attending. Help her express the sentences in Spanish.

1. The days seem long here.

2. I still don't know many of the boys.

3. I know where the cafeteria and the pool are.

4. Many boys don't obey the camp's rules.

5. The counselor appears and disappears without making noise.

6. I still don't know his name.

7. We're producing a short skit.

8. The camp offers many activities.

9. We disappear when the counselor isn't here.

10. I know how to play tennis better.

Chapter 8
Ser and Estar

Spanish has two different verbs, *ser* and *estar,* that both correspond to the English verb "to be." Which one you should use depends on the context.

[1] USES OF SER

Ser is used:

a. to express a characteristic, a description, or an identification.

    (1) Characteristics

La sopa **es buena.**	*The soup is good.*
El profesor **es estricto.**	*The teacher is strict.*

    (2) Description

Martha **es alta.**	*Martha is tall.*
El señor Salas **es rico.**	*Mr. Salas is rich.*

    (3) Identification

¿Quién es?	*Who is it?*
Soy yo.	*It's me.*

b. to express occupation or nationality.

    (1) Occupation

Mi primo **es abogado.**	*My cousin is a lawyer.*
Ellos **son contadores.**	*They are accountants.*

    (2) Nationality

Pedro y Elenita **son españoles.**	*Pedro and Elenita are Spanish.*
Victoria **es peruana.**	*Victoria is Peruvian.*

c. to express time and dates.

    (1) Time

Son las dos.	*It's two o'clock.*
Es medianoche.	*It's midnight.*

(2) Dates

Es el tres de mayo.   *It's May 3.*
Es el primero de abril.   *It's April 1.*

d. with *de,* to express origin, possession, or material.

(1) Origin

El muchacho **es de México.**   *The boy is from Mexico.*
Las naranjas **son de Valencia.**   *The oranges are from Valencia.*

(2) Possession

Ese reloj **es de Carmen.**   *That watch is Carmen's.*
La casa **es de mi tío.**   *The house is my uncle's.*

(3) Material

La blusa **es de seda.**   *The blouse is made of silk.*
El reloj **es de oro.**   *The watch is made of gold.*

NOTE:

1. Adjectives used with *ser* must agree with the subject in number and gender.

Miguel y Adalberto **son mexicanos.**   *Miguel and Adalberto are Mexican.*
Tía Clara **es puertorriqueña** también. *Aunt Clara is Puerto Rican too.*

2. In questions, the adjective usually follows the verb.

¿**Son viejos** los edificios?   *Are the buildings old?*

3. The adjective *feliz* is generally used with *ser.*

Ella **es feliz.**   *She is happy.*

4. The forms of *ser* are summarized in the section on irregular verbs in the Appendix, page 378.

EXERCISE A

After a party at your home, your mother asks you about the friends who attended. Tell her about them using the correct forms of *ser* and the suggested adjectives below.

aburrido	bonito	guapo	responsable
amable	celoso	independiente	simpático
antipático	divertido	inteligente	tacaño

EXAMPLE: Adela es **amable y divertida.**

1. Stephen _____.   *4.* Diana _____.

2. Alicia y Sofía _____.   *5.* Hank _____.

3. Gerardo y Raúl _____.   *6.* Marcos y Elsa _____.

EXERCISE B

After introducing himself and some friends, Lorenzo tells their nation-alities. Using the appropriate form of *ser,* tell what Lorenzo says.

EXAMPLE: Raquel / Chile
            Raquel **es de** Chile. Ella **es chilena**.

1. yo / México   *5.* Inés y yo / México

2. Beatriz / Argentina   *6.* tú (Juan) / Puerto Rico

3. Homero y Hugo / España   *7.* ellas / Perú

4. Gloria / Colombia

EXERCISE C

You are helping a teacher clean out the school's lost and found at the end of the year. You identify the owners of many of the lost objects.

EXAMPLE: el suéter / Belinda
            El suéter **es de** Belinda

1. los anteojos / Enrique

2. el reloj / Berta

3. las llaves / la señora Pérez

4. el diccionario / Roberto

5. los guantes de béisbol / Arturo y Víctor

6. las fotos / Pilar

EXERCISE D

Every student was asked to bring in an object or a picture of an object from another country. Write the question and the answer for each item listed.

EXAMPLE: estas monedas / Rusia
            ¿De dónde son estas monedas?
            Son de Rusia.

1. estas castañuelas / España
2. estas maracas / Puerto Rico
3. esta cámara / Japón
4. estas galletas / Inglaterra
5. esta tortilla / México

EXERCISE E

Enrique goes to a watch repair shop. All the watches there show a different time. Tell what time it is on each clock.

EXAMPLE:

Son las cuatro y once.

1.

2.

3.

4.

5.

6.

7.

8.

9.

10.

11.

12.

EXERCISE F

Answer your new friend's questions.

1. ¿Quién es Ud.?

2. ¿De dónde es Ud.?

3. ¿Cuál es su nacionalidad?

4. ¿Cómo es Ud.?

5. ¿De qué color es su casa?

6. ¿De qué material es su casa?

7. ¿Es Ud. un(a) alumno(a) diligente?

8. ¿Cómo son sus hermanos?

9. ¿Qué es su padre?

10. ¿Cómo son sus amigos?

11. ¿Quién es su mejor amigo(a)?

12. ¿De quién es esta cámara?

13. ¿Qué día es hoy?

14. ¿Cuál es la fecha de hoy?

15. ¿Qué hora es?

EXERCISE G

Complete this letter that Carmen received from a new pen pal, using the appropriate forms of the verb *ser*.

Querida Carmen:

Yo _____ Amelia Mariscal. _____ de un pueblo cerca de Buenos Aires.
　　　1.　　　　　　　　　　　　2.

_____ argentina. Mi padre _____ ingeniero. Nuestra casa _____ muy
　3.　　　　　　　　　　　　4.　　　　　　　　　　　　　　5.

bonita. _____ nueva y _____ de ladrillo. Mi dormitorio _____ muy
　　　　6.　　　　　　　7.　　　　　　　　　　　　　　　8.

grande porque yo _____ la hija mayor de la familia. _____ de color
　　　　　　　　　9.　　　　　　　　　　　　　　　10.

rosado y _____ muy lindo. Los dormitorios de mis hermanos (tengo tres)
　　　　11.

_____ más pequeños. La comida argentina _____ muy sabrosa.
　12.　　　　　　　　　　　　　　　　　　13.

Comemos mucha carne. Yo sé cocinar y a veces yo _____ la cocinera y

14.

mis hermanos _____ los meseros. _____ muy cómico cuando

15.   16.

hacemos esto. Yo creo que mis hermanos _____ guapos. También ellos

17.

_____ fuertes y _____ buenos futbolistas. Ya sabes que en mi país

18.   19.

nosotros _____ aficionados al fútbol. Mis hermanos _____ miembros

20.   21.

de un equipo y juegan bien. Ya _____ las cinco de la tarde y _____ la

22.   23.

hora de mi clase de baile. Escríbeme pronto y cuéntame cómo tú _____ y

24.

cuáles _____ tus pasatiempos favoritos. Hasta pronto.

25.

Amelia

[2] USES OF *ESTAR*

Estar is used:

a. to express location or position.

Madrid **está en España.**	*Madrid is in Spain.*
Mi tío **está en México.**	*My uncle is in Mexico.*
El libro **está en la mesa.**	*The book is on the table.*
¿Dónde **están los niños?**	*Where are the children?*

b. to express a condition or state.

La sopa **está caliente.**	*The soup is hot.*
María **está sentada.**	*María is seated.*
El señor Salas **está triste.**	*Mr. Salas is sad.*
¿Cómo **está Ud.? Estoy** muy bien.	*How are you? I'm very well.*
La ventana **está abierta.**	*The window is open.*

NOTE:

1. **Adjectives used with** *estar* **agree with the subject in number and gender.**

Ana **está ocupada.**	*Ana is busy.*
Los jóvenes **están ocupados.**	*The young people are busy.*

2. In questions, the adjective usually follows the verb.

¿Está ocupada Ana? *Is Ana busy?*

¿Están ocupados los jóvenes? *Are the young people busy?*

3. The forms of *estar* are summarized in the section on irregular verbs in the Appendix, page 377.

EXERCISE H

When Luisa comes home from school, she asks her mother where everyone and everything is. Write Luisa's questions and her mother's responses.

EXAMPLE: los refrescos / el refrigerador
¿Dónde están los refrescos?
Están en el refrigerador.

1. el pastel / el horno

2. el correo / la mesa del comedor

3. mis hermanos / el parque

4. mi blusa roja / el armario

5. la revista «Tú» / el sofá

6. tú / la cocina

7. mi diario / la cama

8. papá / la oficina

9. mis zapatos / el cuarto

EXERCISE I

The mathematics teacher is giving back a test. Tell how the students feel.

EXAMPLE: Marta / nervioso
Marta **está nerviosa.**

1. Gabriel / desilusionado

2. Rita y Linda / contento

3. yo / triste

4. Sergei y José / preocupado

5. Inés y Luigi / nervioso

6. Sofía / sorprendido

EXERCISE J

Alicia is working as a waitress. Write the complaints that she gets about what she serves. Use the suggestions below.

el café	agrio
la ensalada	caliente
la hamburguesa	crudo
el helado	derretido
la leche	duro
el pan	frío
las papas fritas	horrible
el refresco	seco
la sopa	viejo

EXAMPLE: La ensalada **está vieja.**

EXERCISE K

Your coach is upset and is delaying the start of practice because two teammates aren't there. Complete the dialogue with the appropriate forms of *estar.*

ENTRENADOR: ¿Quién _____ ausente hoy?
1.

TÚ: Creo que todos nosotros _____ presentes.
2.

RAFAEL: No. José y Roberto no _____ aquí.
3.

ENTRENADOR: ¿Y dónde _____ ellos? Yo _____ preocupado.
4.   5.

PABLO: Roberto y José _____ sentados debajo de un árbol.
6.

TÚ: ¿Por qué _____ ellos allí?
7.

PABLO: José _____ enfermo y Roberto _____ con él.
8.   9.

(Roberto llega.)

ENTRENADOR: Roberto, ¿cómo _____ José?
10.

ROBERTO: Él _____ enfermo.
11.

(José llega.)

ENTRENADOR: ¿Cómo _____ tú?
12.

JOSÉ: Ahora yo _____ bien. Vamos a jugar.
13.

TÚ: Ahora nosotros _____ contentos porque podemos jugar.
14.

EXERCISE L

Susana is trying to understand how people feel in different circumstances. Answer her questions using the cues provided.

1. ¿Cómo estás cuando recibes una buena nota en un examen? *(contento)*
2. ¿Cómo estás cuando no puedes contestar la pregunta del profesor? *(preocupado)*
3. ¿Cómo estás cuando estás solo(a) en la casa? *(nervioso)*
4. ¿Cómo estás cuando el profesor da un examen de sorpresa? *(enojado)*
5. ¿Cómo estás cuando ganas un partido? *(emocionado)*
6. ¿Cómo estás cuando ves una telenovela? *(triste)*
7. ¿Cómo estás cuando comes demasiado chocolate? *(enfermo)*
8. ¿Cómo estás cuando tus padres te dan un coche nuevo? *(sorprendido)*
9. ¿Cómo estás cuando tu novio(a) sale con otra(o) chica(o)? *(celoso)*
10. ¿Cómo estás después de ayudar en casa? *(cansado)*

MASTERY EXERCISES

EXERCISE M

While standing in line for the movies, you hear these statements. Complete them with the appropriate form of *ser* or *estar*.

1. Guillermo _____ sentado porque _____ cansado.
2. En ese cuarto hace calor porque las ventanas _____ cerradas.
3. No comprendo. ¿Dices que Julio _____ peruano pero no _____ de Perú?
4. La madre de Elena _____ enfermera pero ella _____ en el hospital porque _____ enferma.
5. Los señores Arvida _____ ricos. Sus hijos siempre _____ en otras ciudades.
6. En el verano su ropa _____ de algodón, y en el invierno sus pantalones _____ de lana.

7. Tú _____ pálida hoy. ¿Cómo _____ tú?

8. El señor Pardos trabaja mucho. Siempre _____ muy cansado.

9. Los niños _____ preocupados porque no saben dónde _____ su perro.

10. ¿ _____ lunes hoy? ¿Y cuál _____ la fecha?

11. No traigo reloj. ¿Qué hora _____ ?

12. La motocicleta _____ nueva. _____ de mi hermana.

13. Mañana _____ día de fiesta. Yo _____ feliz.

14. Los colores vivos _____ más bonitos que los colores claros.

15. La película _____ aburrida. Nosotros _____ desilusionados.

EXERCISE N

Express in Spanish Amalia's description of an evening at home.

1. Today is Tuesday. It's October fifth.

2. It's eight o'clock.

3. It's a pleasant evening.

4. My father is very tired.

5. John is seated on the sofa.

6. The dog is near him on the floor.

7. My mother is in the kitchen.

8. She's worried because my grandmother is ill.

9. I'm a good student, but tonight I'm nervous.

10. The math assignment is very difficult.

11. My younger sister is unhappy.

12. Her favorite television program is not tonight.

13. The hot chocolate is delicious, but it's not very hot.

14. This pen is my sister's.

15. She's angry because I'm using her pen.

Chapter 9

Commands

[1] FORMAL COMMANDS OF REGULAR VERBS

a. Formal or polite commands are formed by droppng the final -*o* from the first-person singular of the present tense and adding:

1. -*e* for *Ud.* (singular) and -*en* for *Uds.* (plural) in the case of -*ar* verbs.

2. -*a* for *Ud.* and -*an* for *Uds.* in the case of -*er* or -*ir* verbs.

INFINITIVE	PRESENT TENSE FIRST PERSON SINGULAR	COMMAND FORMS SINGULAR	PLURAL	MEANING
abrir	abro	abra	abran	open
cerrar	cierro	cierre	cierren	close
decir	digo	diga	digan	say, tell
hablar	hablo	hable	hablen	speak
hacer	hago	haga	hagan	do, make
leer	leo	lea	lean	read
perder	pierdo	pierda	pierdan	lose
servir	sirvo	sirva	sirvan	serve
tener	tengo	tenga	tengan	have
traducir	traduzco	traduzca	traduzcan	translate
venir	vengo	venga	vengan	come
ver	veo	vea	vean	see
volver	vuelvo	vuelva	vuelvan	return

NOTE:

1. The vowel of the endings of the command forms is the "opposite" of the vowel endings of the third-person singular form of the present tense: -*e* for -*ar* verbs, and -*a* for -*er* and -*ir* verbs.

2. The subject pronoun *(Ud., Uds.)* follows the verb.

3. In Spanish America, *Uds.* can be either formal or informal.

b. To form the negative command, place *no* before the verb.

No hablen inglés.　　　　*Don't speak English.*
No pierda las llaves.　　　*Don't lose the keys.*

c. Verbs that end in *-zar, -car,* and *-gar* have spelling changes in the command forms. The spelling change in *-zar* verbs occurs because in Spanish, *z* is rarely followed by *e* or *i*. The spelling change in *-car* and *-gar* verbs occurs to keep the original sounds of *c* and *g*.

Study the following examples:

INFINITIVE	PRESENT TENSE FIRST PERSON SINGULAR	COMMAND FORMS SINGULAR	PLURAL	MEANING
empezar	empiezo	empiece	empiecen	*begin*
buscar	busco	busque	busquen	*seek*
jugar	juego	juegue	jueguen	*play*

EXERCISE A

The Santiago family just moved into a new house. Their neighbor invites Mrs. Santiago to her home. Write what she tells Mrs. Santiago to do.

EXAMPLE: venir a mi casa
Venga a mi casa.

1. entrar en la casa

2. cerrar la puerta

3. pasar a la cocina

4. tomar un café

5. aprender a conducir

6. asistir a la reunión de la comunidad conmigo

7. subir al segundo piso

8. leer el periódico del barrio

9. pedir instrucciones a la policía

10. recordar nuestra cita mañana

EXERCISE B

Mrs. Ortega's grandchildren are leaving for camp. Write what she tells them to do.

EXAMPLE: prestar atención al consejero
Presten atención al consejero.

1. no pelear con los otros chicos
2. decir la verdad siempre
3. llamar a casa los domingos
4. no perder sus cosas
5. tener paciencia
6. leer muchos libros
7. escribir cada semana
8. comer bien
9. no correr mucho
10. no beber muchos refrescos

EXERCISE C

You have been hired as a waiter (waitress). Write the instructions that the restaurant manager gives you.

EXAMPLE: saludar a los clientes
            Salude a los clientes.

1. ofrecer los platos especiales del día
2. describir los platos si los clientes preguntan
3. contestar sus preguntas
4. preguntar qué van a tomar
5. poner pan y mantequilla en la mesa en seguida
6. traer la comida rápidamente
7. servir la ensalada primero
8. recordar los postres y el café
9. quitar los platos sucios de la mesa
10. dejar la cuenta en la mesa
11. volver a poner la mesa

EXERCISE D

You are moving into a new house, and the moving van has arrived. Tell the movers where to put your things.

1. Señor, *(subir)* _____ estos cartones al segundo piso.

2. Señores, *(colocar)* _____ el sofá contra esta pared.

3. Señor, *(sacar)* _____ las lámparas de la caja.

4. Señores, no *(maltratar)* _____ los cuadros.

5. Señores, *(poner)* _____ esa caja en la cocina.

6. Señor, no *(dejar)* _____ este sillón aquí.

7. Señores, *(leer)* _____ las etiquetas de las cajas.

8. Señor, *(cerrar)* _____ la puerta.

9. Señor, *(tener)* _____ mucho cuidado con esa mesa.

10. Señores, *(volver)* _____ a colocar el sofá contra la otra pared.

[2] FORMAL COMMANDS OF IRREGULAR VERBS

The following verbs have irregular formal command forms:

INFINITIVE	PRESENT TENSE FIRST PERSON SINGULAR	COMMAND FORMS SINGULAR	PLURAL	MEANING
dar	doy	dé	den	*give*
estar	estoy	esté	estén	*be*
ir	voy	vaya	vayan	*go*
ser	soy	sea	sean	*be*

NOTE:

1. *Dé* has an accent mark to distinguish it from *de* (of).

2. *Esté* and *estén* have accent marks to indicate that the stress falls on the last syllable.

EXERCISE E

Write the instructions your mother gave you when you and your brother stayed at a friend's house.

1. *(ser)* ¡ _____ corteses!

2. *(hacer)* ¡ _____ la cama por la mañana!

3. *(poner)* ¡ _____ la ropa en el armario!

4. *(ir)* ¡ _____ despacio!

5. *(dar)* ¡ _____ las gracias después de comer!

6. *(tener)* ¡ _____ mucho cuidado en la casa!

EXERCISE F

You and some friends are in Sevilla for Carnaval. Write the advice the hotel manager gives you as you tell him your plans.

EXAMPLE: Yo traigo mucho dinero. *(no)*
¡**No traiga** mucho dinero!

1. Nosotros buscamos un guía. *(sí)*

2. Llevamos máscaras en Carnaval. *(sí)*

3. Vamos despacio por las calles. *(sí)*

4. Estamos listos para salir del hotel a las diez. *(sí)*

5. Volvemos muy tarde. *(no)*

6. Conduzco mi coche. *(no)*

7. Hacemos caso de los anuncios. *(sí)*

8. Olvido la dirección del hotel. *(no)*

9. Doy una propina al guía. *(sí)*

10. Somos impacientes. *(no)*

[3] AFFIRMATIVE FAMILIAR COMMANDS (SINGULAR)

a. The affirmative *tú* command of regular verbs and stem-changing verbs is the same as the *Ud.* form of the present tense.

INFINITIVE	PRESENT TENSE *Ud.* FORM	MEANING
abrir	**abre**	*open*
cerrar	**cierra**	*close*
dar	**da**	*give*
hablar	**habla**	*speak*
leer	**lee**	*read*
perder	**pierde**	*lose*
servir	**sirve**	*serve*
ver	**ve**	*see*
volver	**vuelve**	*return*

b. The following verbs have irregular affirmative *tú* commands:

INFINITIVE	COMMANDS *TÚ* FORM	MEANING
decir	di	*say, tell*
hacer	haz	*do, make*
ir	ve	*go*
poner	pon	*put*
salir	sal	*leave, go out*
ser	sé	*be*
tener	ten	*have*
venir	ven	*come*

NOTE:

1. Subject pronouns are usually omitted.

2. The familiar commands are used: (1) between friends and class-mates; (2) by parents and other adults when speaking to young children; (3) in other cases where there is a familiar (not a formal) relationship.

EXERCISE G

Write in Spanish the advice your father gave you on your first day of school.

EXAMPLE: llegar temprano a la escuela
            ¡**Llega** temprano a la escuela!

1. prestar atención en las clases

2. escuchar al maestro

3. preparar la tarea cada noche

4. comenzar la tarea al llegar a casa

5. asistir a la escuela todos los días

6. leer la tarea

7. pedir ayuda al maestro

8. escribir la tarea con cuidado

9. pensar antes de hablar

10. recibir buenas notas

EXERCISE H

You are in the kitchen while your mother hurries to finish preparing a special family meal. Write what she tells you to do.

EXAMPLE: tener paciencia conmigo
               ¡**Ten** paciencia conmigo!

1. ser bueno

2. hacer la ensalada

3. ir a la tienda

4. poner la mesa

5. salir de la cocina

6. venir acá

7. decir «buenas tardes» a los invitados

8. tener la bondad de ayudarme

EXERCISE I

Your friends always ask you for advice. What do you tell them to do in these circumstances?

EXAMPLE: La bicicleta de Roberto no funciona. *(pedir prestada la bicicleta de tu hermano)*
               ¡**Pide** prestada la bicicleta de tu hermano!

1. Gloria quiere resolver los problemas de la atmósfera. *(conservar energía, caminar más)*

2. La novia de Jorge no quiere ir al baile de la escuela. *(ir solo)*

3. Roberto pierde muchas cosas. *(tener más cuidado)*

4. Alicia no va a patinar porque sus amigos no quieren ir. *(ser más independiente)*

5. Sarita trabaja y acaba de recibir su primer cheque. *(poner el dinero en el banco)*

6. Felipe necesita un nuevo guante de béisbol. *(ahorrar el dinero)*

[4] NEGATIVE FAMILIAR COMMANDS (SINGULAR)

a. To form a negative *tú* command, use the stem of the *yo* form of the present tense and add *-es* for *-ar* verbs and *-as* for *-er* and *-ir* verbs.

INFINITIVE	PRESENT TENSE FIRST PERSON SINGULAR	NEGATIVE FAMILIAR COMMAND	MEANING
mirar	**miro**	**no mires**	*don't look*
cerrar	**cierro**	**no cierres**	*don't close*
decir	**digo**	**no digas**	*don't say, tell*
leer	**leo**	**no leas**	*don't read*
perder	**pierdo**	**no pierdas**	*don't lose*
servir	**sirvo**	**no sirvas**	*don't serve*
tener	**tengo**	**no tengas**	*don't have*
ver	**veo**	**no veas**	*don't see*

b. The following verbs have irregular *tú* commands:

dar	**no des**	*don't give*
estar	**no estés**	*don't be*
ir	**no vayas**	*don't go*
ser	**no seas**	*don't be*

c. Verbs that end in *-zar*, *-car*, and *-gar* have spelling changes in the negative familiar command forms. The spelling change in *-zar* verbs occurs because in Spanish, *z* is rarely followed by *e* or *i*. The spelling change in *-car* and *-gar* verbs occurs to keep the original sounds of *c* and *g*.

INFINITIVE	PRESENT TENSE FIRST PERSON SINGULAR	NEGATIVE FAMILIAR COMMAND	MEANING
almorzar	**almuerzo**	**no almuerces**	*don't have lunch*
buscar	**busco**	**no busques**	*don't look for*
llegar	**llego**	**no llegues**	*don't arrive*

EXERCISE J

While you're at the beach, you overhear a parent tell her small child not to do the following things. Write what she says.

EXAMPLE: no tomar el agua del mar
　　　　　　　¡**No tomes** el agua del mar!

1. no poner arena en los zapatos
2. no comer arena
3. no estar en el mar solo
4. no caminar lejos
5. no perder los juguetes
6. no tener miedo del agua
7. no tirar arena
8. no me quitar el dinero
9. no molestar a las personas
10. no dejar la cubeta ahí

EXERCISE K

You are sitting in the dentist's waiting room with your younger brother. What do you tell himto do?

EXAMPLE: no gritar
           ¡No grites!

1. no romper la revista
2. no poner los pies en la silla
3. no ir ahí
4. no decir eso
5. no cerrar esa puerta
6. no salir de la oficina
7. no ser malo

M A S T E R Y   E X E R C I S E S

EXERCISE L

You're visiting a botanical garden. As you enter the gate, you read the sign. What are the missing verbs?

1. *(pagar)* ¡ _____ la entrada en la caja!
2. *(entrar)* ¡No _____ sin pagar!
3. *(mirar)* ¡ _____ las flores!
4. *(tocar)* ¡No _____ las flores!
5. *(andar)* ¡ _____ en los caminos!
6. *(correr)* ¡No _____ en la hierba!
7. *(jugar)* ¡No _____ a la pelota en el jardín!
8. *(respetar)* ¡ _____ a las otras personas!
9. *(gritar)* ¡No _____ en el jardín!
10. *(comer)* ¡ _____ solamente en las mesas!

11. *(almorzar)* ¡No _____ en la hierba!

12. *(poner)* ¡ _____ los papeles en la basura!

13. *(tirar)* ¡No _____ papeles en el jardín!

14. *(gozar)* ¡ _____ de la naturaleza!

15. *(salir)* ¡Por favor, no _____ sin visitar nuestra tienda!

16. *(volver)* ¡Por favor, _____ al jardín pronto!

EXERCISE M

Several friends are helping you set up for a party. Tell them what to do.

1. *(colgar)* ¡Ricardo, _____ los globos ahí!

2. *(poner)* ¡Gladys, _____ los refrescos en esa mesa!

3. *(colocar)* ¡Arturo, no _____ las decoraciones en la puerta!

4. *(traer)* ¡Estela, no _____ el pastel ahora!

5. *(preparar)* ¡Mirta, _____ la limonada ahora!

6. *(sacar)* ¡Ricardo, no _____ los discos todavía!

7. *(dejar)* ¡John, no _____ los platos ahí!

8. *(ir)* ¡Estela, _____ a la tienda para comprar hielo!

9. *(ayudar)* ¡Mirta, _____ a Arturo con las decoraciones!

10. *(abrir)* ¡Gladys, no _____ los regalos!

EXERCISE N

You're on a school trip, and the counselor gives the group the following instructions before leaving the airport in Caracas.

EXAMPLE: venir acá
             ¡**Vengan** acá!

1. poner las maletas en el autobús

2. subir al autobús rápidamente

3. no gritar en el autobús

4. respetar al chófer

5. bajar el equipaje del autobús

6. no perder el pasaporte

7. subir al cuarto en seguida

8. volver en quince minutos

9. no dejar nada de valor en el cuarto
10. no dar la llave a extraños
11. no perder la llave
12. cerrar bien la puerta del cuarto
13. recordar el número del cuarto
14. no olvidar el nombre del hotel
15. no pedir vino en el restaurante
16. no ser irresponsables
17. obedecer todas las reglas
18. no gastar todo el dinero
19. leer bien el itinerario
20. traer la cámara

EXERCISE O

You are directing a school play and are giving the actors instructions. Express the following in Spanish.

1. Everyone, pay attention now.
2. Gloria, speak louder.
3. Rafael, don't lose the ball.
4. Alicia, come closer.
5. John, don't make noises.
6. Everyone, practice the dance.
7. Everyone, listen to the music.
8. Sergio, don't bring food here.
9. Alfredo, wait a minute.
10. Mrs. Beltrán, play the song again, please.
11. Everyone, rest for ten minutes.
12. José, don't put the chairs there.
13. Francisco, repeat that phrase.
14. Jorge, ask the question again.
15. Everyone, don't be so disagreeable.

Chapter 10
Preterite Tense of Regular Verbs

[1] REGULAR -AR VERBS

a. The preterite tense of regular *-ar* verbs is formed by dropping the infinitive ending *-ar* and adding the personal endings *-é, -aste, -ó, -amos, -asteis, -aron.*

	hablar *to speak*	**cerrar** *to close*
yo	habl**é**	cerr**é**
tú	habl**aste**	cerr**aste**
Ud., él, ella	habl**ó**	cerr**ó**
nosotros, -as	habl**amos**	cerr**amos**
vosotros, -as	habl**asteis**	cerr**asteis**
Uds., ellos, ellas	habl**aron**	cerr**aron**

b. The first-person plural ending *(-amos)* is the same as in the present tense: *tomamos* (*we take, we took*).

c. Most verbs that are stem-changing (*o* to *ue*; *e* to *ie*) do not change the stem in the preterite tense: (*cerrar*) Present—*cierro*; Preterite—*cerré.*

d. The preterite tense has the following meanings in English:

Ud. habló   *you spoke, you did speak*

yo cerré   *I closed, I did close*

e. Verbs that end in *-car, -gar,* and *-zar* have a spelling change in the *yo* form. In *-car* and *-gar* verbs, this change occurs to keep the original sound of the *c* and *g*. The change occurs in *-zar* verbs because *z* rarely precedes *e* or *i* in Spanish.

sacar   yo saqué

jugar   yo jugué

empezar   yo empecé

Other verbs that have these changes are:

-car   practicar, tocar, buscar

-gar   llegar, pagar

-zar   comenzar, almorzar

[2] USES OF THE PRETERITE

a. The preterite tense is used to narrate an action or event in the past. It may indicate the beginning or end of the action, or the complete action or event begun and finished in the past.

   (1) Beginning or End

      Joe comenzó a trabajar.   *Joe began to work.*

      Cerraron la tienda.   *They closed the store.*

   (2) Complete Action

      Visité a mi tía ayer.   *I visited my aunt yesterday.* (I went and returned.)

b. Some expressions that are often used with the preterite are:

anoche *last night*	**la semana pasada** *last week*
ayer *yesterday*	**el año pasado** *last year*
anteayer *the day before yesterday*	**el mes pasado** *last month*

EXERCISE A

Alejandro describes what he and his family did last night. Tell what he says.

EXAMPLE: mi padre / jugar al tenis
               Mi padre **jugó** al tenis.

1. yo / estudiar para un examen

2. mi mamá / preparar un pastel

3. mi hermana / limpiar su cuarto

4. Roberto y yo / mirar un programa de televisión

5. Marta y tú / trabajar en la tienda

6. mis hermanos / patinar

EXERCISE B

Laura spent last summer with her family on a farm. What does she say they did there?

EXAMPLE: mi tío / plantar maíz
               Mi tío **plantó** maíz.

1. yo / caminar en el bosque

2. Carlos / ayudar a mi tío

3. mi mamá y mi tía / cocinar mucho

4. mi papá / cortar la hierba

5. mi abuela / cuidar los pollos

6. Ernesto y yo / nadar en un lago

EXERCISE C

Alfonso has just returned from a trip to Spain. Using the words in parentheses, answer the questions Rafael asks him.

1. ¿Qué país visitaste? *(España)*

2. ¿Con quién viajaste? *(mi familia)*

3. ¿Cuánto tiempo pasaron Uds. allí? *(quince días)*

4. ¿Quién pagó el viaje? *(mi padre)*

5. ¿Cómo viajaron Uds.? *(en avión y en autobús)*

6. ¿Alquilaron Uds. un coche allí? *(no)*

7. ¿A qué ciudad llegaron Uds.? *(Madrid)*

8. ¿En qué ciudad terminaste el viaje? *(Málaga)*

9. ¿Entraste en muchos museos? *(sí)*

10. ¿Sacó tu hermano muchas fotos? *(sí)*

EXERCISE D

Complete this letter that Teresa writes to a friend by filling in the appropriate preterite form of the verbs indicated.

Querida Alicia:

Ayer yo _____ en ti varias veces. Yo _____ a escribir esta carta
      1. (pensar)   2. (comenzar)

en muchas ocasiones pero nunca _____ a terminar la carta. Anoche la
                   3. (llegar)

orquesta de la escuela _____ en una competencia. Yo _____ el
          4. (tocar)   5. (tocar)

violín y nosotros. _____ el premio de segundo lugar. El coro
       6. (ganar)

_____ también pero no _____ ningún premio. Todavía me
 7. (cantar)   8. (ganar)

fascina la música y el mes pasado yo_____ a estudiar la guitarra.
               9. (empezar)

Como ves, _____ el violín por un instrumento «menos serio».
10. (cambiar)

La semana pasada yo _____ mi cumpleaños. Mis padres me
11. (celebrar)

_____ muchos regalos bonitos. Mi familia me _____ a cenar
12. (regalar)   13. (llevar)

en un restaurante elegante. Nosotros _____ un buen rato allí. Después,
14. (pasar)

dos amigos me _____ a una discoteca y nosotros _____ hasta la
15. (invitar)   16. (bailar)

medianoche. Yo _____ a casa cansada pero contenta. Al día siguiente
17. (llegar)

yo _____ al tenis con mis hermanos pero ellos _____ .
18. (jugar)   19. (ganar)

¿Cómo _____ tú tu cumpleaños? ¿ _____ tú algún lugar
20. (pasar)   21. (visitar)

divertido? ¿A quién _____ ? Yo _____ la foto que tu padre
22. (invitar)   23. (buscar)

_____ de nosotras en la fiesta, pero no la _____ .
24. (sacar)   25. (encontrar)

Hasta pronto.

Teresa

EXERCISE E

Tell whether or not you and your friends did these things yesterday.

EXAMPLE: escuchar discos
            Mi amigo Pedro **escuchó** discos ayer.
    OR: Yo **no escuché** discos ayer.

1. practicar un deporte
2. trabajar mucho
3. descansar por la tarde
4. lavar el carro
5. usar la aspiradora
6. sacar fotografías
7. buscar un disco nuevo
8. almorzar en el centro

EXERCISE F

Answer these questions that a friend asks while you're riding the school bus together one morning.

1. ¿Qué programa de televisión miraste anoche?
2. ¿Hablaste con tus amigos por teléfono anoche?
3. ¿Qué música tocaste?
4. ¿Estudiaron juntos tú y Alicia para el examen?
5. ¿Prepararon Uds. la escena para la clase de español?
6. ¿Terminaste la carta a tu amigo por correspondencia?
7. ¿Preguntaste a tus padres si puedes cenar conmigo esta noche?
8. ¿Qué desayunaste hoy?

EXERCISE G

Gloria is showing her yearbook to a cousin. Write what the person in each picture did.

EXAMPLE:

Lorenzo sacó fotografías.

1. Yo _____ .

2. Gilberto y Anita _____ .

3. Ricardo _____ .

4. Juan y yo _____ .

5. Sarita _____ .

[3] REGULAR *-ER* AND *-IR* VERBS

a. The preterite tense of regular *-er* and *-ir* verbs is formed by dropping the infinitive ending *-er* or *-ir* and adding the personal endings *-í, -iste, -ió, -imos, -isteis, -ieron.*

	perder *to lose*	**abrir** *to open*
yo	perd*í*	abr*í*
tú	perd*iste*	abr*iste*
Ud., él, ella	perd*ió*	abr*ió*
nosotros, -as	perd*imos*	abr*imos*
vosotros, -as	perd*isteis*	abr*isteis*
Uds., ellos, ellas	perd*ieron*	abr*ieron*

b. The preterite endings are the same for *-er* and *-ir* verbs.

c. In *-ir* verbs, the first-person plural ending (*-imos*) is the same as in the present tense. In *-er* verbs, however, the endings are different.

viv*imos*   *we live*   viv*imos*   *we lived*
beb*emos*   *we drink*   beb*imos*   *we drank*

d. The accent mark is omitted over the following forms of *ver*: *vi, vio.*

e. Stem-changing verbs ending in *-er* do not change the stem vowel in the preterite tense. Stem-changing verbs ending in *-ir* have special stem changes in the preterite and are discussed in Chapter 11.

EXERCISE H

Raúl and some friends are telling what they had for dinner last night. Write what they say.

EXAMPLE: Rosa / arroz con frijoles
            Rosa **comió** arroz con frijoles.

1. Luis y Daniel / pescado

2. yo / arroz con pollo

3. Alicia / una ensalada

4. Bobby y yo / hamburguesas

5. tú / chuletas de cerdo

6. ellos / paella

EXERCISE I

The students are selecting their courses for the following year. What did they decide to study?

EXAMPLE: Tomás / francés
Tomás **decidió estudiar** francés.

1. Lola / literatura

2. Carmen y Mary / baile

3. yo / biología

4. José y yo / música

5. tú / química

6. Jane / geografía

EXERCISE J

You're talking to a new friend who spent part of her life in the Dominican Republic. Write the questions you ask her about her background.

EXAMPLE: dónde / aprender el español
¿Dónde **aprendiste** el español?

1. cuándo / vivir en Santo Domingo

2. a qué escuela / asistir

3. cuándo / volver a los Estados Unidos

4. cuándo / decidir volver aquí

5. por qué / salir de Santo Domingo

EXERCISE K

Complete this letter that Ramona, who is visiting acquaintances in Mexico, writes to a friend back in her hometown.

Querida Gabriela:

Anoche yo _____ a una fiesta en casa de mi amiga Lourdes. Ellos
               1. (asistir)

_____ el cumpleaños de su hermana menor. Muchas personas
2. (celebrar)

_____ a la fiesta y la hermana de Lourdes _____ muchos regalos.
  3 (asistir)   4. (recibir)

La fiesta _____ a las nueve de la noche. Muchas personas no
          5. (comenzar)

_____ hasta las diez. Un grupo de mariachis _____
  6. (llegar)   7. (cantar)

«Las mañanitas» a la hermana de Lourdes. Yo no _____ todas las
                                                8. (entender)

palabras, pero me _____ mucho y _____ dos canciones más.
                   9. (gustar)   10. (aprender)

Cuando _____ los mariachis, el padre de Lourdes _____ una
        11. (terminar)   12. (colgar)

piñata y todos nosotros _____ de romperla. Un joven guapo
                        13. (tratar)

_____ la piñata.
  14. (romper)

Nosotros _____ y _____ muy bien. La mamá de Lourdes y sus
         15. (comer)   16. (beber)

tías _____ unos platillos muy sabrosos. Yo _____ tacos de
     17. (preparar)   18. (comer)

pollo y tamales. La mamá de Lourdes _____ enseñarme a preparar
                                     19. (prometer)

los tamales. Yo _____ a casa a las doce y media de la noche.
                20. (volver)

Hasta pronto.

Ramona

EXERCISE L

Answer these questions from your older sister. Use the cues provided.

1. ¿A qué hora saliste de la casa anoche? *(7:00)*

2. ¿Con quién asististe al concierto? *(Manuela)*

3. ¿Qué decidieron Uds. hacer después del concierto? *(ir a un restaurante)*

4. ¿Dónde comieron Uds.? *(el Café Colón)*

5. ¿Qué comiste? *(una hamburguesa)*

6. ¿A qué hora prometiste estar en la casa? *(11:00)*

7. ¿Cómo volviste a casa? *(en taxi)*

8. ¿A qué hora abriste la puerta de la casa? *(11:30)*

MASTERY EXERCISES

EXERCISE M

Describe what you and a friend did during a weekend trip to another city. Use the suggestions below.

asistir a un concierto	gastar mucho dinero
caminar por la ciudad	jugar al tenis (boliche . . .)
comer en un restaurante español	perder la cartera
comprar unos discos	ver a unos amigos
correr en una carrera	visitar el museo

EXERCISE N

While visiting Costa Rica, you meet a girl who used to be an exchange student at your school. Tell her about yourself and the other people you both knew there.

EXAMPLE: el señor Álvarez / dejar de enseñar
El señor Álvarez **dejó** de enseñar.

1. Miriam / volver a vivir en Puerto Rico

2. Jorge y Pedro / asistir a la misma universidad

3. Eddy / abrir una tienda de juguetes

4. tu professor de inglés / escribir un libro de poemas

5. yo / ver a Daniel en España

6. Malika y yo / viajar a Europa

7. las hermanas Silva / correr en muchas carreras

8. Janet / recibir una beca

9. Alicia y Berta / aprender el japonés

10. la señora Oyama / salir de la escuela

EXERCISE O

You have to give an oral report about your trip abroad last summer. Express in Spanish what you plan to say.

1. Last summer I spent one month in Europe.

2. My friends and I visited three countries.

3. We flew to Madrid.

4. We decided to travel by bus and bicycle in each country.

5. I learned to ride a bicycle very well.

6. I saw many interesting monuments.

7. I met young people in each city.

8. Many times they invited us to eat dinner in their homes.

9. Pablo lost his passport in Paris.

10. He left his passport at the bank when he changed a traveler's check.

11. The police found his passport.

12. They returned the passport to Pablo.

13. In Madrid, I understood the people when they spoke Spanish, but I answered in English.

14. I looked for a Spanish dictionary.

15. I forgot to bring my dictionary with me.

16. I paid five thousand pesetas for the dictionary.

17. I also took many pictures in each city.

18. We returned home tired but happy.

19. We learned a great deal during the trip.

20. We became acquainted with many nice young people.

Chapter 11

Verbs Irregular in the Preterite Tense

[1] PRETERITE TENSE OF -*IR* STEM-CHANGING VERBS

a. Stem-changing verbs ending in -*ir* change the stem vowel *e* to *i* and *o* to *u* in the third-person singular and plural of the preterite tense.

	servir *to serve*	**dormir** *to sleep*
yo	serví	dormí
tú	serviste	dormiste
Ud., él, ella	s*i*rvió	d*u*rmió
nosotros, -as	servimos	dormimos
vosotros, -as	servisteis	dormisteis
Uds., ellos, ellas	s*i*rvieron	d*u*rmieron

b. Other verbs that change *e* to *i* are:

medir *to measure*	referir *to tell*	sentir *to feel*
pedir *to ask for*	reñir *to argue*	vestir *to dress*
preferir *to prefer*	repetir *to repeat*	

Other verbs that change *o* to *u* are:

morir *to die*	podrir *to rot*

c. Verbs ending in -*ar* or -*er* that are stem-changing don't change the stem vowel in the preterite tense.

pensar *to think:* pensé, pensaste, pensó,
pensamos, pensasteis, pensaron

volver *to return:* volví, volviste, volvió,
volvimos, volvisteis, volvieron

EXERCISE A

Luis tells what he and his friends preferred to do yesterday. Write what he says.

EXAMPLE: Paul y yo / ir al cine
Paul y yo **preferimos** ir al cine.

1. Enrique / ir a la piscina

2. tú / ver a tus amigos

3. Abdul y Mateo / montar en bicicleta

4. Jean y yo / ir a la playa

5. mi hermano / ver una película

6. Marta / mirar la televisión

7. ellos / jugar al fútbol

EXERCISE B

You overhear your mother on the phone telling a friend how late everyone slept. Write in Spanish what she says.

EXAMPLE: mi esposo y yo / 7:30
            Mi esposo y yo **dormimos hasta** las siete y media

1. Alejandro / 12:00

2. María y Elena / 10:30

3. tú / 8:15

4. Gregorio y Felipe / 11:00

5. yo / 7:00

6. mi padre / 5:00

EXERCISE C

Carmen is writing in her diary about the night she stayed at Raquel's house. Fill in the appropriate preterite forms of the verbs given.

Yo _____ pasar la noche en casa de Raquel porque nosotras _____
    1. (decidir)   *2. (volver)*

tarde del teatro. Antes de ir al teatro, nosotras _____ en un restaurante
                                                   3. (comer)

francés. Yo _____ sopa de cebollas y me _____ mucho. Raquel
        4. (pedir)   *5. (gustar)*

_____ caracoles pero no le _____ . Ella _____ no volver a ese
6. (pedir)   *7. (gustar)*   *8. (resolver)*

restaurante. A veces Raquel es antipática. Ella _____ al mesero una vez
                                           9. (reñir)

y luego le _____ su orden. Yo no _____ bien en su casa pero
        10. (repetir)   *11. (dormir)*

Raquel _____ profundamente toda la noche.
      12. (dormir)

[2] VERBS THAT CHANGE *I* TO *Y* IN THE PRETERITE

a. *-er* and *-ir* verbs whose stems end in a vowel change the endings of the preterite tense from *-ió* to *-yó* in the third-person singular and from *-ieron* to *-yeron* in the third-person plural. The endings for all other persons take an accent on the *-i*.

caer *to fall*			
yo	caí	nosotros, -as	caímos
tú	caíste	vosotros, -as	caísteis
Ud., él, ella	*cayó*	Uds., ellos, ellas	*cayeron*

b. Verbs like *caer:*

construir *to build*   leer *to read*

creer *to believe*   oír *to hear*

distribuir *to distribute*   poseer *to possess; to own*

incluir *to include*

EXERCISE D

Some friends are telling what they heard on the radio last night. Write what they say.

EXAMPLE: nosotros / las noticias
Nosotros **oímos** las noticias.

1. tú / el tiempo

2. Tiffany / un debate

3. Felipe y Nicolás / un partido de fútbol

4. yo / música

5. ellos / un concierto

6. Beverly y yo / un concurso

EXERCISE E

The students in the woodworking class tell what they built. Write what they say.

EXAMPLE: Esteban / una mesa
Esteban **construyó** una mesa.

1. yo / una lámpara
2. ellos / un librero
3. Sarita / un marco
4. tú / un banco
5. Chun y Susan / una caja
6. Juan y yo / una silla

EXERCISE F

Some neighbors are discussing an incident that took place nearby. Write what they say.

EXAMPLE: yo / creer que mi hijo / cerrar la puerta
Yo **creí** que mi hijo **cerró** la puerta.

1. mi esposo / oír las noticias en el radio del carro
2. los señores Delgado / construir esa casa el año pasado
3. yo / leer las noticias en el periódico
4. la policía / incluir a mi hermano en la investigación
5. nosotros / creer / que un meteoro / caer en la casa
6. La explosión / destruir toda la casa de los señores Delgado y / romper las ventanas de mi casa

[3] *I*-STEM VERBS IN THE PRETERITE

The following verbs have irregular stems and endings in the preterite:

	hacer *to do;* *to make*	querer *to want;* *to love*	venir *to come*
yo	hice	quise	vine
tú	hiciste	quisiste	viniste
Ud., él, ella	hizo	quiso	vino
nosotros, -as	hicimos	quisimos	vinimos
vosotros, -as	hicisteis	quisisteis	vinisteis
Uds., ellos, ellas	hicieron	quisieron	vinieron

NOTE: The preterite endings of *i*-stem verbs do not have accent marks.

EXERCISE G

Mrs. Montes organized a potluck dinner. She tells who made each dish. Write what she says.

EXAMPLE: Silvia / el pastel de chocolate
Silvia **hizo** el pastel de chocolate.

1. yo / la ensalada

2. los señores Rivas / la paella

3. Carmen / las legumbres

4. tú / el té helado

5. Rosa y yo / el arroz con pollo

6. Uds. / el flan

EXERCISE H

Roberto is not speaking to any of his friends because they didn't want to do what he wanted to do. Tell what his friends wanted to do.

EXAMPLE: Jaime / montar en bicicleta
Jaime **quiso** montar en bicicleta.

1. Yolanda / ir al cine

2. Kenji / estudiar

3. tú / sacar fotografías

4. Eduardo y Patricia / mirar la televisión

5. Gabriel y yo / jugar al voleibol

6. Tony / descansar

EXERCISE I

Caterina tells her cousin how the members of her family came to her grandparents' anniversary party. Write what she says.

EXAMPLE: mi hermana / en taxi
Mi hermana **vino** en taxi.

1. mis tíos / en autobús

2. el hermano de mi abuela / en tren

3. mis hermanos y yo / en coche

4. mi tía / en avión

5. mis padres / en coche

6. tú / a pie

7. mi madrina / en motocicleta

EXERCISE J

Answer these questions that a friend asks you. Use the words in parentheses.

1. ¿Hiciste la tarea anoche? *(sí)*

2. ¿Vinieron Carlos y Juanita a la escuela hoy? *(no)*

3. ¿Qué quiso hacer Alfredo el sábado pasado? *(ir de compras)*

4. ¿Cuándo vinieron tus primos a verte? *(el agosto pasado)*

5. ¿Cómo vino Berta a la escuela hoy? *(en taxi)*

6. ¿Por qué vino ella en taxi? *(perder el autobús)*

7. ¿Qué hizo tu mamá para cenar anoche? *(pollo)*

[4] *U*-STEM VERBS IN THE PRETERITE

The following verbs have irregular stems and endings in the preterite:

INFINITIVE	STEM	PRETERITE FORMS
andar	anduv	anduve, anduviste, anduvo anduvimos, anduvisteis, anduvieron
estar	estuv	estuve, estuviste, estuvo estuvimos, estuvisteis, estuvieron
poder	pud	pude, pudiste, pudo pudimos, pudisteis, pudieron
poner	pus	puse, pusiste, puso pusimos, pusisteis, pusieron
saber	sup	supe, supiste, supo supimos, supisteis, supieron
tener	tuv	tuve, tuviste, tuvo tuvimos, tuvisteis, tuvieron

NOTE: The preterite endings of *u*-stem verbs do not have accent marks.

[5] THE VERBS *DAR, SER,* AND *IR*

The verbs *dar, ser,* and *ir* are also irregular in the preterite. *Dar* takes the endings of regular *-er, -ir* verbs, but without a written accent in the first- and third-person singular forms. *Ser* and *ir* have the same forms in the preterite.

dar *to give*   di, diste, dio, dimos, disteis, dieron

ser *to be*
ir *to go* } fui, fuiste, fue, fuimos, fuisteis, fueron

EXERCISE K

Gerardo describes what he and a friend did last Saturday. Complete the statements with the correct forms of the preterite tense.

El sábado pasado Enrique y yo _____ al centro. Nosotros _____ allí
    1. (ir)   2. (estar)

porque yo _____ que comprar una nueva raqueta de tenis. Nosotros no
      3. (tener)

_____ encontrar la tienda que recomendó un amigo de Enrique. Este
4. (poder)

amigo le _____ un papel con el nombre y la dirección de la tienda a
      5. (dar)

Enrique, pero él no _____ recordar dónde _____ ese papel. Enrique
          6. (poder)   7. (poner)

_____ que llamar por teléfono a su amigo y luego nosotros _____
8. (tener)   9. (ir)

a la tienda. Yo le _____ las gracias a Enrique por su ayuda.
          10. (dar)

EXERCISE L

Conchita and some friends are talking about what they did during the spring vacation. Tell what they say, using the preterite tense.

EXAMPLE: yo / hacer un viaje en autobús
        Yo **hice** un viaje en autobús.

1. Bonnie / andar en la playa

2. Paul y Eduardo / ir a Puerto Rico

3. nosotros / dar muchos paseos en el parque

4. tú / tener que trabajar

5. yo / estar en casa de una prima

6. Uds. / poder divertirse en casa

EXERCISE M

Answer the questions that a friend asks you about a party he didn't attend at Lorenzo's home.

1. ¿Con quién fuiste a la fiesta?
2. ¿Quiénes estuvieron allí?
3. ¿Supo Lorenzo por qué yo no fui a la fiesta?
4. ¿Cómo fuiste a casa de Lorenzo?
5. ¿Cómo fue la música?
6. ¿Pudiste bailar con Estela?
7. ¿Fueron Uds. al jardín de la casa?
8. ¿Tuviste que volver a casa temprano?
9. ¿Estuviste en casa a esa hora?
10. ¿Quién puso las decoraciones?

MASTERY EXERCISES

EXERCISE N

Your sister has just returned from an exchange program in Colombia. Answer the questions a friend asks you about her trip.

1. ¿Cuánto tiempo estuvo ella en Colombia?
2. ¿A quién pidió ella permiso para ir?
3. ¿Hizo ella el viaje sola?
4. ¿Con quién fue a Colombia?
5. ¿Cómo fue la familia con que vivió?
6. ¿Pudiste pedirle muchos regalos?
7. ¿Pudo ella traer muchas cosas?
8. ¿Qué quiso ella hacer allí?
9. ¿Tuviste que ir al aeropuerto cuando llegó?
10. ¿Quién más fue a recibirla al aeropuerto?
11. ¿Cómo supiste la hora de su llegada?

12. ¿Durmió ella en el avión?

13. ¿Quién vino con ella?

14. ¿Tuvo ella alguna dificultad en Colombia?

15. ¿Qué ciudad de Colombia prefirió ella?

EXERCISE O

Complete the latest entry in Laura's diary, using the correct forms of the preterite tense.

Hoy por la mañana yo _____ en casa de mi amiga Gloria. Su padre
       1. (estar)

_____ una casita de muñecas para su hermana menor, Teresa.
2. (construir)

_____ una sorpresa para la niña. Teresa y yo _____ los muebles en
  3. (ser)   *4. (poner)*

la casa. Después nosotras _____ al centro para comprar otros muebles.
              5. (ir)

Nosotras _____ por muchas tiendas hasta que nosotras _____ con
     6. (andar)   *7. (dar)*

unos muebles bonitos. Teresa _____ comprar todos los muebles pero
                    8. (preferir)

nosotras no _____ encontrar una mesita para el comedor. Ella
      9. (poder)

_____ un catálogo de muebles y _____ una mesita bonita. Antes de
10. (leer)   *11. (pedir)*

salir de la casa, Teresa y Gloria _____ las ventanitas de la casita. Ellas
                       12. (medir)

_____ tela e _____ cortinas para todos los cuartos de la casita.
13. (comprar)   *14. (hacer)*

Yo quería comprar un regalito para Teresa pero no _____ encontrar
                                  15. (poder)

nada. Cuando regresamos a casa, Teresa _____ a llorar. La casita de
                         16. (ponerse)

muñecas _____ de la mesa al suelo. Yo _____ mucho lo que pasó.
      17. (caer)   *18. (sentir)*

El perro _____ la casa al correr a la puerta. La madre de Teresa
       19. (destruir)

_____ al perro y el perro _____ que estar en el jardín. Yo
20. (reñir)   *21. (tener)*

_____ a casa a las ocho de la noche.
22. (venir)

EXERCISE P

Express in Spanish what Elisa tells a friend about her date with Jamal.

1. I wasn't nervous.
2. The weather was bad.
3. Jamal and I went to the movies.
4. I put my wallet in my purse.
5. I couldn't find my keys.
6. We walked to the movie theater.
7. We had to wait in line.
8. I read the posters about the film.
9. Jamal preferred to see another film.
10. We quarreled.
11. We had to sit in the second row of the theater.
12. The ticket included a box of popcorn.
13. I gave Jamal some popcorn.
14. He asked for more popcorn.
15. He slept in the theater.
16. It was a terrible movie.
17. After the movie, I went home.
18. Jamal wanted to go with me.
19. I preferred to return alone.
20. He went to a party.

Chapter 12
Imperfect Tense

[1] REGULAR VERBS

a. The imperfect tense of regular verbs is formed by dropping the infinitive ending *(-ar, -er, -ir)*, and adding the following endings:

INFINITIVE	STEM	IMPERFECT ENDINGS
mostrar	mostr	-aba, -abas, -aba, -ábamos, -abais, -aban
volver	volv	-ía, -ías, -ía, -íamos, -íais, -ían
abrir	abr	-ía, -ías, -ía, -íamos, -íais, -ían

b. Verbs that are stem-changing in the present tense do not change the stem vowel in the imperfect.

c. The first- and third-person singular forms are the same. Subject pronouns are used if necessary to clarify the meaning of the verb.

EXERCISE A

At a high-school reunion, some friends are remembering where they used to eat lunch when they were students. Write what they say.

EXAMPLE: Shaquille / la cafetería / siempre
Shaquille **almorzaba en** la cafetería siempre.

1. Luis y Yoko / el parque / a veces

2. tú / el restaurante / de vez en cuando

3. Jack y yo / casa / siempre

4. yo / la clase de arte / todos los días

5. ellos / el gimnasio / con frecuencia

6. nosotros / el patio de la escuela / a veces

7. mis primos / mi casa

EXERCISE B

David and some friends have given up eating sweets. What did they used to eat?

EXAMPLE: Pedro / helado todos los días
Pedro **comía** helado todos los días.

1. Pascal / muchos chocolates

2. Yolanda / pastel en cada comida

3. Carol y yo / dulces todos los días

4. Arturo y Nick / flan con frecuencia

5. tú / helado después de las clases

6. María / jalea de guayaba

EXERCISE C

A group of friends are telling where they used to live. Write what they say.

EXAMPLE: Juan / Nevada
            Juan **vivía en** Nevada.

1. yo / Tejas

2. Ana / California

3. los hermanos Casero / Honduras

4. tú / la Florida

5. Fabiana y yo / San Juan

6. Uds. / Nueva York

EXERCISE D

Javier describes what life was like when he was younger. Write what he says.

EXAMPLE: nosotros / vivir en una casa grande
            Nosotros **vivíamos** en una casa grande.

1. yo / tener un perro

2. mis hermanos / jugar al fútbol conmigo

3. mi mamá / no trabajar

4. toda la familia / visitar a los abuelos los domingos

5. mi abuela / preparar comidas deliciosas

6. mis amigos y yo / correr en la calle

7. tú / hacer muchas bromas

8. mi papá / tener un automóvil convertible

9. mi hermano mayor / querer aprender a conducir

10. nosotros / salir de la ciudad con frecuencia

EXERCISE E

Your little brother asks your grandfather questions about his life. Answer his questions in the imperfect, using the cues provided.

1. ¿Dónde vivías cuando tenías mi edad? *(en un pueblo)*

2. ¿Con quién vivías? *(mis padres y hermanos)*

3. ¿Jugabas al béisbol a veces? *(sí)*

4. ¿Conocías a mi abuela cuando Uds. estaban en la escuela? *(no)*

5. ¿Asistían Uds. a la misma escuela? *(no)*

6. ¿Tenías una bicicleta? *(sí)*

7. ¿Cómo celebrabas tu cumpleaños? *(una fiesta)*

8. ¿Te daban muchos regalos? *(sí)*

9. ¿Nadaban tú y tus amigos en una piscina? *(un lago)*

10. ¿De qué tenías miedo? *(nada)*

[2] VERBS IRREGULAR IN THE IMPERFECT TENSE

There are three irregular verbs in the imperfect tense: *ir*, *ser*, and *ver*.

INFINITIVE	IMPERFECT ENDINGS
ir	iba, ibas, iba, íbamos, ibais, iban
ser	era, eras, era, éramos, erais, eran
ver	veía, veías, veía, veíamos, veíais, veían

EXERCISE F

Write where these people used to go in the summer.

EXAMPLE: José / a la playa
José **iba** a la playa.

1. tú / a las montañas

2. mi hermana y yo / al campamento

3. Hugo / a casa de sus abuelos

4. yo / al campo

5. Rodolfo y César / a la escuela

6. Ud. / al extranjero

EXERCISE G

Write what these people were like when they were younger.

EXAMPLE: Gladys / muy alta
            Gladys **era** muy alta.

1. yo / tímido

2. Patricia / bonita

3. los niños / traviesos

4. tú / cariñoso

5. Nilda y Victoria / muy enérgicas

6. Esteban y yo / consentidos

EXERCISE H

Write the types of programs these people used to watch.

EXAMPLE: mi mamá / telenovelas todos los días
            Mi mamá **veía** telenovelas todos los días.

1. Enrique / las películas policíacas los sábados

2. tú / los deportes los lunes

3. mi papá y yo / el reportaje deportivo cada noche

4. Kyoko y Pilar / las comedias

5. Pat y Mike / las noticias cada noche

6. Uds. / los programas de ciencia ficción cada semana

EXERCISE I

Tell who used to do these things. Write about each activity using the imperfect tense.

ayudar a mi madre siempre
ir al circo en la primavera
ir de compras con sus amigas los sábados
jugar al tenis cada sábado
practicar con el equipo por la tarde
vender limonada en el verano
ver los concursos cada noche

1. Mi abuela _____.

2. Yo _____.

3. Mis hermanos y yo _____.

4. Mis amigos _____.

5. Tú _____.

6. Mi hermana _____.

7. Mi prima _____.

[3] USES OF THE IMPERFECT TENSE

The imperfect tense is used:

a. to express what used to happen.

Íbamos a México todos los veranos.	*We would go (used to go) to Mexico every summer.*
Yo tocaba la guitarra.	*I played (used to play) the guitar.*

b. to express what happened repeatedly in the past.

Yo trabajaba a menudo durante las vacaciones.	*I often worked (used to work) during vacation.*
Pablo **me llamaba** mucho.	*Pablo called (used to call) me a lot.*

c. to describe what was going on at a particular time.

Leía el periódico durante el concierto.	*I read (was reading) the newspaper during the concert.*

d. to describe simultaneous actions in the past. *Mientras* is usually used to connect the two actions.

Yo **escribía** una carta **mientras** escuchaba la radio.	*I wrote a letter while I listened to the radio.*

e. to describe what was going on in the past (imperfect) when something else began or ended (preterite). *Cuando* usually links the two actions.

Yo **escribía** una carta **cuando** Carlos entró.	*I was writing a letter when Carlos entered.*

f. to describe persons or things in the past.

Jane **era** alta y bonita.	*Jane was tall and pretty.*
Los aviones **eran** muy grandes.	*The planes were very large.*

g. to express the time of day (hour) in the past.

Eran las once.	*It was eleven o'clock.*

EXERCISE J

The weather often affects what people do. Felipe's talking about the things he and his friends used to do in different kinds of weather. Write what he says, using the imperfect tense.

EXAMPLE:

Yo **iba a la playa cuando hacía sol.**

1. Alicia y Melique _____ .

2. Federico, John y yo _____ .

3. Tú _____ .

4. Yo _____ .

5. El equipo _____ .

EXERCISE K

Answer the questions that a new friend asks you about your childhood. Use the imperfect tense and the cues provided.

1. ¿Acompañabas a tu mamá a las tiendas? *(a veces)*
2. ¿Obedecías a tus padres? *(siempre)*
3. ¿Buscabas a tu mamá todos los días? *(sí)*
4. ¿Llorabas a menudo? *(sí)*
5. ¿Eras un niño (una niña) exigente? *(sí)*
6. ¿Poseían tú y tus hermanos muchos juguetes? *(no)*
7. ¿Gritabas mucho? *(no)*
8. ¿Dividían tus hermanos su dinero contigo? *(no)*
9. ¿Quitabas sus juguetes a los otros niños? *(sí)*
10. ¿Caías enfermo(a) a menudo? *(no)*

EXERCISE L

Someone played a prank in school, and the principal wants to know what everyone was doing at that time. Use the suggestions below to tell what these people were doing.

comer en la cafetería
estar en la clase de biología
estudiar con Beto
hablar con el profesor de español

hacer gimnasia
ir a la oficina
leer en la biblioteca
ver una película en la clase de historia

1. Juan _____ .
2. Peggy y yo _____ .
3. Eduardo y Mai-Li _____ .
4. Tú _____ .
5. Ellas _____ .
6. Yo _____ .
7. Adela _____ .
8. Tú y Yolanda _____ .

EXERCISE M

Something interrupted what various people were doing. Relate each pair of events in a complete sentence.

EXAMPLE: yo / hablar por teléfono / mi padre / llegar
Yo **hablaba** por teléfono **cuando** mi padre **llegó**.

1. Elena / bañarse / el teléfono / sonar
2. mi madre / cocinar / ella ver un ratoncito
3. yo / mirar la televisión / yo / oír un ruido
4. Gordon y yo / correr en el parque / empezar a llover
5. Ellos / dormir / el perro / ladrar

6. tú / leer un libro / la alarma / sonar

7. Janice y José / subir al árbol / una rama / caer

8. mi hermano / dormir profundamente / el despertador / sonar

EXERCISE N

Who was your hero (heroine) when you were younger? Use the imperfect tense in a series of sentences describing this person.

MASTERY EXERCISES

EXERCISE O

Rewrite this story in the imperfect tense.

Es la una de la mañana y todo el mundo duerme profundamente menos yo. Yo no puedo dormirme. No sé por qué. No estoy preocupado. No estoy enfermo.

Estoy ansioso porque pasado mañana voy a esquiar con mis amigos. Nosotros tenemos todo preparado y no me falta nada. Me gusta salir con ellos. Ya son las dos y media. Continúo despierto. Quiero tomar un vaso de leche caliente pero no tengo ganas de salir de la cama. Voy a contar ovejas—mi abuela dice que eso siempre le ayuda a dormir. Cuento ovejas pero después de quince minutos pierdo la cuenta.

Quiero gritar y llorar de la frustración. Ya son las cuatro. Trato de leer pero no puedo fijarme en el cuento. Siempre soy así la noche antes de mi cumpleaños.

EXERCISE P

Answer the questions that you are asked when you return from summer camp.

1. ¿Tenías muchos amigos en el campamento?

2. ¿Qué hacían durante el día?

3. ¿Cuándo nadaban Uds.?

4. ¿Cómo se llamaba tu consejero?

5. ¿Cómo era?

6. ¿Qué deportes practicabas?

7. ¿Adónde ibas después de cenar?

8. ¿Con quién pasabas mucho tiempo?

9. ¿Gastabas mucho dinero en los videojuegos?

10. ¿Qué hacían Uds. cuando llovía?

EXERCISE Q

Express in Spanish what Diego's father tells him about his youth.

1. When I was your age I was very responsible.

2. I used to study and work.

3. I wanted to buy a car.

4. I had to save my money.

5. I had a girlfriend.

6. Her name was Diana.

7. She was sixteen years old when I met her.

8. She was very pretty, and she liked to dance.

9. I preferred to play football.

10. We used to go to a lot of parties and football games.

11. I used to see Diana on Saturdays.

12. We couldn't go out alone.

13. Diana's younger sister used to go with us.

14. She was very spoiled and cried a lot when I didn't pay attention to her.

15. Diana's parents were very strict.

16. I couldn't save any money for my car because I was always paying for Diana and her sister.

17. I was unhappy, but I liked Diana a lot.

18. We were very good friends, and I used to write to her when she was away at college.

19. Those were the good days.

Chapter 13
Future Tense

[1] *IR A* + INFINITIVE

An action in the future can be expressed in Spanish by the present tense of *ir* followed by the preposition *a* and the infinitive of the verb that indicates the future action.

Voy a estudiar más tarde.   *I'm going to study later.*
¿Qué vas a hacer?   *What are you going to do?*

EXERCISE A

Jorge can never guess what his friends are going to do. Write what Jorge guesses and what his friends are actually going to do.

EXAMPLE: Luis / jugar al tenis / trabajar
Luis **va a** jugar al tenis.
No, Luis **va a** trabajar.

1. Sergei / descansar / escuchar música
2. tú y Antonio / jugar al boliche / jugar al tenis
3. María / cocinar / tocar el piano
4. tú / ayudar a Felipe / leer un libro
5. Uds. / ver televisión / lavar los platos
6. Paco / dormir / estudiar

EXERCISE B

It's the end of the school year. Write six sentences in which you tell what you, your family, and your friends are going to do during the summer vacation.

EXERCISE C

The weather often affects our plans. Tell what you and your friends are going to do under these weather conditions.

EXAMPLE: si hace fresco
Si hace fresco, **vamos a montar** en bicicleta.

1. Si hace sol _____ .   2. Si hace frío _____ .

3. Si llueve _____ .

4. Si hace calor _____ .

5. Si nieva _____ .

[2] FUTURE TENSE OF REGULAR VERBS

a. The future tense of regular verbs is formed by adding the following personal endings to the infinitive form of the verb.

	hablar	comer	vivir
yo	hablar**é**	comer**é**	vivir**é**
tú	hablar**ás**	comer**ás**	vivir**ás**
Ud., él, ella	hablar**á**	comer**á**	vivir**á**
nosotros, -as	hablar**emos**	comer**emos**	vivir**emos**
vosotros, -as	hablar**éis**	comer**éis**	vivir**éis**
Uds., ellos, ellas	hablar**án**	comer**án**	vivir**án**

b. In English, the future tense is expressed by means of the helping verb *will* or *shall*.

Visitaré a mis primos el domingo. *I shall visit my cousins on Sunday.*

¿**Viajarás** a México pronto? *Will you visit Mexico soon?*

c. All the endings have an accent mark except *-emos.*

EXERCISE D

Write what these people will do next summer.

EXAMPLE: Bernardo / trabajar en una oficina
Bernardo **trabajará** en una oficina.

1. Eva / visitar a sus primos en el campo

2. mi hermana y yo / aprender a conducir

3. Fumi y Mario / jugar al tenis

4. mis padres / ir a Santo Domingo

5. yo / tomar una clase de baile

6. Elena y Teodoro / viajar a Costa Rica

7. tú / asistir a la universidad

8. Kim / ayudar a su padre en la tienda

9. Rosalía / participar en un concurso

10. nosotros / vivir cerca de la playa

EXERCISE E

Write when these people will do these things.

EXAMPLE: Elisa / volver a las montañas / el próximo invierno
Elisa **volverá** a las montañas el próximo invierno.

1. Alicia y yo / preparar la cena / esta noche

2. Simon / lavar el coche / pasado mañana

3. yo / ir a la biblioteca / mañana

4. los niños / jugar en un partido / el sábado que viene

5. tú / dar un paseo en el parque / por la tarde

6. Silvia y Amalia / correr en una carrera / en septiembre

7. el maestro / escribir una carta de recomendación / más tarde

EXERCISE F

You're saying good-bye to your best friend before going on vacation with your family to Mexico. Answer your friend's questions.

1. ¿Cuánto tiempo estarán Uds. en México? (*un mes*)

2. ¿Cuántas ciudades visitarás? (*tres*)

3. ¿Quién conducirá el coche? (*mis padres*)

4. ¿Qué cosas verás allí? (*monumentos y playas*)

5. ¿Me escribirás? (*sí*)

6. ¿Conocerán Uds. las playas de Acapulco también? (*sí*)

7. ¿Dormirás la siesta todos los días? (*sí*)

8. ¿Cuándo volverán Uds.? (*en agosto*)

[3] VERBS IRREGULAR IN THE FUTURE TENSE

Some verbs form the future tense by adding the future personal endings *(-é, -ás, -á, -emos, -éis, -án)* to an irregular stem.

a. Verbs like *poder* drop the *e* of the infinitive and then add the endings of the future tense.

poder: **podr** -é, -ás, -á, -emos, -éis, -án
Like **poder**:   haber, querer, saber

b. In verbs like *poner*, the *e* (or *i*) of the infinitive is replaced by a *d*, and the endings of the future tense are added.

poner: pondr -é, -ás, -á, -emos, -éis, -án
Like **poner**:   salir, tener, venir

c. The verbs *decir* and *hacer* drop two letters to form an irregular future stem.

decir: dir -é, -ás, -á, -emos, -éis, -án
hacer: har -é, -ás, -á, -emos, -éis, -án

EXERCISE G

Upon arrival in Buenos Aires, a group of students take a bus to their hotel. They're excited about what they'll be able to do in Argentina. Write what they say.

EXAMPLE: nosotros / poder conocer el barrio italiano
Nosotros **podremos** conocer el barrio italiano.

1. yo / poder conocer muchos lugares

2. Elena / poder ir de compras

3. Spiros y Estela / poder aprender a bailar el tango

4. tú / poder asistir a la ópera

5. Raúl / poder conocer las pampas argentinas

6. Diana y yo / poder ver a muchos gauchos

7. Uds. / poder tomar fotografías

EXERCISE H

Raquel writes to a friend and tells her about her plans. Complete her note with the appropriate forms of the future tense of the verbs indicated.

Querida Elena:

¡Buenas noticias! Mi familia _____ un viaje a tu ciudad el mes que viene.
                             1. (hacer)

Yo _____ el viaje con ellos. Yo no _____ la fecha exacta en que
    2. (hacer)   *3.* (saber)

nosotros _____ hasta la próxima semana, pero yo _____ verte
          4. (salir)   *5.* (querer)

durante mi visita. ¿ _____ tú ir a verme al hotel? Creo que Gloria y
  6. (poder)

María _____ también. Nosotras _____ mucho que contar. Yo
   7. (venir)   **8.** (tener)

_____ el placer de invitarte a almorzar. Al saber la fecha de mi llegada yo
 9. (tener)

te la _____ en otra carta o te la _____ por teléfono.
    10. (poner)   **11.** (decir)

Hasta pronto,

Raquel

EXERCISE I

You and some friends are talking about the future. Where will you be in twenty years? Answer these questions.

1. ¿Tendrás un trabajo bueno?

2. ¿Ganarás mucho dinero?

3. ¿Saldrás todavía con tus amigos?

4. ¿Vendrás a ver a tus amigos de la juventud?

5. ¿Sabrás hablar español?

6. ¿Querrás vivir en otra ciudad?

7. ¿Harás muchos viajes a Europa?

8. ¿Pondrás mucho dinero en el banco?

9. ¿Qué dirás de tus amigos?

EXERCISE J

You're the stage manager for a school play. Using the verbs indicated, write what each of your crew members will do.

EXAMPLE: Yo no **podré** hacer todas las cosas.

1. Claude _____ la mesa al lado del sofá.
         (poner)

2. Miguel y Luz _____ que ayudar a Gerardo.
              (tener)

3. El director _____ todo listo a las seis.
            (querer)

4. Todos nosotros _____ los adornos.
              (hacer)

5. Elena _____ dónde poner las flores.
   (saber)

6. Tú _____ a buscar una lámpara.
   (salir)

7. Los actores _____ aquí a las seis y cuarto.
   (venir)

8. Nosotros no _____ descansar hasta más tarde.
   (poder)

M A S T E R Y   E X E R C I S E S

EXERCISE K

José is the youngest child in the family, and he loves to reaffirm what his parents say his brothers and sisters will do. Write what his parents say and then what José says.

EXAMPLE: Marcos / sacar la basura
            Marcos **va a sacar** la basura.
            Marcos s**acará** la basura.

1. Pablo / lavar el coche

2. Anita / hacer la ensalada

3. Gregory / vender su bicicleta

4. Susan / poner la mesa

5. José, tú / ayudar a Susana

6. Gregory y Pablo / venir a casa temprano

7. Paul y yo / descansar

EXERCISE L

On New Year's Eve, Mr. Moore is talking with you about what will happen during the coming year. Write what he says.

EXAMPLE: Gabriel / terminar sus estudios
            Gabriel **terminará** sus estudios.

1. Lorenzo / poder comprar un coche

2. Lorenzo y Gabriel / tener que buscar un trabajo

3. tú / hacer un viaje a Puerto Rico

4. Alicia y yo / salir a menudo

5. yo / venir a casa temprano

6. mis padres / vivir en otro estado

EXERCISE M

Help an American exchange student in Caracas to communicate with his host family. Express what he wants to say in Spanish.

1. I'll leave Atlanta on Saturday morning.

2. I'll make the trip by plane.

3. I'm going to bring two suitcases.

4. Will you meet me at the airport?

5. How will I know you?

6. Will we take a taxi to your house?

7. Are we going to go directly to your house?

8. I'll have to exchange money.

9. I'll have to call my parents upon arriving.

10. We'll spend six weeks together.

11. My friends will want your address.

12. It will be fun.

Chapter 14

Reflexive Verbs

[1] REFLEXIVE VERBS IN SIMPLE TENSES

a. A reflexive verb requires a reflexive pronoun *(me, te, se, nos, os, se)* that refers the action of the verb back to the subject.

Yo me lavo.	*I wash myself.*
Ellos se visten.	*They dress themselves. (They get dressed.)*

b. Reflexive pronouns generally precede the verb in the simple tenses.

PRESENT TENSE	
yo me lavo	nosotros (-as) nos lavamos
tú te lavas	vosotros (-as) os laváis
Ud., él, ella se lava	Uds., ellos, ellas se lavan

PRETERITE TENSE	
yo me lavé	nosotros (-as) nos lavamos
tú te lavaste	vosotros (-as) os lavasteis
Ud., él, ella se lavó	Uds., ellos, ellas se lavaron

IMPERFECT TENSE	
yo me lavaba	nosotros (-as) nos lavábamos
tú te lavabas	vosotros (-as) os lavasteis
Ud., él, ella se lavaba	Uds., ellos, ellas se lavaban

FUTURE TENSE	
yo me lavaré	nosotros (-as) nos lavaremos
tú te lavarás	vosotros (-as) os lavaréis
Ud., él, ella se lavará	Uds., ellos, ellas se lavarán

c. When a reflexive verb is used as an infinitive, the reflexive pronoun is attached to the end of the infinitive or placed before the conjugated verb. Both forms are accepted.

Voy a bañar**me**. **Me** voy a bañar.	*I'm going to take a bath.*

Queremos levantar**nos** ahora. **Nos** queremos levantar ahora.	*We want to get up now.*

d. Common reflexive verbs:

acostarse (ue) *to go to bed*

afeitarse *to shave*

bañarse *to take a bath, bathe*

cepillarse *to brush* (one's teeth, hair, or clothes)

desayunarse *to have breakfast*

despertarse (ie) *to wake up*

divertirse (ie) *to enjoy oneself, have a good time*

dormirse (ue) *to fall asleep*

irse *to go away*

lavarse *to wash oneself*

levantarse *to get up*

llamarse *to be named, be called*

peinarse *to comb one's hair*

ponerse *to put on* (clothing)

quedarse *to stay, remain*

quitarse *to take off* (clothing)

sentarse (ie) *to sit down*

vestirse (i) *to get dressed*

NOTE:

1. Some verbs that are reflexive in Spanish are translated nonreflexively in English.

nos quedamos *we remain*   él se va *he goes away*

2. Some reflexive verbs are stem-changing. In the end vocabulary, the stem change is indicated after the verb.

sentarse (ie) me siento *I sit down*

vestirse (i) me visto *I get dressed*

EXERCISE A

Lola thinks that her family has many idiosyncrasies. Write what she says.

EXAMPLE: mi hermano / peinarse sin peine
           Mi hermano **se peina** sin peine.

1. mi abuelo / lavarse las manos cincuenta veces al día

2. mi papá / afeitarse mientras bañarse

3. mis hermanas / bañarse por la mañana y por la noche

4. yo / ponerse perfume cinco veces al día

5. Berta y yo / ponerse la misma ropa

6. tú / vestirse en la oscuridad

EXERCISE B

Rita has been baby-sitting her neighbor's children. Answer the questions Rita is asked when the neighbor returns home.

EXAMPLE: ¿Se lavaron las manos? *(no)*
No, **no se lavaron** las manos.

1. ¿Se puso Juan la pijama sin problema? *(sí)*

2. ¿Se bañaron Angela y Elena? *(no)*

3. ¿Se acostó Juan a las ocho? *(sí)*

4. ¿Se durmió delante de la televisión? *(no)*

5. ¿Se peinó Elena antes de acostarse? *(sí)*

6. ¿Te lavaste las manos? *(sí)*

7. ¿Se despertó Juan alguna vez? *(no)*

8. ¿Te dormiste cuando los niños se acostaron? *(no)*

EXERCISE C

Luis is at a camp reunion, reminiscing with his friends about the things they used to do. Write what he says, using the imperfect tense.

EXAMPLE: yo / levantarse temprano
Yo **me levantaba** temprano.

1. Abraham y Sergio / despertarse a las seis

2. tú / vestirse rápidamente

3. el consejero / cepillarse los dientes después de cada comida

4. Paco y yo / nunca desayunarse

5. Alberto / dormirse en la cama y no quitarse la ropa

6. nosotros / divertirse en el lago

EXERCISE D

You are on vacation. Write five sentences in which you describe how you spend one day. Use the verbs suggested below.

acostarse	despertarse	dormirse	peinarse	quedarse
desayunarse	divertirse	lavarse	ponerse	vestirse

EXERCISE E

Using the cues provided, write what these people will do.

EXAMPLE: Esteban tiene hambre por la mañana. *(desayunarse)*
           Él **se desayunará.**

1. La señora Singh está cansada. *(acostarse)*
2. Tú vas a ver un programa en la televisión. *(sentarse en el sillón)*
3. Los niños van a comer ahora. *(lavarse las manos)*
4. Richie acaba de jugar al béisbol. *(bañarse)*
5. Marta va a salir con sus amigas. *(peinarse bien)*
6. Yo tengo frío. *(ponerse un suéter)*
7. Llueve mucho y no queremos salir. *(quedarse en casa)*
8. Vemos un programa aburrido en la televisión. *(dormirse en el sofá)*
9. Luz oye el despertador. *(levantarse rápidamente)*
10. Tus tíos tienen un bebé recién nacido. *(llamarse Francisco)*

[2] REFLEXIVE COMMANDS

In affirmative commands, reflexive pronouns follow the verb and are attached to it. In negative commands, reflexive pronouns precede the verb. Affirmative reflexive commands with more than two syllables have a written accent over the stressed vowel.

AFFIRMATIVE COMMANDS	NEGATIVE COMMANDS
(tú) ¡Lávate! (Uds.) ¡Lávense!	(tú) ¡No te laves! (Uds.) ¡No se laven!
(Ud.) ¡Lávese!	(Ud.) ¡No se lave!

EXERCISE F

Your parents are away, and your older sister is in charge. Write in Spanish the commands she gives you.

EXAMPLE: bañarse ahora
           ¡**Báñate** ahora!

1. cepillarse los dientes
2. acostarse temprano
3. quitarse los zapatos

4. ponerse ropa limpia
5. quedarse en la casa

EXERCISE G

While you rehearse a school play, the teacher gives you directions. Write what she says you shouldn't do.

EXAMPLE: levantarse de la silla ahora
            ¡**No te levantes** de la silla ahora!

1. peinarse en este momento
2. sentarse en el sofá
3. ponerse el sombrero todavía
4. quitarse el suéter hasta más tarde
5. irse de la escena

EXERCISE H

A teacher walking through the school cafeteria tells a group of students to do the following things. Write what she says.

EXAMPLE: quedarse en la cafetería
            ¡**Quédense** en la cafetería!

1. desayunarse en silencio
2. quitarse los anteojos de sol
3. sentarse en las sillas
4. lavarse las manos
5. quedarse donde están ahora

EXERCISE I

What does she tell them they shouldn't do?

EXAMPLE: irse de la cafetería
            ¡**No se vayan** de la cafetería!

1. desayunarse en el piso
2. ponerse los anteojos de sol
3. peinarse aquí
4. quedarse cerca de la ventana
5. quitarse los zapatos
6. sentarse en la mesa

M A S T E R Y   E X E R C I S E S

EXERCISE J

**Rosa, Annette, Theresa, and Mary are sharing a hotel room on an
overnight school trip. Complete their dialogue using the appropriate
form of the reflexive verbs.**

ROSA: _____, muchachas. Ya son las siete de la mañana.
  1. (despertarse)

MARY: ¿Quién _____ primero?
  2. (bañarse)

THERESA: La persona que _____ primero puede _____
  3. (levantarse)   **4.** (bañarse)
  primero.

ROSA: Bueno, mientras yo _____, Uds. _____ .
  5. (bañarse)   **6.** (peinarse)

MARY: Buena idea. Annette, _____ . Vamos a llegar tarde.
  7. (levantarse)

ANNETTE: Tengo mucho sueño. Vuelvo a _____ mientras Uds.
  8. (dormirse)

  _____ .
  9. (vestirse)

THERESA: ¡No _____ otra vez, Annette! Tenemos que
  10. (dormirse)

  _____ a las ocho.
  11. (desayunarse)

ANNETTE: Bueno, ahora yo _____ .
  12. (levantarse)

MARY: Theresa, ¿qué _____ hoy?
  13. (ponerse)

THERESA: Hace calor. Rosa y yo decidimos _____ pantalones
  14. (ponerse)
  cortos. ¿Y tú?

MARY: Yo _____ lo mismo.
  15. (ponerse)

ROSA: ¡Annette, no _____ aquí! _____ en el cuarto de
  16. (peinarse)   **17.** (peinarse)

  baño, por favor. Y mientras estás allí, _____
  18. (bañarse)

  y _____ la cara. Después yo _____ la cara
  19. (lavarse)   **20.** (lavarse)

  y _____ también.
  21. (peinarse)

THERESA: ¡Mary, _____ esa blusa! Es mía. ¡ _____ otra blusa!
22. (quitarse) · · · · · · · · · · · · · · 23. (ponerse)

MARY: Bueno, yo voy a _____ esta blusa blanca.
24. (ponerse)

ROSA: Annette, no _____ en esa silla, por favor. Mi ropa está allí.
25. (sentarse)

ANNETTE: Yo no quiero salir. Prefiero _____ aquí. Todavía tengo
26. (quedarse)

sueño y hay buenos programas en la televisión por la mañana.

MARY: De ninguna manera, Annette. _____ ahora porque
27. (vestirse)

nosotras estamos listas y _____ .
28. (irse)

EXERCISE K

Express in Spanish Mirta's description of a new friend.

1. Her name is Susan.
2. She likes to stay at home.
3. She and her sisters enjoy themselves in the garden.
4. Susan wakes up at seven o'clock.
5. Her family has breakfast together every day.
6. She bathes and dresses rapidly.
7. She and I prefer to comb our hair after we get dressed.
8. She and I fall asleep in history class sometimes.
9. She sits at the first desk.
10. The teacher tells her: "Wake up!"
11. She tells me: "Don't fall asleep in this class again!"
12. When we wake up, we leave the room to wash our faces.
13. She wears pretty clothes.
14. She always asks: "What are you going to wear tomorrow?"
15. We have a good time together.
16. Her mother always says: "Don't go to bed late!"
17. She and her sisters are going away.

Chapter 15
Common Idiomatic Expressions with Verbs

Many Spanish verbs are used in idiomatic expressions. A list of common expressions follows:

[1] EXPRESSIONS WITH *HACER*

¿Qué tiempo hace? *How's the weather?*
¿Qué tiempo hace en julio? *How's the weather in July?*

hacer buen / mal tiempo *to be good / bad weather*
Hace mal tiempo hoy. *Today the weather is bad.*

hacer (mucho) frío / calor / fresco *to be (very) cold / warm / cool* (weather)
Hizo mucho frío anoche. *It was very cold last night.*

hacer (mucho) sol *to be (very) sunny*
Hace mucho sol por la tarde. *It's very sunny in the afternoon.*

hacer (mucho) viento *to be (very) windy*
Hace viento. *It's windy.*

hacer el favor de + infinitive *please . . .*
Haga el favor de abrir la ventana. *Please open the window.*

hacer un viaje *to take a trip*
Hacen un viaje cada año. *They take a trip each year.*

hacer una pregunta *to ask a question*
El niño hace muchas preguntas. *The boy asks many questions.*

hacer una visita *to pay a visit*
Ella hizo una visita a su abuela. *She paid a visit to her grandmother.*

EXERCISE A

Tell what you like to do in different kinds of weather. Use the suggestions below.

andar en el parque	ir al cine	mirar la televisión
correr en el parque	jugar al tenis	nadar en la piscina
ir a las montañas	leer un libro	quedarse en casa

EXAMPLE: hacer buen tiempo
Cuando **hace** buen tiempo **me gusta andar en el parque.**

1. hacer sol
2. hacer mucho viento
3. hacer mal tiempo
4. hacer mucho calor
5. hacer fresco
6. hacer mucho frío

EXERCISE B

Describe the weather in each of the drawings below.

EXAMPLE:

1.

Hace mucho viento.

2.

3.

4.

5.

EXERCISE C

Use an idiomatic expression with hacer to tell what these people do.

1. Moses no comprende un problema de la clase de matemáticas.
   Él _____ .
2. Alicia y Ramona se visten para ir a la escuela.

Ellas preguntan _____ .

3. Los señores Ortiz quieren conocer Chile.

Ellos _____ .

4. Yo estoy en la biblioteca y quiero estudiar, pero unos jóvenes hablan en voz alta.

Yo digo _____ .

5. Tú tienes ganas de ver a tus primos.

Tú _____ .

[2] EXPRESSIONS WITH *TENER*

¿Qué tiene Ud.? *What's the matter with you?*	
¿Qué tiene Ud. ahora?	*What's the matter with you now?*

tener... años to be ... years old
¿Cuántos años tiene Juan?	*How old is Juan?*
Juan tiene diez años.	*Juan is ten years old.*

tener (mucho) calor *to be (very) warm* (persons)
¿Tiene Ud. calor?	*Are you warm?*

tener cuidado *to be careful*
¡Ten cuidado en la playa!	*Be careful at the beach!*

tener dolor de cabeza *to have a headache*
Ella tiene dolor de cabeza.	*She has a headache.*

tener dolor de muelas *to have a toothache*
Él tiene dolor de muelas.	*He has a toothache.*

tener (mucho) frío *to be (very) cold* (persons)
Los niños tienen frío.	*The children are cold.*

tener ganas de *to feel like, want to*
Tengo ganas de gritar.	*I feel like screaming.*

tener (mucha) hambre *to be (very) hungry*
No tengo hambre.	*I'm not hungry.*

tener la bondad de + infinitive *to be kind enough to*
Tenga la bondad de cerrar la puerta.	*Be kind enough to close the door.*

tener miedo de *to be afraid of*
Tienen miedo del mar.	*They're afraid of the sea.*

tener (mucha) sed *to be (very) thirsty*
Tenemos sed ahora.	*We're thirsty now.*

tener (mucho) sueño   *to be (very) sleepy*
¿Tienen Uds. sueño?   *Are you sleepy?*

tener prisa   *to be in a hurry*
¡No tengas prisa!   *Don't be in a hurry!*

tener que + infinitive   *to have to, must*
Mi padre tiene que trabajar.   *My father has to work.*

tener razón / no tener razón   *to be right / to be wrong*
Mary siempre tiene razón.   *Mary is always right.*
Jamal no tiene razón.   *Jamal is wrong.*

EXERCISE D

Using an expression with *tener,* tell why these people do what they do.

EXAMPLE: Llevo pantalones cortos hoy.
            Yo **tengo calor**.

1. Pilar va al dentista.

2. Tú usas un suéter.

3. Yo busco otra respuesta a la pregunta.

4. Vamos a la playa.

5. Ellos comen una manzana.

6. Juan se acuesta.

7. El niño grita.

8. Ud. bebe una limonada.

9. Estudio ocho horas para un examen.

10. El señor corre.

11. Al no ver autos, el niño cruza la calle.

12. La madre toma dos aspirinas.

EXERCISE E

Use the expressions with *tener* in parentheses to complete Martín's dialogue with the school nurse.

ENFERMERA: Hola, Martín. ¿ _____ ?
                         1. (qué tener)

MARTÍN: _____ .
                2. (tener dolor de cabeza)

ENFERMERA: ¿ _____ ?
                3. (tener fiebre)

MARTÍN: No creo. _____ y a veces _____ .
4. (tener frío)   5. (tener calor)

ENFERMERA: ¿Quieres comer algo?

MARTÍN: No, gracias. _____ .
6. (no tener hambre)

ENFERMERA: ¿ _____ beber algo?
7. (tener ganas de)

MARTÍN: Sí, _____ .
8. (tener sed)

ENFERMERA: Yo _____ llamar a tu mamá.
9. (tener que)

MARTÍN: Ud. _____ . Yo _____ ir a casa.
10. (tener razón)   11. (tener ganas de)

ENFERMERA: _____ darme tu número de teléfono.
12. (tener la bondad de)

MARTÍN: Es el 555-0021.

ENFERMERA: Está bien. Tú _____ esperar a tu madre. Ella viene por ti.
13. (tener que)

MARTÍN: Muchas gracias. Ahora yo _____ .
14. (tener sueño)

[3] OTHER IDIOMATIC VERBAL EXPRESSIONS

acabar de + infinitive   *to have just*
Él acaba de llegar.   *He has just arrived.*

dar la hora   *to strike the hour*
El reloj da las tres.   *The clock strikes three.*

dar las gracias   *to thank*
Damos las gracias al profesor.   *We thank the teacher.*

dar un paseo   *to take a walk*
Doy un paseo en el parque cada día.   *I take a walk in the park every day.*

darse la mano   *to shake hands*
Nos damos la mano.   *We shake hands.*

dejar caer   *to drop*
El niño deja caer la leche.   *The child drops the milk.*

dejar de + infinitive   *to fail to; to stop; to neglect to*
John deja de estudiar.   *John stops studying.*

echar al correo   *to mail*
Echo la carta al correo.   *I mail the letter.*

echar de menos   *to miss* (a person or thing)
Echo de menos a mis primos.   *I miss my cousins.*

estar de acuerdo   *to agree*
Estamos de acuerdo.   *We agree.*

guardar cama   *to stay in bed*
Él guarda cama por dos días.   *He's staying in bed for two days.*

llegar a ser   *to become; to get to be*
Quiero llegar a ser médico.   *I want to become a doctor.*

pensar + infinitive   *to intend to*
Pienso hacer un viaje.   *I intend to take a trip.*

ponerse + adjective   *to become; to turn*
El niño se puso triste.   *The child became sad.*

querer decir
¿Qué quiere decir «dinero»?   *What does "dinero" mean?*

sacar una fotografía   *to take a picture*
Pedro saca muchas fotografías.   *Peter takes many pictures.*

EXERCISE F

Several friends are commenting on various topics. Select the expression from those listed below and write its appropriate form in the space provided.

dar	dejar caer	estar de acuerdo	ponerse
dar las gracias	dejar de	guardar cama	querer decir
darse la mano	echar de menos	llegar a ser	sacar fotografías
dar un paseo	echarla al correo	pensar	

1. Luis está enfermo. Él _____ por tres días.

2. Cuando mis padres no están en casa, mi hermana menor los _____ .

3. Estoy contento porque trabajo en un hospital. Quiero _____ médico.

4. Cuando conoces a una persona, es correcto _____ .

5. Escribí esta carta. Ahora voy a _____ .

6. Roy y yo tenemos las mismas ideas. Nosotros _____ .

7. Yo voy a jugar al tenis mañana. ¿Qué _____ tú hacer?

8. Jorge no quiere ponerse gordo. Él _____ comer dulces.

9. Mi tía me dio este reloj. Ahora tengo que _____ a ella.

10. Phyllis tiene una cámara nueva. Le fascina _____ .

11. Yo no pasé el examen de conducir y _____ furioso.

12. Felipe no comprende nada. Él siempre pregunta: «¿Qué _____ eso?»

13. Hace buen tiempo y necesito ejercicio. Voy a _____ en el parque.

14. ¡No le des ese vaso de cristal a Jaime! Él _____ todo.

15. ¿Qué hora es? El reloj _____ la una y media.

EXERCISE G

Answer these questions a friend asks you.

1. ¿Sacas muchas fotografías cuando haces un viaje?

2. ¿Guardas cama cuando estás enfermo(a)?

3. ¿Te pones nervioso(a) antes de un examen?

4. ¿Echas de menos a tus amigo(a)s durante las vacaciones?

5. ¿Acabas de comprar ese suéter?

6. ¿Dejas de estudiar cuando tus amigo(a)s te llaman por teléfono?

7. ¿Das un paseo cada noche?

8. ¿Das las gracias a tu madre cuando ella sirve la cena?

9. ¿Piensas trabajar durante el verano?

10. ¿Qué haces cuando conoces a una persona?

MASTERY EXERCISES

EXERCISE H

The teacher asks the class to rewrite these sentences using an expression with *dar*, *hacer*, *tener*, or *querer*.

EXAMPLE: **Le duele** el estómago.
Tiene dolor de estómago.

1. Desea ir al cine esta noche.

2. Tú **debes** estudiar.

3. Abra la puerta, **por favor**.

4. ¿Qué **significa** esta palabra?

5. Ellos **caminan** por el parque.

6. **¿Qué edad tienes?**

7. **Me duele** la cabeza.

EXERCISE I

Carmen is spending a few weeks at a nature camp. Complete this letter with the appropriate idiomatic expressions.

Querida Susana:

Yo _____ volver de un paseo formidable. Casi todos los días
    1. (to have just)

hacemos lomismo. El grupo _____ en el bosque y vemos muchas
            2. (to take a walk)

cosas interesantes. Cuando _____ salimos muy temprano y
           3. (the weather is good)

no volvemos hasta muy tarde. Yo _____ usar un sombrero,
         4. (to have to)

especialmente cuando _____ . Tengo mi cámara conmigo y yo
        5. (it's very sunny)

_____ . Un día una chica _____ mi cámara y
6. (to take many pictures)   **7.** (to drop)

yo _____ furiosa. La cámara está bien y ella y yo _____ en
  8. (to become)   **9.** (to agree)

que fue un accidente. Nosotras _____ y ahora somos buenas
          10. (to shake hands)

amigas. Por lo general, _____ aquí. Por la mañana y por
        11. (the weather is good)

la tarde _____ . Nosotras _____ llevar un suéter con nosotras
  12. (it's cold)   **13.** (to have to)

cuando salimos. También cuando nosotras _____ a otro sitio
          14. (to take a trip)

llevamos comida y bebidas para no _____ ni _____ .
         15. (to be hungry) **16.** (to be thirsty)

Las actividades son fuertes y a las ocho de la noche yo ya _____ .
              17. (to be sleepy)

Yo _____ a mis amigas pero Uds. pueden _____ a este
  18. (to miss)   **19.** (to pay a visit)

campamento. Ahora yo _____ porque quiero _____
        20. (to be in a hurry)   **21.** (to mail)

esta carta. _____ contestar esta carta.
    22. (please)

                Cariñosamente,

                Carmen

EXERCISE J

A friend's helping you study for a Spanish test. He asks how you would say various things in Spanish. Tell him.

EXAMPLE: How would you ask someone if he's thirsty?
¿Tiene Ud. sed?

1. How would you ask someone how the weather is?
2. How would ask someone if she's cold?
3. How would you ask someone if he has a toothache?
4. How would you ask someone if it's windy today?
5. How would you ask someone if she's hungry?
6. How would you tell someone that he's wrong?
7. How would you ask someone how old she is?
8. How would you tell someone that today it's sunny?
9. How would you tell your mother that you're thirsty?
10. How would you tell someone that the weather's fine?
11. How would you ask a sick man what's the matter with him?
12. How would you ask someone what the word *algodón* means?
13. How would you ask someone to please close the door?
14. How would you ask your friends if they're planning to take a trip?
15. How would you tell your father that your younger brother is sleepy?
16. How would you tell a friend to be careful?
17. How would you tell someone that you are in a hurry?
18. How would you tell a friend that you feel like taking a walk?
19. How would you tell a friend that he has to leave?
20. How would you tell someone that you agree?
21. How would you tell someone that you want to become a teacher?
22. How would you tell someone that you have to stay in bed?
23. How would you ask a friend if she misses her sister?
24. How would you tell your mother that you have just eaten?
25. How would you ask a friend why she becomes nervous?

Chapter 16
Negation

[1] NEGATIVES

a. The most common negative is *no*, which always precedes the conjugated verb.

Yo **no** leo el libro.   *I don't read the book.*

¿**No** escribiste la carta?   *Didn't you write the letter?*

EXERCISE A

Pablo is answering a friend's questions about where the students in his class are from. Write what he says.

EXAMPLE: ¿Es Marta de México? *(Venezuela)*
              No, Marta **no es** de México. Ella **es** de Venezuela.

1. ¿Son Juan y Xavier de Puerto Rico? *(España)*

2. ¿Es Alberto de la República Dominicana? *(Colombia)*

3. ¿Es Laura de Guatemala? *(Costa Rica)*

4. ¿Son Rafael y Linda de la Argentina? *(Chile)*

5. ¿Eres tú de los Estados Unidos? *(Nicaragua)*

EXERCISE B

You and your friends are in your basement. Your mother wants to know what you're doing. Answer her questions.

EXAMPLE: ¿Miran Uds. la televisión?
              No, no miramos la televisión.

1. ¿Juegan Uds. al ajedrez?

2. ¿Leen Uds. el periódico?

3. ¿Come Enrique helado?

4. ¿Hablas tú por teléfono?

5. ¿Preparas tú la tarea para mañana?

6. ¿Arreglan Uds. el cuarto?

7. ¿Practicas tú el diálogo con Luis?

EXERCISE C

From the list below, tell five things you are not going to do this weekend.

caminar en el parque	jugar al fútbol	ver una película
estudiar en la biblioteca	lavar el coche	visitar a los abuelos
ir a la playa	nadar	

EXAMPLE: **No voy a ir a la playa.**

b. Other negatives are:

nada   *nothing, (not) anything*

nadie   *no one, nobody, (not) anyone*

ni... ni   *neither... nor; not . . . either . . . or . . .*

ninguno (-a)   *no, none, (not) any*

no   *no, not*

nunca   *never, (not) ever*

tampoco   *neither, not either*

c. A double negative is acceptable in Spanish. In fact, this construction occurs frequently. If one of the negatives is *no*, it precedes the verb. If *no* is omitted, the other negative must precede the verb.

No veo **nada.**
Nada veo. } *I don't see anything.*

Él **no** juega **nunca.**
El **nunca** juega. } *He never plays.*

d. *Nadie* can be used as the subject or the object of the verb. When it is the object of the verb, it is preceded by the preposition *a*.

Nadie entra.
No entra **nadie.** } *No one enters.*

BUT

No veo **a nadie.**   *I don't see anyone (anybody).*

A nadie veo.   *I see no one (nobody).*

e. *Ninguno* drops the final *-o* and takes a written accent over the *u* if it comes immediately before a masculine singular noun. If a preposition comes between *ninguno* and the noun, the full form is used.

Ningún alumno está ausente.   *No pupil is absent.*

Ninguno de los alumnos está ausente.   *None of the pupils is absent.*
Ninguna casa tiene ascensor.   *No house has an elevator.*

EXERCISE D

Sarita's telling her mother the chores that her friends never do. Tell what she says.

EXAMPLE: ayudar en casa *(Juanita)*
           Juanita nunca ayuda en casa.

1. sacar la basura *(Raquel)*

2. ir de compras *(Jorge y Pedro)*

3. lavar el coche *(Alejandro)*

4. preparar la ensalada *(Beatriz y Alex)*

5. pasar la aspiradora *(Tomás y Víctor)*

6. sacar al perro *(Oyuki)*

7. poner la mesa *(Esteban)*

8. secar los platos *(Lola y Emilio)*

EXERCISE E

During a camping trip, your friend tries your patience with her questions. Answer them in Spanish, using a form of *ninguno,* **if possible, or** *nada.*

EXAMPLE: ¿Cuántos videojuegos tienes?
           No tengo **ninguno**.

1. ¿Ves los pájaros?   *4.* ¿Llevas la mochila?

2. ¿Tienes una lamparita?   *5.* ¿Preparas la cena?

3. ¿Lees el mapa?   *6.* ¿Necesitas mi ayuda?

EXERCISE F

Mr. Perales is complaining to his wife about his day at work. Tell what he says.

EXAMPLE: saludar a los jefes
           Nadie saluda a los jefes.

1. contestar el teléfono
2. ayudar a la secretaria
3. llegar a tiempo
4. tomar una hora de almuerzo
5. arreglar su escritorio
6. recibir a los clientes
7. hablar en voz baja

EXERCISE G

During a date, Theresa finds Juan very distracted. Give Juan's answers to her questions.

EXAMPLE: ¿A quién miras?
            No miro a nadie.

1. ¿A quién hablas?
2. ¿A quiénes buscas?
3. ¿A quién esperas?

4. ¿A quién admiras?
5. ¿A quiénes respondes?

EXERCISE H

Maria's helping her mother prepare a shopping list. Tell what she says to her mother.

EXAMPLE: pan
            No tenemos ningún pan.

1. fruta
2. chocolate
3. helado
4. queso

5. cebolla
6. mantequilla
7. pastel

EXERCISE I

Lupe is comparing herself to a popular actress she just saw on a talk show. Tell what she says.

EXAMPLE: No le gusta el color rojo.
            No me gusta el color rojo **tampoco.**

1. Nunca se levanta temprano.
2. No come carne.
3. No le gusta decir adiós.
4. Nunca usa paraguas.
5. No fuma.

EXERCISE J

César is describing a new neighbor. Tell what he says about him.

EXAMPLE: jugar al béisbol o al fútbol
Él **no juega ni** al béisbol **ni** al fútbol.

1. leer periódicos o revistas
2. jugar a las damas o al ajedrez
3. ver películas o documentales
4. correr o caminar a la escuela
5. coleccionar estampillas o monedas
6. dibujar o pintar

EXERCISE K

Pedro describes a dream he had. Complete his description with the appropriate negative expressions.

Roberto y yo estamos en una fiesta. Estamos sentados en el sofá porque

_____ conocemos _____ . _____ nos habla. La fiesta es muy aburrida.
  1.   **2.**   **3.**

Tenemos hambre pero _____ hay _____ de comer. Por fin una chica sale
          4.   **5.**

de la cocina con unos platos en la mano pero ella _____ nos ofrece
          6.

_____ . Roberto y yo vamos a la mesa y vemos que _____ hay _____
 7.   **8.**   **9.**

plato bueno. A nosotros _____ nos gustan _____ los tacos _____ los
          10.   **11.**   **12.**

frijoles. Queremos salir pero _____ encontramos _____ puerta. _____
          13.   **14.**   **15.**

contesta nuestras preguntas. _____ chico quiere ayudarnos. Yo _____
          16.   **17.**

puedo salir de allí y Roberto _____ puede salir _____ . Le digo a Roberto
  18. 19.

voy a aceptar una invitación a una fiesta donde que _____ voy a aceptar una
  20.

invitación a una fiesta donde _____ conozco_____ . En ese momento
  21. 22.

oigo una voz que me pregunta: —Pedro, ¿ _____ vas a comer con tus
  23.

compañeros en la cafetería? Entonces me despierto y digo: —_____
  24.

vuelvo a dormirme en la clase otra vez.

[2] NEGATIVE EXPRESSIONS

Some useful negative expressions are:

Creo que no. *I don't think so.*

De nada. *You're welcome.*

en ningún lado
en ninguna parte } *nowhere*

Mejor no. *Better not.*

Ni yo tampoco. *Me neither.*

No es así. *It's not so.*

No es para tanto. *It's not such a big deal.*

No hay más remedio *It can't be helped*

No importa. *It doesn't matter.*

No lo creo. *I don't believe it.*

¡No me digas! *Don't tell me! (You don't say!)*

No me gusta nada. *I don't like it at all.*

No puede ser. *It can't be.*

No puedo más. *I can't take it anymore.*

¿No te parece? *Don't you think so?*

¿Por qué no? *Why not?*

EXERCISE L

Several friends are sitting around and making plans. Using the following expressions, react to their statements.

De nada.   No lo creo.   No puede ser.
Ni yo tampoco.   No me gusta nada.   ¿Por qué no?
No es para tanto.

EXAMPLE: Juan dice: —Cuando mis primos dicen «gracias» yo nunca sé
           qué contestar.
           Tú dices: **—Debes decir «de nada».**

1. Roberto dice: —Yo no tengo clases mañana.

   Tú dices:

2. Luis dice: —Después de estos días de lluvia, dicen que va a hacer buen

   tiempo mañana.

   Tú dices:

3. Laura dice: —Si vamos a la playa podemos practicar el esquí acuático.

   Tú dices:

4. Esteban dice: —Mañana es el cumpleaños de Lázaro.

   Tú dices:

5. Anita dice: —Lázaro tiene un coche de último modelo.

   Tú dices:

6. Tomás dice: Vamos a llamar a Lázaro por teléfono.

   Tú dices:

EXERCISE M

**Poor Enrique spent the summer working while his friends went to
Mexico. Using the expressions given, write appropriate responses that
Enrique would make as his friends tell him about their trip.**

Creo que no.   No hay más remedio.   No me gusta nada.
En ningún lado.   No lo creo.   No puedo más.
No es para tanto.   No me digas.

EXAMPLE: Raúl dice: —¡En el avión nos sentamos en primera clase!
           Enrique dice: **—No es para tanto.**

1. Joaquín dice: —Encontramos a tu maestra de español en un restaurante.

   Enrique dice:

2. Felipe dice: —Cuando fuimos a pescar, yo pesqué un pez de cien libras.

   Enrique dice:

3. Laura dice: —Visitamos muchos museos.

   Enrique dice:

4. Alfredo dice: —Vamos a volver a México el verano que viene. ¿Vas con nosotros?

   Enrique dice:

5. Héctor dice: —¿Vas a trabajar otra vez durante el verano?

   Enrique dice:

6. Alicia dice: —Me encanta la música de los mariachis. ¿Sabes dónde venden discos de esta música?

   Enrique dice:

7. Ofelia dice: —Tienes que ver las fotos que sacamos durante el viaje.

   Enrique dice:

M A S T E R Y   E X E R C I S E S

EXERCISE N

An exchange student asks you some questions in Spanish. Answer using a negative word or expression.

1. ¿Están cerradas las tiendas hoy?

   No, _____ de las tiendas está cerrada hoy.

2. ¿Visitaste el museo de arte?

   No visité _____ museo de arte.

3. ¿Vas al concierto o al cine?

   No voy _____ al concierto _____ al cine.

4. ¿Cuándo juegas al tenis?

   _____ juego al tenis.

5. ¿Quién habla español en tu casa?

   _____ habla español en mi casa.

6. ¿A quién acompañas después de las clases?

   No acompaño _____ después de las clases.

7. ¿Qué haces por la noche?

No hago _____ por la noche.

8. ¿Lees algún libro interesante?

No leo _____ libro interesante.

9. ¿Te gustan las películas de ciencia ficción?

No, _____ veo esas películas.

EXERCISE O

You're telling a friend about your school and classes. Express the following in Spanish.

1. No school is open today.
2. We never have tests on Mondays.
3. I never ask questions in any of my classes.
4. No one goes to Spanish class without the homework.
5. You can't speak to anyone in class.
6. None of the tests are very difficult.
7. We don't have a football team or a baseball team.
8. The other teams never win.
9. I'm not a member of any team.
10. We never see any movies in school.
11. No one likes to eat in the school cafeteria.
12. The teachers are never absent.

Part two

Noun and Pronoun
Structures

Chapter 17

Nouns and Articles

[1] GENDER OF NOUNS

a. All nouns in Spanish are either masculine or feminine. Nouns ending in *-o* and nouns referring to male beings are generally masculine. Nouns ending in *-a*, *-d*, or *-ión* and nouns referring to female beings are generally feminine.

MASCULINE	FEMININE
el libro *the book* **el padre** *the father*	**la pluma** *the pen* **la madre** *the mother* **la ciudad** *the city* **la lección** *the lesson*

b. The gender of other nouns must be learned individually.

MASCULINE	FEMININE
el lápiz *the pencil* **el papel** *the paper*	**la flor** *the flower* **la sal** *the salt*

c. The articles used before masculine singular nouns are *el* (the) and *un* (a, an). The articles used before feminine singular nouns are *la* (the) and *una* (a, an).

MASCULINE	FEMININE
el hombre *the man* **un cuadro** *a picture*	**la mujer** *the woman* **una silla** *a chair*

d. The article is generally repeated before each noun in a series.

Come **una** naranja y **un** huevo.   *He eats an orange and an egg.*

Compra **la** leche y **el** pan.   *He buys the milk and the bread.*

EXERCISE A

Enrique tells his little cousin the names of the kinds of food they see at the supermarket. Write what Enrique says.

EXAMPLE:

la leche

1.

2.

3.

4.

5.

6.

7.

8.

9.

10.

11.

12.

13.

14.

15.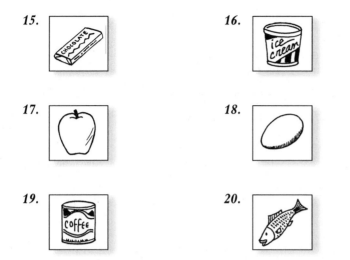

EXERCISE B

School has begun, and Carolina is preparing a shopping list of the
school supplies she will need. Help her prepare the list.

EXAMPLE:

un bolígrafo

1.

2.

3.

4.

5.

6.

7.

EXERCISE C

Jorge and his cousin Javier have been figuring out their family tree. Identify the relationships among the following members of their families.

EXAMPLE: Jorge es **el primo** de Javier.

1. Alfonso es _____ de Rafael.

2. Alberto es _____ de Jorge.

3. Anabel es _____ de Carmen.

4. Fernando es _____ de Jorge.

5. Alberto es _____ de Anabel y Javier.

6. Anabel es _____ de Javier.

7. Luis es _____ de Javier.

8. Rafael es _____ de Cristina.

9. Marta es _____ de Rafael y Alberto.

10. Cristina es _____ de Javier y Anabel.

11. Anabel es _____ de Luis y Marta.

12. Alfonso es _____ de Luis y Marta.

EXERCISE D

Alejandro is thinking about the gifts he plans to give his friends for the holidays. Identify the items he includes on his list.

EXAMPLE:

una pelota de voleibol

1.

2.

3.

4.

5.

6.

7.

8.

[2] PLURAL OF NOUNS

a. Nouns ending in a vowel form the plural by adding *-s*.

SINGULAR	PLURAL
el libro *the book*	**los libros** *the books*
la pluma *the pen*	**las plumas** *the pens*
un amigo *a friend*	**unos amigos** *some friends*
una clase *a class*	**unas clases** *some classes*

b. Nouns ending in a consonant form the plural by adding *-es*.

SINGULAR	PLURAL
el profesor *the teacher*	**los profesores** *the teachers*
la ciudad *the city*	**las ciudades** *the cities*

c. Nouns ending in *-z* change *z* to *c* before adding *-es*.

SINGULAR	PLURAL
el lápiz *the pencil* **la actriz** *the actress*	**los lápices** *the pencils* **las actrices** *the actresses*

d. An accent mark is added or dropped in nouns ending in *n* or *s* to keep the original stress.

SINGULAR	PLURAL
el joven	los jóvenes
el examen	los exámenes
el inglés	los ingleses
la lección	las lecciones

NOTE:

1. The articles *el* and *la* become *los* and *las* when used with plural nouns.

2. The plural forms of the indefinite articles are *unos* and *unas;* they mean *some, a few, several.*

EXERCISE E

Before going to summer camp, Rose studies a list of recommended articles of clothing. Tell how many of each item she should pack.

EXAMPLE: blusa *(2)*
   dos blusas

1. falda *(2)*

2. pantalón largo *(5)*

3. camiseta *(6)*

4. pañuelo *(10)*

5. traje de baño *(3)*

6. calcetín blanco *(8)*

7. pantalón corto *(7)*

8. suéter *(2)*

9. chaqueta *(2)*

10. juego de ropa interior *(6)*

EXERCISE F

You're helping your Spanish teacher review a writing exercise submitted by students in another class. Read each one and then indicate what that person likes or dislikes.

EXAMPLE: Me gusta el tenis. También me gusta nadar.
   A Roberto **le gustan los deportes**.

1. Me gusta ver las noticias. También me gusta ver las telenovelas.

A Sue le _____ .

2. Me gusta el inglés. También me gusta pasar muchas horas en la biblioteca.

A Ivan le _____ .

3. Me gusta el gato de Jorge. También me gusta el perro de mi abuelo.

A Clara le _____ .

4. Me gustan los videojuegos. También me gustan los juegos computarizados.

A Lorenzo le _____ .

5. Me gusta «Tom Sawyer». También me gusta «Jane Eyre».

A Laurie le _____ .

6. Me gusta escuchar la radio. También me gustan mucho los conciertos.

A Gabriel le _____ .

[3] FORMS OF THE ARTICLES

a. There are four definite articles in Spanish corresponding to English *the.*

	SINGULAR	PLURAL
MASCULINE	**el**	**los**
FEMININE	**la**	**las**

NOTE: Feminine nouns that begin with a stressed *a* sound (*a-* or *ha-*) take the articles *el* and *un* in the singular. In the plural, the articles are *las* and *unas*.

el agua *water*	**las** aguas *waters*	
un agua	**unas** aguas	

el aula *classroom* **las** aulas *classrooms*
un aula **unas** aulas

el hacha *ax* **las** hachas *axes*
un hacha **unas** hachas

BUT

la amiga ⎫
la alumna ⎭ (initial *a* is not stressed)

b. There are four indefinite articles in Spanish corresponding to English *a (an), some, several, a few.*

	SINGULAR	PLURAL
MASCULINE	**un**	**unos**
FEMININE	**una**	**unas**

un amigo   *a friend*   **unos** amigos   *some friends*
una blusa   *a blouse*   **unas** blusas   *several blouses*

[4] USES OF THE ARTICLES

The definite article is used:

a. before the names of languages and other subjects of study (*asignaturas*), unless the subjects of study follow *hablar, en,* or *de.*

El inglés es una lengua.	*English is a language.*
Estudio **el** español.	*I study Spanish.*
La química es difícil.	*Chemistry is difficult.*

BUT

Él **habla** español.	*He speaks Spanish.*
Escriben **en** alemán.	*They write in German.*
Mi libro **de** historia está en el escritorio.	*My history book is on the desk.*

b. before titles (except when speaking directly to a person).

El señor Gómez no está aquí.	*Mr. Gómez is not here.*
La doctora Álvarez sabe mucho.	*Dr. Álvarez knows a lot.*

BUT

Buenos días, señora Molina.	*Good morning, Mrs. Molina.*

c. before the words *escuela, clase,* and *iglesia* when they follow a preposition.

Voy **a la** escuela.	*I'm going to school.*
Están **en la** iglesia.	*They are in church.*

d. before certain geographic names.

la América Central	*Central America*
la América del Norte	*North America*
la América del Sur	*South America*
la Argentina	*Argentina*
la Florida	*Florida*
el Canadá	*Canada*
los Estados Unidos	*the United States*
el Perú	*Peru*

BUT

Alemania	*Germany*	Inglaterra	*England*
España	*Spain*	Italia	*Italy*
Europa	*Europe*	México	*Mexico*
Francia	*France*	Rusia	*Russia*

NOTE: Current informal usage tends to omit the definite article before the names of countries.

Vivo en Estados Unidos   *I live in the United States.*

e. before the days of the week, to express the English word *on*.

No voy a la escuela **los** domingos.   *I don't go to school on Sundays.*

f. The indefinite article is used to express the English word *a (an)*.

Tengo **un** hermano.   *I have a brother.*

g. The indefinite article is omitted before a noun expressing nationality, profession, or occupation when it follows the verb *ser*.

Pablo **es** francés.	*Paul is a Frenchman (is French).*
Ese hombre **es** zapatero.	*That man is a shoemaker.*
Ella va a **ser** médico.	*She's going to be a doctor.*

BUT

If the noun is modified, the indefinite article is used.

Deseo ser **un** médico bueno.   *I want to be a good doctor.*

EXERCISE G

Answer the questions a new student asks you. Use the cues provided.

1. ¿Eres francés (francesa)? *(español / española)*
2. ¿Qué asignaturas estudias? *(inglés, biológía, historia)*
3. ¿Cómo se llama tu profesora de inglés? *(Miss McCarthy)*
4. ¿En qué aula tienes la clase de historia? *(210)*
5. ¿Qué deportes te gustan? *(tenis, natación)*
6. ¿En que día vas al laboratorio en la clase de biología? *(jueves)*
7. ¿A qué hora de la noche te acuestas? *(10:30)*
8. ¿Qué país de la América del Sur deseas visitar? *(Perú, Argentina)*
9. ¿Sabes escribir en español? *(no)*
10. ¿Qué es tu padre? *(ingeniero)*

EXERCISE H

Use the correct form of the articles to complete this letter that Jorge received from a friend living in Mexico. Some sentences may not need an article.

Mientras estamos en _____ escuela prestamos atención al maestro y
                            1.

contestamos en _____ español. _____ miércoles tomé una lección de
               2.   **3.**

_____ música. Aprendo a tocar _____ guitarra. El profesor es _____
4.   **5.**   **6.**

argentino y es _____ guitarrista profesional. Durante las vacaciones él
               7.

viaja por _____ México, _____ Venezuela y _____ Estados Unidos.
          8.   **9.**   **10.**

Se llama _____ señor Rivas. Su padre es _____ guitarrista también.
         11.   **12.**

La clase es difícil porque _____ señor Rivas prefiere hablar en _____
                           13.   **14.**

español, pero aprendo así _____ español mientras asisto a la clase de _____
                          15.   **16.**

música. _____ sábado vamos a un concierto de _____ música flamenca.
        17.   **18.**

MASTERY EXERCISES

EXERCISE I

Describe the contents of a time capsule that you and a friend are preparing.

EXAMPLE: **una pelota de béisbol**

EXERCISE J

Roberto is telling a friend about his Spanish teacher. Tell what he says.

EXAMPLE: ella / vivir / Estados Unidos
Ella **vive en los** Estados Unidos.

1. ella / ser / señora Flores

2. ella / ser / América del Sur

3. Buenos Aires / estar / Argentina

4. ser / argentina

5. ser / profesora buena

6. hablar / italiano y español

7. su esposo / ser / médico

8. ellos / pasar el verano / Canadá

9. ella / dar un examen / viernes

10. corregir los exámenes / pluma verde

EXERCISE K

You're preparing a short autobiographical speech for your Spanish class. Express the following in Spanish.

1. I'm American, but I was born in Canada.
2. My parents are Argentinean.
3. They're from Argentina.
4. I'm a good student.
5. I attend high school.
6. I'm studying Spanish, English, biology, mathematics, and art.
7. I'm learning a lot in school.
8. The math class is my favorite class.
9. I'm going to be a pilot.
10. I want to be a good pilot.
11. On Saturdays, I get up late.
12. A few friends and I are going to the park.
13. It's a big park.
14. Several teams play soccer there on Saturday mornings.
15. Mr. Morales is a coach.

Chapter 18
Pronouns

[1] SUBJECT PRONOUNS

SINGULAR	PLURAL
yo *I*	**nosotros, -as** *we*
tú *you* (familiar)	**vosotros, -as** *you* (familiar)
usted (Ud.) *you*	**ustedes (Uds.)** *you*
él *he*	**ellos** *they* (masculine)
ella *she*	**ellas** *they* (feminine)

Subject pronouns are not used in Spanish as often as in English. Normally the verb ending indicates the subject. Spanish subject pronouns are used for clarity, emphasis, and politeness.

Él dibuja mientras **ella** escribe cartas.   *He draws while she writes letters.*

No entres: **yo** debo entrar primero.   *Don't enter: I should enter first.*

Pase. Tome asiento.   *Enter. Have a seat.*

NOTE:

1. Even though subject pronouns are usually omitted, *usted, (Ud.)*, and *ustedes (Uds.)* are regularly used.

2. The *vosotros* (familiar plural) form is used in Spain but rarely in Spanish America, where the *ustedes* form is preferred.

3. The English pronoun *it* is not expressed as a subject in Spanish.

¿Dónde está? Está allí.   *Where is it? It's over there.*

¿Qué es? Es un libro.   *What is it? It's a book.*

EXERCISE A

Arturo is asking you the nationalities of some of his new classmates. Write your answers in Spanish, using the correct subject pronouns.

EXAMPLE: Enrique / Guatemala
       Él es de Guatemala.

1. Rosa / Puerto Rico

2. Jacques y Pierre / Francia

3. David / España

4. Kyung Mi y Mi Soo / Corea

5. Arturo / Chile

6. Arturo y Miriam / Colombia

7. Pietro / Italia

EXERCISE B

A new student asks you the following questions. Use the correct subject pronouns in your answers.

1. ¿Cómo te llamas?

2. ¿Dónde vives?

3. ¿Quién es ese chico?

4. ¿Adónde van tú y tus amigos por la tarde?

5. ¿Qué hacen Uds. allí?

6. ¿Quiénes son esos señores?

7. ¿Podemos tú y yo estudiar juntos?

8. ¿Dónde juegan al tenis tus amigos?

9. ¿Quieres ver una película esta noche?

10. ¿Qué clases vas a tomar el año próximo?

[2] PREPOSITIONAL PRONOUNS

Prepositions, which will be more fully explained in the next chapter, are words that define a relationship to a person, place, or thing. When a personal pronoun follows a preposition, it takes the following forms:

SINGULAR	PLURAL
mí *me*	**nosotros, -as** *us*
ti *you* (familiar)	**vosotros, -as** *you* (familiar)
usted (Ud.) *you*	**ustedes (Uds.)** *you*
él *him, it*	**ellos** *them* (masculine)
ella *her, it*	**ellas** *them* (feminine)

a. Prepositional pronouns are used as the objects of a preposition and always follow the preposition.

No es para **mí**; es para **ella**.   *It's not for me; it's for her.*

b. The pronouns *mí* and *ti* combine with the preposition *con* as follows:

conmigo *with me*   contigo *with you*

NOTE:

1. Prepositional pronouns are identical to subject pronouns, except for *mí* and *ti*.

2. The forms *conmigo* and *contigo* do not change in gender and number.

3. The familiar plural form *vosotros, -as* is used in Spain but rarely in Spanish America, where the form *ustedes (Uds.)* is preferred.

c. Common prepositions

a *to, at*	**entre** *between, among*
cerca de near	**hacia** *toward*
con *with*	**para** *for*
contra *against*	**por** *for*
de of, from	**sin** *without*
en *in, on*	**sobre** *on top of, over*

EXERCISE C

While visiting Mexico, you and a friend are in a department store. Your friend wants to know for whom you're buying gifts. Answer her questions, using prepositional pronouns in your responses.

EXAMPLE: ¿Es el cinturón para tu papá?
             Sí, el cinturón **es** para **él**.

1. ¿Es la bolsa para tu mamá?

2. ¿Son los guantes para tus tías?

3. Los zapatos son para ti, ¿verdad?

4. ¿Son las botas para tu hermano?

5. ¿Es la estatua para Jaime?

6. ¿Son los libros para César y Arturo?

7. Los aretes son para mí, ¿verdad?

8. ¿Son los discos para nosotros?

EXERCISE D

Before Alfredo goes to the movies, he wants to know what his younger brother is going to do. Answer Alfredo's questions, using the appropriate prepositional pronoun and the cue provided.

EXAMPLE: ¿Vas al parque con Luis? *(no)*
No, no voy al parque con **él.**

1. ¿Vas al centro con mamá? *(no)*

2. ¿Vas a la piscina con Beto y Anita? *(no)*

3. ¿Vas al estadio con Víctor? *(no)*

4. ¿Vas al museo con Gloria y Antonia? *(no)*

5. ¿Vas al supermercado con papá? *(no)*

6. ¿Vas a la biblioteca con tus amigos? *(no)*

7. ¿Vas al cine conmigo? *(sí)*

EXERCISE E

Your little cousin is asking you a lot of questions while you're baby-sitting her in the park. Answer her questions, using the correct pronoun.

EXAMPLE: ¿Viven muchos animales en el parque?
Sí, muchos animales viven en **él.**

OR: **No**, muchos animales **no** viven en **él.**

1. ¿Reman muchas personas en el lago?

2. ¿Juegan muchos niños cerca de la piscina?

3. ¿Andan tus amigos por el parque?

4. ¿Estamos lejos del carrusel ahora?

5. ¿Te gusta sentarte en los bancos?

6. ¿Te subes a las atracciones conmigo?

7. ¿Venden globos en la entrada?

8. ¿Crecen flores debajo de las piedras?

9. ¿Mueren las plantas sin agua?

10. ¿Vuelan los pájaros sobre las nubes?

11. ¿Viven muchas personas en el edificio?

[*3*] DIRECT OBJECT PRONOUNS

a. Direct object pronouns tell who or what receives the action of the verb. Direct object pronouns replace direct objects and agree with them in gender and number.

SINGULAR	PLURAL
me *me*	**nos** *us*
te *you* (fam.)	**os** *you* (fam.)
le *him, you*	**los** *them, you* (m.)
lo *him, you* (formal, m.); *it* (m.)	
la *her, you* (formal, f.); *it* (f.)	**las** *them, you* (f.)

NOTE:

1. Either *le* or *lo* may be used to express *him*.

2. The plural form of both *le* and *lo* is *los.*

b. The direct object pronoun is usually placed directly before the verb.

¿Quién pronuncia **las palabras**?	*Who pronounces the words?*
El profesor **las** pronuncia.	*The teacher pronounces them.*
¿Tiene **el libro** Albert?	*Does Albert have the book?*
Albert no **lo** tiene.	*Albert doesn't have it.*

c. The direct object pronoun precedes the main verb or is attached to an infinitive.

Nos van a visitar.	
Van a visitar**nos**.	*They're going to visit us.*
Ella no **la** desea ver.	*She doesn't want to see it/her/you*
Ella no desea ver**la**.	*(formal).*

d. Direct object pronouns follow the affirmative command, but they come immediately before the verb in the negative command.

Bórre**la**.	*Erase it.*
BUT	
No **la** borre.	*Don't erase it.*

NOTE: When the direct object pronoun follows the affirmative command, an accent mark is normally required on the stressed vowel of the verb in order to keep the original stress. If the affirmative command has only one syllable *(pon)*, no accent mark is required *(ponlo)*.

EXERCISE F

Julio describes to his mother what happens in his Spanish class. His little brother repeats everything he says, with a slight variation. Tell what his brother says.

EXAMPLE: La maestra enseña la lección.
La maestra **la** enseña.

1. La clase saluda a la profesora.
2. Ella tiene un periódico español.
3. La maestra muestra los anuncios a la clase.
4. Teresa lee un anuncio en voz alta.
5. Roberto mira las fotos.
6. La profesora ayuda a Ahmed.
7. Beatriz y Lorenzo no comprenden un párrafo.
8. Fernando explica unas palabras.

EXERCISE G

Answer your friend's questions in Spanish, using the correct direct object pronoun.

EXAMPLE: ¿Lees el periódico todos los días?
Sí, **lo leo** todos los días.
 OR: **No, no lo leo** todos los días.

1. ¿Vas a ayudar a Peter?
2. ¿Quieres esta hamburguesa?
3. ¿Compró las flores Sarita?
4. ¿Van a vender la casa tus abuelos?
5. ¿Lavas tu ropa los sábados?
6. ¿Escribes tus cartas en español?

EXERCISE H

The Spanish Club is planning a party. Tell what one of the co-presidents tells the members to do.

EXAMPLE: Jorge / poner las banderas allí.
Jorge, **ponlas** allí.

1. Sarita / preparar la limonada
2. Rafael y Emma / comprar los refrescos
3. Gabriel / quitar las sillas
4. Simón e Hilda / traer los vasos
5. Estela / invitar a los profesores
6. Gustavo / mandar las invitaciones
7. Alejandro / revisar la música

EXERCISE I

Using the seven statements in Exercise H, tell what the other co-president tells the members not to do.

EXAMPLE: Jorge, ponlas allí.
Jorge, **no las pongas** allí.

EXERCISE J

Answer the questions that a new friend asks you. Use a direct object pronoun in your responses.

EXAMPLE: ¿Usas un diccionario en tu clase?
Sí, **lo uso** en mi clase.
OR: No, **no lo uso** en mi clase.

1. ¿Tienes el dinero?
2. ¿Contestas las preguntas correctamente?
3. ¿Me comprendes cuando hablo rápidamente?
4. ¿Esperas recibir regalos para la Navidad?
5. ¿Recibes buenas notas en todas tus clases?
6. ¿Piensas celebrar tu cumpleaños este mes?
7. ¿Lees el periódico todos los días?
8. ¿Perdiste tu cartera recientemente?

9. ¿Llevas un abrigo en el invierno?

10. ¿Aprendes a bailar el tango?

11. ¿Vas a comer la hamburguesa?

12. ¿Preparas las tareas por la noche?

13. ¿Estudias la química este año?

14. ¿Ayudan los profesores a los alumnos?

15. ¿Escuchas a la profesora?

[4] INDIRECT OBJECT PRONOUNS

a. Indirect objects tell to whom or for whom the action of the verb is performed. Indirect object pronouns replace indirect objects and agree with them in gender and number.

SINGULAR	PLURAL

me *to me*
te *to you* (fam.)
le *to you* (formal)
     to him, to her
	nos *to us*
	os *to you* (fam.)
	les *to you* (formal)
	     to them (m. and f.)

NOTE:

1. The forms *le* and *les* are used as both masculine and feminine indirect object pronouns.

2. If the meaning is not clear or if we wish to add emphasis, a phrase with *a + a prepositional* pronoun may be used in addition to the indirect object pronouns.

   (Clarity)   Yo les hablo **a ellos**.   *I speak to them.*

   (Emphasis)   **A mí** me gusta comer.   *I like to eat.*

   Sentences with both indirect object and indirect object pronoun are very common in Spanish.

3. The forms *me, te, nos,* and *os* are also used for direct object pronouns and for reflexive pronouns.

4. The indirect object pronoun may be identified in English by the preposition *to + a person.* The *to* may be expressed or implied.

   Les da el dinero.   *He gives the money to them.*
                            (He gives them the money.)

b. The indirect object pronoun is usually placed before the verb.

Ana **le** habla.	*Ana speaks to him/her/you* (formal).
Ella **me** escribe una carta.	*She writes a letter to me.*
	(She writes me a letter.)

c. When a verb is followed by an infinitive, indirect object pronouns precede the verb or are attached to the infinitive.

¿**Me** quieres decir la verdad? }
¿Quieres decir**me** la verdad? } *Do you want to tell me the truth?*

d. The indirect object pronoun is attached to the end of an affirmative command, but is placed before a negative command.

Escríbe**me** una carta.	*Write a letter to me.*
	(Write me a letter.)

BUT

No **me** escribas una carta.	*Don't write a letter to me.*
	(Don't write me a letter.)

NOTE: When the indirect object pronoun follows and is attached to the affirmative command, an accent mark is normally required on the stressed vowel of the verb in order to keep the original stress.

EXERCISE K

Rogelio is telling a friend what gifts he is giving to various people. Tell what he says.

EXAMPLE: a mi abuela / flores
Le doy flores a mi abuela.

1. a mis tíos / dulces

2. a Luisa / un pañuelo

3. a Pablo / un disco

4. a mis primas / una muñeca

5. a Martín / un juego electrónico

6. a ti / un cartel

EXERCISE L

Tomás's father is very proud of the trophy his son won and wants to show it to everyone, but Tomás already did that. Tell what Tomás tells his father.

EXAMPLE: Quiero mostrarle el trofeo a tu abuelo.
Ya le mostré el trofeo a **mi** abuelo.

1. Quiero mostrarles el trofeo a tus hermanos.
2. Quiero mostrarle el trofeo a tu tío.
3. Quiero mostrarles el trofeo a tus padrinos.
4. Quiero mostrarle el trofeo al profesor.
5. Quiero mostrarle el trofeo a tu mamá.
6. Quiero mostrarles el trofeo a todos mis amigos.

EXERCISE M

Phil is telling a friend what to do for various people before leaving for camp.

EXAMPLE: a Alejandro / devolver la raqueta de tenis
Debes devolverle la raqueta de tenis a Alejandro.

1. a mí / comprar otro disco
2. a Billy / prestar los patines
3. a Sarita y a Pilar / pedir una disculpa
4. a la profesora / escribir una carta
5. a Miguel y a mí / invitar a comer
6. a tu hermana / pagar los diez dólares
7. a Vicente y a Dan / hablar
8. a tus padres / pedir dinero

EXERCISE N

Using an indirect object pronoun, express your boss's instructions to you on your first day of work as a waiter.

EXAMPLE: dar el menú a los clientes
¡**Dales** el menú!

1. llevar agua a la señora
2. dar otra cuchara al niño

3. pedir la orden a los jóvenes

4. quitar el menú a los niños

5. llevar la hamburguesa al señor

6. servir el postre a las señoras

7. ofrecer más café a esa señorita

8. dar la cuenta a los hombres

9. traer el dinero a mí

EXERCISE O

Sarita and her sister are preparing to leave for a study-abroad program. Write what their father tells them.

EXAMPLES: a mí / llamar cada domingo
   Llámenme cada domingo.

   a sus amigas / no hablar por teléfono
   No les hablen a sus amigas por teléfono.

1. a mí / escribir todos los días

2. a nosotros / no comprar regalos

3. a Gloria / no buscar revistas de telenovelas

4. a su profesora / mandar una tarjeta

5. a Arturo y a Felipe / no traer recuerdos

6. a mí / no llamar todos los días

7. a tus hermanos / no prometer nada

8. a su abuela / comprar un regalo

EXERCISE P

Answer the questions that an exchange student asks you. Use the appropriate indirect object pronoun in each of your answers.

1. ¿Pides dinero a tu abuelo?

2. ¿Quién te presta dinero?

3. ¿Quién enseña a los alumnos?

4. ¿Haces tú muchas preguntas al profesor?

5. ¿Escribes a tus primos que viven lejos?

6. ¿Haces favores a tus compañeros?

7. ¿Prometen Uds. a sus padres estudiar diligentemente?

8. ¿Contestas tú al maestro correctamente?

9. ¿Pides muchos regalos a tu tío?

10. ¿Ofreces tu ayuda a tu papá cuando él conduce el carro?

11. ¿Das regalos a tu mamá con frecuencia?

12. ¿Te hablan tus amigos por la mañana?

13. ¿Muestras tus buenas notas a tus amigos?

14. ¿El maestro les da a Uds. muchos exámenes?

15. ¿Siempre dices la verdad a tus padres?

[5] THE VERB GUSTAR

a. *Gustar* (to please) is used to express "to like."

Me gusta la comida.	*I like the food.* *(Literally: The food pleases me.)*
Te gustan las manzanas.	*You like the apples.* *(Literally: The apples please you.)*
Nos gusta jugar a las damas.	*We like to play checkers.* *(Literally: To play checkers pleases us.)*

b. *Gustar* is preceded by an indirect object pronoun. The form of *gustar* agrees with the subject, which generally follows it.

Te **gusta el libro.**	*You like the book.*
Te **gustan los libros.**	*You like the books.*
Nos **gusta la revista.**	*We like the magazine.*
Nos **gustan las revistas.**	*We like the magazines.*
Les **gusta** leer.	*They like to read.*

> NOTE: If the thing liked is not a noun but an action (expressed by a verb in the infinitive), *gustar* is used in the third person singular.

Me gusta leer y escribir.	*I like to read and write.*

c. To clarify the indirect object pronouns *le* and *les*, or to give emphasis, the indirect object normally precedes the indirect object pronoun.

A Josefa no le gusta cantar.	*Josefa doesn't like to sing.*
A los niños les gusta correr.	*The children like to run.*

| A José **le** gusta el helado. | *Joseph likes the ice cream.* |
| A mí **no me** gusta saltar. | *I don't like to jump.* |

[6] OTHER VERBS LIKE *GUSTAR*

encantar
fascinar $\Big\}$ *to delight* (Used for things that someone likes a lot or loves.)

Me encantan las películas. *I love movies.*

parecer *to seem*

La comida **me parece** buena. *The food seems good to me.*

doler *to be painful, to cause sorrow*
faltar *to be lacking, to need*
tocar (a uno) *to be one's turn*

NOTE: **Since *parecer* is usually followed by an adjective, the adjective must agree in number and gender with the item described.**

| **La blusa** me parece **bonita**. | *The blouse seems pretty to me.* |
| **Las noches** me parecen **largas**. | *The nights seem long to me.* |

EXERCISE Q

Tell whether you like or dislike each of the following activities.

EXAMPLE:

Me gusta bailar.
OR: **No me gusta bailar.**

1.

2.

EXERCISE R

You've taken a young cousin to an amusement park, and it's now time to eat. Based on the illustrations, ask him what he likes and write his responses as indicated.

EXAMPLE:

¿Te gusta el helado?
Sí, me gusta el helado.

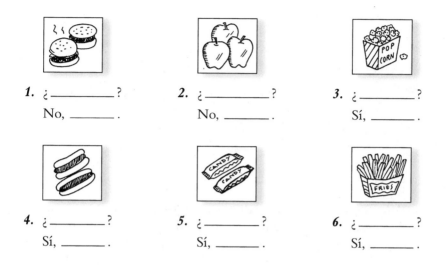

1. ¿_____?
No, _____.

2. ¿_____?
No, _____.

3. ¿_____?
Sí, _____.

4. ¿_____?
Sí, _____.

5. ¿_____?
Sí, _____.

6. ¿_____?
Sí, _____.

EXERCISE S

You and your friends are talking about your likes and dislikes. Tell what is said.

EXAMPLE: a Gloria / gustar / ir al cine
            A Gloria **le gusta** ir al cine.

1. a ti / no gustar / los dibujos animados
2. a ustedes / gustar / las comedias
3. a mí / no gustar / los documentales
4. a Estela / gustar / comer en un restaurante
5. a Felipe y a mí / encantar / los tacos de pollo
6. a ellas / encantar / las telenovelas
7. a Gonzalo / no gustar / las noticias
8. a ellos / encantar / mirar los partidos de fútbol
9. a nosotros / no gustar / las novelas largas
10. a ella / encantar / cocinar

EXERCISE T

After your school's varsity soccer practice, you and your friends are describing what hurts. Tell what you and they say.

EXAMPLE: a Ramón / las piernas
            A Ramón **le duelen** las piernas.

1. a mí / los ojos

2. a Vinnie / la espalda

3. a Juan y a mí / la cabeza

4. a Gunther / los oídos

5. a Clara y a Antonia / las manos

6. a Esteban / la garganta

EXERCISE U

As the Pérez family sits down to dinner with their guests, Mrs. Pérez notices that certain things are missing from the table. Tell what she says.

EXAMPLE: a tu papá / un cuchillo
             A tu papá **le falta** un cuchillo.

1. a tus abuelos / la ensalada

2. a mí / una cucharita

3. a Eduardo y a Lourdes / un vaso

4. a ti / un plato

5. a nosotros / la sal y la pimienta

6. a Carlos / un tenedor y una cuchara

7. a Uds. / la servilleta

EXERCISE V

Marisol is telling her mother what she and various classmates think of their math class. Tell what she says.

EXAMPLE: a mí / Beto / muy inteligente
             A mí, Beto **me parece** muy inteligente.

1. al profesor / la clase / perezoso

2. a Griselda y a Gladys / el maestro / estricto

3. a Tomás / las tareas / difícil

4. a Luz y a mí / los exámenes / justo

5. a Angel / los alumnos / simpático

6. a mí / la clase / aburrido

MASTERY EXERCISES

EXERCISE W

Complete this letter that Roberto writes to a new pen pal, stating in Spanish the words or expressions given beneath the blanks.

Querido amigo:

_____ me llamo Roberto Casares. Mi familia y _____ vivimos en
   1. (I)   *2.* (I)

Chicago, una ciudad grande de los Estados Unidos. _____ practicar los
                                                3. (I like)

deportes, especialmente el béisbol. _____ practico casi todos los días. Soy
                                     4. (it)

miembro de un equipo que se llama «Los cuervos». Tengo muchos amigos

en el equipo y _____ ganar partidos. Mi familia no es grande. Mi
                        5. (they like)

hermano Alfredo comparte el cuarto _____ . _____ es un chico
                                 6. (with me)   *7.* (he)

bueno, pero nunca puedo estar en el cuarto _____ . Hay un
                                      8. (without him)

televisor en nuestro cuarto, pero _____ los dibujos animados.
                                    9. (he loves)

_____ muy cómicos y _____ mira todos los sábados
 10. (they seem to him)   *11.* (them)

por la mañana cuando _____ dormir. Muchas veces yo dejo de hablar
                        12. (I like)

_____ porque él no _____ respeta. Él tiene once años y
 13. (with him)   *14.* (me)

_____ molestar _____ . Es difícil salir con mis amigos sin _____ .
 15. (he loves)   *16.* (me)   *17.* (him)

Siempre quiere acompañar _____ cuando salgo con _____ .
                         18. (us)   *19.* (them)

Tengo una amiga especial. _____ se llama Connie. Yo _____ admiro
                           20. (she)   *21.* (her)

mucho. Pasamos mucho tiempo juntos: _____ caminar en el parque y
                                  22. (we like)

sacar fotografías. Ella _____ guarda en un álbum. Ella hizo copias para
                        23. (them)

_____ de todas las fotos que sacamos. Ella _____ en otro álbum
 24. (me)   *25.* (put them)

y _____ el álbum como regalo.
    26. (gave me)

¡ _____ pronto! La foto del equipo es para _____ . ¡No
  27. (write to me)   *28. (you)*

_____ enseñes a tus amigos!
  29. (it)

Hasta pronto,

Roberto

EXERCISE X

José found an old board game. Express the following in Spanish.

1. José found it *(the game)*.
2. He showed the game to his friends.
3. He invited them to play with him.
4. He explained the rules to them.
5. He told them: "Follow them *(the rules)*!"
6. José loves to win.
7. His friends don't like to lose.
8. He told Carlos: "The red is for you; the black is for them."
9. They told him: "It's not your turn now."
10. Now it's our turn.
11. The game seemed boring to Juan.
12. Juan doesn't like this game a lot.
13. Juan doesn't want to play with them.
14. He told them: "You can play without me."
15. They need (are lacking) three points to win.

Chapter 19
Prepositions

Prepositions are words that relate a noun or pronoun to some other word in the sentence.

Yo voy a la tienda.	*I'm going to the store.*
Ella estudia con George.	*She studies with George.*
Trabajo en la biblioteca.	*I work in the library.*

[1] USES OF THE PREPOSITION A

a. The preposition *a* is used to indicate destination or direction.

Vamos a la fiesta.	*We're going to the party.*
Llegamos temprano a la escuela.	*We arrived at school early.*
El café está a la derecha.	*The café is to the right.*

NOTE:

1. The preposition *a* (to) combines with *el* (the) to form the contraction *al* (to the).

María va al mercado.	*María goes to the market.*
El profesor habla al alumno.	*The teacher speaks to the student.*

2. The preposition *a* never combines with the other articles *(la, los, las)* to form a single word.

Rosa va a la tienda.	*Rosa goes to the store.*
El profesor habla a los alumnos.	*The teacher speaks to the students.*

3. In some expressions, *a* plus the definite article is used where there's no equivalent in English.

Juegan al béisbol.	*They play baseball.*

EXERCISE A

Tell where you're going, based on the drawings.

EXAMPLE:

Voy a la piscina.

b. The preposition *a* is required before the direct object of a verb if the direct object is a person, a personalized group, a pet, or something personified.

Ana visita **a** Peter.   *Ana visits Peter.*

El niño ve **al** hombre.   *The boy sees the man.*

Pablo invita **a** sus amigos.   *Pablo invites his friends.*

Lola saca **al** perro.   *Lola takes the dog out.*

BUT

Ana visita la escuela.   *Ana visits the school.*

El niño ve la pelota.   *The boy sees the ball.*

c. The preposition *a* is required before the pronouns *¿quién?, ¿quiénes?, nadie,* and *alguien,* when they refer to a person.

No conoce **a** nadie.   *He doesn't know anyone.*

Vio **a** alguien en la calle.   *He saw someone in the street.*

¿**A** quién defendemos?   *Whom do we defend?*

NOTE:

1. When used before a direct object, the preposition *a* (personal *a*) has no equivalent in English. When used before an indirect object, it is translated as "to."

Veo **a** mi prima.   *I see my cousin.*

Hablo **a** mi prima.   *I speak to my cousin.*

2. The personal *a* is not used after the verb *tener* (to have).

Tiene una hermana bonita.   *He has a pretty sister.*

Tengo muchos amigos.   *I have many friends.*

EXERCISE B

You and a friend are attending a civic function. Tell your friend who's talking to whom.

EXAMPLE: el alcalde / los ciudadanos
                   El alcalde **habla a** los ciudadanos.

1. el médico / la enfermera

2. el profesor / los alumnos

3. el zapatero / el cliente

4. la señorita Vargas / los señores Polaski

5. Veronique / las amigas

6. Luis y Fernando / la chica

7. tú y yo / el alcalde

8. mi madre / la profesora

EXERCISE C

Complete this letter that Cristina writes to her friend while visiting Spain. Use the personal *a* or the contraction *al* only when needed.

Querida Gloria:

Mientras espero _____ mozo para bajar la maleta, te escribo estas pocas

1.

palabras. Durante mi viaje vi _____ muchos lugares bonitos e interesantes.

2.

También tuve la oportunidad de conocer _____ muchos jóvenes españoles.

3.

Un día visité _____ mi familia en Sevilla.   Mi prima invitó _____ otros

4.
5.

parientes y _____ unos amigos a una cena en su casa.   Me divertí mucho.

6.

Ahora salgo para Barcelona donde quiero ver _____ Enrique.   Él estudió

7.

en mi escuela el año pasado. Tiene _____ muchos amigos.   Pienso llamar

8.

_____ mis padres esta noche.   Oigo _____ alguien en la puerta.

9.
10.

Adiós por ahora.

Cristina

EXERCISE D

Tell your plans for this evening. Use *a* or *al* when needed.

EXAMPLE: ver la televisión
Pienso ver la televisión.

1. escuchar / el grupo «Coquí»

2. hablar / el vecino

3. jugar / las damas

4. llamar / Elsa

5. esperar / mis padres

6. oír / una cinta

7. acompañar / mi madre

EXERCISE E

Use complete sentences and the cues in parentheses to answer the questions that your new friend asks you.

1. ¿A quiénes saludas por la mañana? *(los vecinos)*

2. ¿A quién ayudas tú? *(mis amigos)*

3. ¿Respetan los jóvenes a sus padres? *(sí)*

4. ¿A quién admiras más? *(el presidente)*

5. ¿Tienes muchos primos y amigos? *(sí)*

6. ¿A quién esperas tú al salir de la escuela? *(nadie)*

7. ¿Cuándo visitas al dentista? *(cada año)*

8. ¿Escuchas a los maestros en tu escuela? *(sí)*

9. ¿A quién buscas cuando tienes un problema? *(mi hermana)*

10. ¿Amas tú a toda tu familia? *(sí)*

d. The preposition *a* is used in time expressions to indicate "at."

¿A qué hora es la fiesta?	*At what time is the party?*
Es **a** las ocho.	*It's at 8 o'clock.*
Llego **a** la una.	*I arrive at one o'clock.*

EXERCISE F

While vacationing in Puerto Rico, Javier wants to know at what time different activities will take place. Using the cues provided, answer his questions.

EXAMPLE: ¿A qué hora es la excursión en barco? *(2:00)*
             Es **a las dos.**

1. ¿A qué hora es el desayuno? *(7:30)*

2. ¿A qué hora es la clase de natación? *(9:00)*

3. ¿A qué hora vamos a comer el almuerzo? *(1:00)*

4. ¿A qué hora vamos al Viejo San Juan? *(4:00)*

5. ¿A qué hora quieres cenar? *(8:00)*

6. ¿A qué hora comienza el baile? *(10:30)*

[2] USES OF THE PREPOSITION *DE*

a. The preposition *de* corresponds to *of, from,* or *about* in English.

¿**De** qué hablas?	*What are you speaking about?*
Hablo **de** la fiesta.	*I'm speaking about the party.*
Recibo cartas **de** Juan.	*I receive letters from Juan.*
Sacan fotos **de** los niños.	*They take photos of the children.*

NOTE:

1. The preposition *de* (of, from) combines with *el* (the) to form *del* (of the, from the, about).

El Sr. Pérez es el presidente **del** país.	*Mr. Pérez is the president of the country.*
Ana recibe dinero **del** jefe.	*Ana receives money from the boss.*

2. The preposition *de* never combines with the other articles *(la, los, las)* to form a single word.

¿Recibe Ud. cartas **de** las muchachas?	*Do you receive letters from the girls?*

EXERCISE G

A group of friends went to see a movie. Say what they're talking about afterwards.

EXAMPLE: Alejandro / la película
Alejandro **habla de** la película.

1. Elena / los actores

2. Esteban y Flor / el cuento

3. Ernie / el reparto

4. Beto y Antonio / los carros antiguos

5. Aisha y Marcel / la ropa

6. Alicia / el fin

7. Hiroshi y Pedro / las escenas cómicas

8. yo / la actriz principal

EXERCISE H

You and a friend are visiting his grandmother. Say what she tells you to do.

EXAMPLE: cerrar las ventanas / el comedor
¡**Cierren** las ventanas **del** comedor!

1. traer flores / el jardín

2. sacar las fotos / los nietos

3. oír el ruido / la calle

4. abrir la puerta / la sala

5. salir / la casa

b. In Spanish, possession is expressed as follows: *noun* (thing possessed) followed by *de* plus *noun* (possessor). This is equivalent to the English possessive expressed with *of.* In Spanish, there is no apostrophe to show possession.

el libro **de** Alberto { *the book of Alberto*
{ *Alberto's book*

la cámara **de** la muchacha { *the camera of the girl*
{ *the girl's camera*

los lápices **de** los alumnos { *the pencils of the students*
{ *the student's pencils*

c. *¿De quién?, ¿De quiénes?* (Whose?) are used to ask *to whom* something belongs.

¿**De quién** son las plumas? *Whose (sing.) pens are they?*

¿**De quiénes** son las fotos? *To whom (pl.) do the photos belong?*

EXERCISE I

Tell whom the following items belong to.

EXAMPLE: los anteojos / el maestro
Son los anteojos **del** maestro.

1. la mochila / la alumna
2. el diccionario / Isaac
3. los tenis / los chicos
4. el reloj / el director
5. la cámara / mi hermano
6. la bandera / la escuela
7. las tarjetas / Beatriz y Charlotte
8. la calculadora / el señor Rivas
9. las fotos / Javier
10. las estampillas / la secretaria

EXERCISE J

A friend is helping you clean up the living room. Tell her who owns the various things she finds.

EXAMPLE: ¿De quién son las historietas? *(mi hermano menor)*
Son de mi hermano menor.

1. ¿De quién son las llaves? *(mi mamá)*
2. ¿De quién es el pasaporte? *(el novio de mi hermana)*
3. ¿De quién son las revistas? *(la amiga de mi mamá)*
4. ¿De quién es el suéter? *(el primo de Juan)*
5. ¿De quién es la novela? *(el profesor de inglés)*
6. ¿De quién es el bolígrafo? *(mi papa)*

d. A *de* phrase may also function as an adjective.

la clase **de** biología	*the biology class*
un reloj **de** oro	*a gold watch*

EXERCISE K

Juanita is playing a game with her little cousin. He has to identify an object or person based on the clues Juanita gives him. Help him get the correct answers.

EXAMPLES: Juan Pardo / el padre
el padre **de** Juan

un examen / matemática
un examen **de** matemática

1. un reloj bueno y caro / oro
2. un libro de palabras en inglés y español / diccionario
3. una bandera roja, blanca y azul / los Estados Unidos
4. julio y agosto / meses
5. martes y jueves / días
6. la primavera y el otoño / estaciones
7. a, be, ce, de / letras
8. Beto Suárez Olmeda / Tomás Ramos Olmeda *(primo)*

e. The phrase *de + la mañana (la tarde, la noche)* is used following a specific hour to indicate A.M. or P.M.

Son las diez **de la mañana.**	*It's 10:00 A.M.*
Te veo a las dos **de la tarde.**	*I'll see you at 2:00 P.M.*

EXERCISE L

Tell at what time you usually do the following activities. Be sure to include the Spanish equivalent of A.M. or P.M. in your response.

EXAMPLE: desayunarte
Me desayuno a las siete de la mañana.

1. despertarte
2. almorzar
3. entrar en la escuela
4. salir del colegio
5. cenar con tu familia
6. lavar los platos
7. jugar con tus amigos
8. acostarte
9. apagar la luz

f. *De* is also used together with other prepositions to indicate location.

El jardín está **detrás de** la casa.	*The garden is behind the house.*
Las flores están **dentro del** florero.	*The flowers are in the vase.*

EXERCISE M

Use the expressions below to tell where the buildings in the pictures are located.

a la derecha de	dentro de	enfrente de
al lado de	detrás de	a la izquierda de
cerca de		

EXAMPLE:

El teatro está **al lado de la iglesia.**

1.

El museo está _____ .

2.

La escuela está _____ .

3.

El supermercado está _____ .

4.

La piscina está _____ .

5.

El hotel está _____ .

6.

La estatua está _____ .

[3] PREPOSITIONS WITH INFINITIVES

a. In Spanish, the infinitive is the only verb form that may follow a preposition. The following prepositions and prepositional phrases are commonly used before an infinitive:

a *to, at*	después de *after*
al *upon, on*	en vez de *instead of*
antes de *before*	sin *without*
de *of, to*	

Al salir de la casa, él cerró la puerta.	*Upon leaving the house, he closed the door.*
Ella corrió **en vez de caminar.**	*She ran instead of walking.*
Pensó **antes de contestar.**	*She thought before answering.*

EXERCISE N

Combine a suggestion from each of the columns below and tell what you and your friends do in various situations. (Use all the words in the first column.)

al	cenar	mi amiga	contar el secreto
antes de	estudiar	mi amigo	decir gracias
después de	ir al cine	mis amigos	hablar por teléfono
en vez de	pedir permiso	mis amigos y yo	mirar la televisión
sin	pensar	yo	salir de la casa
	recibir un regalo		tomar un refresco

EXAMPLE: **Sin pensar, mi amigo contó el secreto.**

b. The preposition *a* is required before any infinitive that follows a verb of (1) beginning, (2) movement, (3) teaching/learning, or (4) helping.

   (1) **Beginning**

      comenzar a + *infinitive*
      empezar a + *infinitive*   }   *to begin to + verb*

      Comienzan a cantar.   *They begin to sing.*
      Empezamos a correr.   *We began to run.*

   (2) **Movement**

      ir a + *infinitive*   *to go to + verb*
      Va a tocar el piano.   *She's going to play the piano.*

correr a + *infinitive* *to run to* + *verb*
Corren a cerrar las ventanas.   *They run to close the windows.*

venir a + *infinitive* *to come to* + *verb*
Vengo a verte.   *I'm coming to see you.*

(3) Teaching/Learning

enseñar a + *infinitive* *to teach to* + *verb*
El maestro nos **enseña a leer.**   *The teacher teaches us to read.*

aprender a + *infinitive* *to learn to* + *verb*
Aprendemos a hablar español.   *We're learning to speak Spanish.*

(4) Helping

ayudar a + *infinitive* *to help (to)* + *verb*
Ella me **ayuda a bailar.**   *She helps me dance.*

EXERCISE O

Gladys describes an afternoon with some friends. Put what she says in complete sentences. Be sure to include the preposition.

EXAMPLE: dos jóvenes españoles / venir / almorzar conmigo
              Dos jóvenes españoles **vienen a almorzar** conmigo.

1. yo / ir / esperarlos en el restaurante

2. yo / correr / llegar temprano al restaurante

3. el mesero / correr / poner la mesa

4. nosotros / empezar / comer en seguida

5. mis amigos / aprender / hablar inglés

6. yo / ir / hacer un viaje a España

7. ellos / ayudarme / pronunciar las palabras

8. yo / enseñarles / cantar en inglés

EXERCISE P

Using a verb from column A and an expression from column B, tell what these people are doing.

A	B
aprender	contar el dinero
ayudar	decirme las noticias
comenzar	lavar el carro

A (cont'd)	B (cont'd)
correr	limpiar la casa
empezar	patinar en hielo
enseñar	pronunciar bien
ir	trabajar por la tarde
venir	ver el accidente

EXAMPLE: Tú **comienzas** a **trabajar por la tarde.**

1. Yo _____ .

2. Mi hermano _____ .

3. Mis padres _____ .

4. Mi hermana _____ .

5. Mis amigos _____ .

6. Mi madre _____ .

7. Mi profesor _____ .

c. The preposition *de* is required before any infinitive that comes after one of thefollowing four verbs:

acabar de + *infinitive*   *to have just*
Acaban de cenar.   *They've just eaten dinner.*

cesar de + *infinitive*   *to stop*
Cesó de llover.   *It stopped raining.*

dejar de + *infinitive*   *to quit, stop*
Juan **dejó de darme** el dinero.   *Juan stopped giving me the money.*

tratar de + *infinitive*   *to try to*
Trataron de llamarme.   *They tried to call me.*

EXERCISE Q

Tell what these people have just done.

EXAMPLE: yo / ver un partido de fútbol
           Yo **acabo de ver** un partido de fútbol.

1. Gerardo / jugar al tenis

2. mi mamá / ir de compras

3. mis hermanas / salir con sus amigas

4. Tommy y Enrique / lavar el carro

5. Alicia y yo / hablar por teléfono

EXERCISE R

You're working as a counselor in a day camp. Using the cues, tell the children to stop doing the following.

EXAMPLE: correr *(Uds.)*
    ¡**Dejen de** correr!

1. gritar *(tú)*

2. pelear *(Ana y Kyoko)*

3. hablar *(tú—Carlos)*

4. tirar la pelota *(Bárbara y Juan)*

5. silbar *(tú—Isabel)*

EXERCISE S

Help Ricardo write a note to a friend in Venezuela.

EXAMPLE: las clases / acabar / terminar
    Las clases **acaban de** terminar.

1. yo / acabar / recibir mi licencia de conducir

2. Jorge / dejar / tomar clases de conducir

3. él / tratar / pasar el examen varias veces

4. Jorge y yo / cesar / ser amigos

5. Jorge / no tratar / llamarme

d. The following verbs are used without a preposition before an infinitive:

deber *ought to, must*	pensar *to intend*
dejar *to let, allow*	poder *to be able, can*
desear *to wish, desire*	preferir *to prefer*
esperar *to hope, expect to*	prometer *to promise*
necesitar *to need*	querer *to want, wish to*
oír *to hear*	saber *to know how to*

Debo ir a la escuela hoy.   *I ought to go to school today.*
No **pueden salir** ahora.   *They can't go out now.*
Él **promete ser** bueno.   *He promises to be good.*
Ella **sabe jugar** al ajedrez.   *She knows how to play chess.*

NOTE: Remember that the verb *dejar* changes meaning when it's followed by the preposition *de*.

¡Déjenme entrar!   *Let me in!*

Ya **dejó de** llover.   *It already stopped raining.*

EXERCISE T

Answer these questions that a new friend asks you.

1. ¿Qué prefieres, caminar en el parque o ir de compras?
2. ¿Qué debes hacer para mañana?
3. ¿Necesitas pedirles permiso a tus padres antes de salir?
4. ¿Qué esperas hacer este fin de semana?
5. ¿Puedes acompañarme a un concierto el sábado?
6. ¿Deseas comer en un restaurante argentino?
7. ¿Sabes tocar la guitarra?
8. ¿Prometes llamarme por teléfono mañana?
9. ¿Piensas ir a la fiesta de Marisol?
10. ¿Con quién esperas ir a la fiesta?

EXERCISE U

Your teacher is telling your class what should happen when she's absent. Write eight sentences telling what she says, using the suggestions provided in the three columns below.

EXAMPLE: **Yo debo dejar una lección interesante.**

la clase	deber	aprender la lección
todos	desear	cooperar con el maestro
Uds.	esperar	dejar una lección interesante
yo	necesitar	estudiar mucho
	pensar	prestar atención
	poder	repasar la lección
	preferir	sentarse en su propio asiento
	prometer	ser amables
	querer	trabajar en grupos
		traer los libros a la clase
		volver al día siguiente

[4] COMMON EXPRESSIONS WITH PREPOSITIONS

al aire libre   *outdoors, in the open air*
A los niños les gusta jugar **al aire libre**.   *The children like to play outdoors.*

a menudo   *often*
Veo a mis primos **a menudo**.   *I see my cousins often.*

a pie   *on foot*
Él va a la escuela **a pie**.   *He goes to school on foot.*

a tiempo   *on time*
El tren llega **a tiempo**.   *The train arrives on time.*

a veces   *sometimes*
A veces me gusta dormir la siesta.   *Sometimes I like to take a nap.*

con cuidado   *carefully*
Escribo la tarea **con cuidado**.   *I write the assignment carefully.*

de memoria   *by heart*
Él sabe la dirección **de memoria**.   *He knows the address by heart.*

De nada.   *You're welcome.*
Muchas gracias. **De nada**.   *Thanks a lot. You're welcome.*

de nuevo   *again*
Escribí la oración **de nuevo**.   *I wrote the sentence again.*

de pie   *standing*
Todos están **de pie**.   *Everyone is standing.*

de pronto
de repente   }   *suddenly*
De repente empezó a llover.   *Sudddenly, it started to rain.*

en punto   *sharp*
Es la una **en punto**.   *It's one o'clock sharp.*

en serio   *seriously*
Él toma todo **en serio**.   *He takes everything seriously.*

en venta   *for sale*
El coche de mi tío está **en venta**.   *My uncle's car is for sale.*

en vez de   *instead of*
Ella descansó **en vez de** trabajar.   *She rested instead of working.*

EXERCISE V

Norma is describing a camping trip in her diary. Write the expressions that are needed to complete the entry in her diary.

El club de la escuela va a acampar _____ . _____ van a la playa
                                            1. (often)   **2.** (sometimes)

_____ ir a las montañas. No importa, porque a mí me gusta estar
3. (instead of)

_____ . El autobús siempre sale de la escuela _____ : a las siete
4. (outdoors)   **5.** (on time)

de la mañana _____ . En el autobús la consejera del club explicó
               6. (sharp)

_____ las reglas _____ . Ya las sé _____ . Ella toma
7. (again)   **8.** (carefully)   **9.** (by heart)

_____ su responsabilidad. Ella viajó _____ _____
10. (seriously)   **11.** (standing)   **12.** (instead of)

sentarse.

Cuando llegamos a la playa, fuimos al campamento _____
                                           13. (on foot)

_____ comenzó a hacer mucho frío. Gladys me prestó un suéter.
14. (suddenly)

Le di las gracias y ella contestó: —_____ .
                                       15. (you're welcome)

M A S T E R Y E X E R C I S E S

EXERCISE W

Read this story. Select the preposition that should be used in each sentence. Note that in some cases a preposition may not be needed.

A una señora le gusta andar _____ pie cuando va _____ mercado
                              1. (a/de)   **2.** (al/a la)

todos los días. _____ menudo lleva _____ su hija _____ ella.
              3. (A/De)   **4.** (a/)   **5.** (a/con)

Prefiere _____ estar _____ aire libre, especialmente cuando cesa
        6. (a/)   **7.** (en el/al)

_____ llover. _____ veces pasa por el parque en vez _____
8. (a/de)   **9.** (De/A)   **10.** (a/de)

tomar una ruta más directa _____ centro. Un día _____ salir de su
                        11. (al/a la)   **12.** (al/a)

casa _____ ocho y media _____ mañana, ella comenzó
    13. (a los/a las)   **14.** (del/de la)

_____ andar por el parque. Cerca _____ entrada vio _____
15. (a/de)   **16.** (del/de la)   **17.** (a/)

la niña _____ vecino. Corrió _____ ayudarla. Trató _____
      18. (del/de la)   19. (a/)   20. (/de)

hablarle _____ niña pero la niña empezó _____ llorar.
      21. (al/a la)   22. (a/de)

_____ fin la niña dijo: —Yo no debo _____ hablarle _____
23. (Al/A la)   24. (a/)   25. (/a)

usted porque no la conozco _____ usted—. La señora prometió
              26. (a/)

_____ ayudar _____ niña _____ encontrar la casa
27. (a/)   28. (al/a la)   29. (a/)

_____ tía. Después _____ andar por unos minutos la señora le
30. (del/de la)   31. (de/)

preguntó: —¿Qué hora es?— La niña contestó: —Yo no sé _____
                                32. (/a)

decir la hora—. La señora prometió _____ enseñarle _____
                  33. (de/)   34. (/a)

decir la hora. _____ repente la niña dejó _____ andar.
      35. (De/A)   36. (/de)

Vio _____ un perro.
   37. (a/)

EXERCISE X

Simón is a new neighbor who has just moved to your area from Colombia. Answer his questions.

1. ¿Hace calor en los meses del verano?
2. ¿A qué hora salen los niños a jugar?
3. ¿De qué color es tu motocicleta?
4. ¿A qué hora del día tienes la lección de tenis?
5. ¿Escuchas los discos de tus amigos?
6. ¿Cuál es el periódico más popular de la ciudad?
7. ¿Viven tus compañeros de escuela cerca de aquí?
8. ¿Cuáles son los colores de la escuela?
9. ¿A qué hora empiezas a trabajar?
10. ¿Quién es el profesor de historia?

EXERCISE Y

Carl is helping his sister study for a Spanish test. He asks her how to say a variety of things in Spanish. Express her answers.

EXAMPLE: How would you say that you're learning to speak Spanish?
Aprendo a hablar español.

1. How would you ask a young lady if she plays tennis?
2. How would you ask your teacher if she is going to explain the assignment?
3. How would you say that it is John's sweater?
4. How would you say that they can go to the movies tonight?
5. How would you ask whose bicycle it is?
6. How would you ask if it stopped snowing?
7. How would you say that he intends to go to the pool tomorrow?
8. How would you ask if they prefer to go to the beach or to the mountains?
9. How would you say that the watch is made of gold?
10. How would you say that you have just read a good book?
11. How would you say that you are trying to call Alicia's brother?
12. How would you ask what they do upon getting up?
13. How would you say that you are starting to go to the gym every day?
14. How would you ask if you should pay before or after eating?
15. How would you say that she is coming to see Antonia's friends?

Part three

Adjective / Adverb and Related Structures

Chapter 20
Adjectives

[1] AGREEMENT OF ADJECTIVES

Adjectives describe nouns and agree in number (singular or plural) and gender (masculine or feminine) with the nouns they modify.

a. Adjectives ending in *-o* change *-o* to *-a* when describing a feminine singular noun.

Carlos es alto.	*Carlos is tall.*
María es alta.	*María is tall.*

b. Adjectives ending in *-e* remain the same when describing a feminine singular noun.

Él es valiente.	*He's brave.*
Ella es valiente.	*She's brave.*
El muchacho es inteligente.	*The boy is intelligent.*
La muchacha es inteligente.	*The girl is intelligent.*

c. Adjectives of nationality that end in a consonant add an *-a* when describing a feminine singular noun.

Paul es francés.	*Paul is French.*
Claire es francesa.	*Claire is French.*

d. The plural of adjectives, like the plural of nouns, is formed by adding *-s* if the adjective ends in a vowel, or *-es* or *-as* if the adjective ends in a consonant.

SINGULAR	PLURAL
Carlos es alto. María es alta.	Carlos y Pedro son altos. María y Anita son altas.
El muchacho es inteligente. La muchacha es inteligente.	Los muchachos son inteligentes. Las muchachas son inteligentes.
Paul es francés. Claire es francesa.	Paul y Pascal son franceses. Claire y Paulette son francesas.

NOTE:

1. Adjectives ending in -*o* have four forms.

   rico, rica, ricos, ricas

2. Adjectives ending in -*e* (or a consonant) have two forms, one for the singular and one for the plural.

SINGULAR	PLURAL	MEANING
cortés	**corteses**	*courteous*
débil	**débiles**	*weak*
fuerte	**fuertes**	*strong*

3. Adjectives of nationality ending in a consonant have four forms.

   español, española, españoles, españolas

4. Adjectives of nationality with an accent mark on the last syllable drop the accent mark in the feminine singular and in both plural forms.

   alemán, alemana, alemanes, alemanas   *German*

   francés, francesa, franceses, francesas   *French*

   inglés, inglesa, ingleses, inglesas   *English*

5. Adjectives that modify two or more nouns of different gender use the masculine plural.

   Yassir y Alice son altos.   *Yassir and Alice are tall.*

   Yassir y Alice son españoles.   *Yassir and Alice are Spanish.*

EXERCISE A

Gregorio, an exchange student in your school, is describing his new friends to you. Tell what he says about them.

EXAMPLE: Javier / interesante
            Javier **es interesante.**

1. Jeffrey / fuerte
2. Cathy / bonito
3. Gloria y Claudia / colombiano
4. Inés / cortés
5. Marco / simpático
6. Pauline / francés

7. Enrique y Lourdes / alto

8. Omar / responsable

9. Las hermanas Dini / popular

10. Kyoko y Mei Ling / divertido

EXERCISE B

At a regional meeting of new exchange students in your area, you introduce them and tell their nationalities.

EXAMPLE: Fritz / alemán
Fritz **es alemán.**

1. Salvador / español

2. Gina / italiano

3. Edson y Milton / brasileño

4. Yoko / japonés

5. Claudine y Marie / francés

6. Sara / inglés

7. José y Pilar / puertorriqueño

8. Brigitte y Eva / alemán

EXERCISE C

How would you describe your friends? Using the adjectives below, write six sentences about your friends or classmates.

alto	cortés	guapo	responsable
bajo	diligente	independiente	serio
cómico	divertido	inteligente	simpático

EXAMPLE: Elena y Migdalia son **guapas** y **responsables.**

EXERCISE D

Write six sentences describing the differences between you and your siblings or best friend. Use the adjectives below.

alegre	diligente	gordo	perezoso
cómico	divertido	independiente	quieto
delgado	generoso	melancólico	serio

EXAMPLE: Yo soy **cómico** y mi hermana es **seria.**

[2] POSITION OF ADJECTIVES

a. Descriptive adjectives generally follow the noun they describe.

una chica **guapa**	*a pretty girl*
un niño **bueno**	*a good boy*
un señor **mexicano**	*a Mexican man*

b. Adjectives expressing number or quantity generally come before the noun.

algunos chicos	*some boys*
cada año	*each year*
mucho dinero	*much money*
tres muchachas	*three girls*

EXERCISE E

You're talking to a blind date on the telephone. Answer his or her questions.

1. ¿Eres alto(a) o bajo(a)?
2. ¿De qué color tienes los ojos?
3. ¿Y el pelo?
4. ¿Tienes el pelo largo o corto?
5. ¿Eres divertido(a) o serio(a)?
6. ¿Eres paciente?
7. ¿Tienes muchos amigos?
8. ¿Cuántas clases tomas?
9. ¿Son aburridas las clases?
10. ¿Es grande tu familia?
11. ¿Cuántos hermanos y hermanas tienes?

EXERCISE F

Prepare a list of things you need to redecorate your bedroom.

EXAMPLE: una cama / doble
una cama **doble**

1. un escritorio / grande
2. una silla / cómodo

3. butaca / rojo, dos

4. una alfombra / negro

5. unas cortinas / bonito

6. lámpara / tres, bueno

7. un estante / fuerte

8. una mesa / pequeño, redondo

9. almohada / duro, tres

10. un televisor / nuevo

EXERCISE G

Make a list of things you see in the beautiful garden outside your window.

EXAMPLE: jardín / uno, bonito
            un jardín **bonito**

1. rosa / tres, rojo

2. geranio / alguno, rosado, rojo

3. planta / mucho, verde

4. árbol / dos, viejo

5. pájaro / uno, alegre

6. clavel / mucho, blanco

7. insecto / mucho, feo

EXERCISE H

While vacationing in Germany, Lisa wrote to her pen pal in Costa Rica. Complete Lisa's letter by choosing the appropriate adjectives from the list of choices for each paragraph. Notice that adjectives in each group are listed alphabetically.

nos. 1–8	*nos. 9–16*	*nos. 17–22*
bello	antiguo	alemán
bonito	cómico	divertido
colombiano	formidable	nuevo
dos	interesante	otro
grande	libre	sincero
idéntico	mucho	tres
moderno	serio	
nuevo	simpático	

Querida Lucía:

Hay _____ alumnos _____ en mi clase de matemáticas. Ellos tienen
    1.   *2.*

quince años y son hermanos, pero no son gemelos _____ . Se llaman Lola
                                             3.

y Luis. Vienen de Bogotá, Colombia, y son _____ . Ahora viven en un
                                          4.

_____ apartamento _____ y _____ cerca de un jardín _____ .
  5.   *6.*   *7.*   *8.*

Lola es muy _____, pero Luis es más _____. Lola dice que los deportes
             9.   *10.*

son _____ , pero Luis prefiere pasar su tiempo _____ en la biblioteca
   11.   *12.*

porque le gustan las novelas _____. A mí me gusta pasar _____horas
                        13.   *14.*

con ellos porque son muy _____ y _____ .
                       15.   *16.*

Mañana vamos a ver una película _____ . En_____ carta te escribo
                              17.   *18.*

más de mis amigos _____ y de sus _____ perros _____ .
                   19.   *20.*   *21.*

                                 Tu amiga _____ ,
                                         22.

                                 Luisa

[3] SHORTENING OF ADJECTIVES

a. The following adjectives drop the final -*o* when used before a masculine singular noun:

uno	*one, a, an*	un amigo	*one (a) friend*
bueno	*good*	un buen amigo	*a good friend*
malo	*bad*	un mal año	*a bad year*
primero	*first*	el primer día	*the first day*
tercero	*third*	el tercer piso	*the third floor*
alguno	*some*	algún día	*some day*
ninguno	*no, not any*	ningún dinero	*no money*

NOTE:

1. The complete form of the adjective is used when:

    (a) it follows a masculine singular noun.
    un muchacho malo   *a bad boy*

(b) it modifies a feminine or plural noun.
una muchacha buena   *a good girl*
algunos libros   *some books*

(c) a preposition comes between the adjective and the noun.
el primero de junio   *June 1*

2. The adjectives *alguno* and *ninguno* require an accent mark when the
   -o is dropped: *algún, ningún.*

b. *Ciento* becomes *cien* before any plural noun and before the numbers
   mil (thousand) and *millón* (million). The short form is not used with
   multiples of *ciento (doscientos, trescientos, etc.)* or in combination with
   any other number *(ciento diez)*:

cien libros (muchachas)   *one (a) hundred books (girls)*
cien mil años   *one (a) hundred thousand years*
cien millones de dólares   *one (a) hundred million dollars*

BUT

cuatrocientos alumnos   *four hundred students*
cuatrocientas personas   *four hundred people*
ciento veintiséis dólares   *one (a) hundred twenty-six dollars*

c. *Santo* becomes *San* before the name of a male saint, unless the
   name begins with *To-* or *Do-*.

San Francisco   *Saint Francis*
San José   *Saint Joseph*

BUT

Santo Tomás   *Saint Thomas*
Santo Domingo   *Saint Dominic*

NOTE: The feminine form of *santo* is *santa.*
Santa María   *Saint Mary*

d. *Grande* becomes *gran* before a singular noun and means "great."
   When *grande* follows the noun, it means "large" or "big."

un gran hombre   *a great man*
una gran mujer   *a great woman*

BUT

una casa grande   *a large house*

EXERCISE I

Select the correct form of each adjective in parentheses to complete Adriana's description of her cousin Esteban.

Esteban es mi primo, pero somos _____ amigos también.
                                    1. (buen / buenos)

Él es el _____ hijo de mis tíos Pedro y Beatriz. Yo soy la
         2. (primer / primero)

_____ hija de mis padres. Vivimos en el mismo edificio: yo
3. (primer / primera)

vivo en el _____ piso y mis tíos viven en el _____ .
            4. (primer / primera)   *5. (tercer / tercero)*

_____ amigos creen que Esteban y yo somos hermanos.
6. (Algún / Algunos)

Cuando yo tengo _____ _____ día, Esteban es la
                  7. (un / uno)   *8. (mal / malo)*

_____ persona con quien hablo. Este verano pensamos hacer
9. (primer / primera)

un viaje juntos a _____ Francisco y a _____ Monica.
                   10. (San / Santo)   *11. (San / Santa)*

Yo tengo _____ dinero ahorrado, pero Esteban no tiene
         12. (algún / alguno)

_____ dinero todavía. Necesitamos _____ setenta
13. (ningún / ninguno)   *14. (cien / ciento)*

y cinco dólares. Yo tengo ya _____ dólares en el banco. Mi tía
                             15. (cien / ciento)

dice que Esteban no puede ahorrar ni _____ centavo. Su cumpleaños
                                      16. (un / uno)

es el _____ de julio. Siempre recibe _____
      17. (primer / primero)   *18. (algún / algunos)*

regalos de dinero. Va a ser _____ verano _____ si no hago
                            19. (un / uno)   *20. (mal / malo)*

_____ excursión.
21. (ningún / ninguna)

EXERCISE J

Roberto has just learned that many Spanish speakers are named after a saint. Write the name of the saint after whom Roberto's friends were named.

1. Guillermo	*6.* Juan
2. Cecilia	*7.* Tomás
3. Fernando	*8.* Teresa
4. Luis	*9.* María
5. Domingo	*10.* Alfonso

MASTERY EXERCISES

EXERCISE K

Gloria shows you her closet. Describe some of the things you see, using the adjectives below.

cien	largo	pequeño
grande	negro	sucio
japonés	nuevo	viejo

EXAMPLE:

nuevo
un sombrero nuevo

EXERCISE L

Express in Spanish what Ricardo says about his summer vacation.

1. Today is the first of August.
2. The long vacation now seems very short.
3. During the third week, my family and I took a short trip.
4. We visited the beautiful mountains in the north.
5. We spent many happy hours walking in the big woods.
6. I liked to look at the great blue sky through the tall green trees.
7. At night there were many bright stars in the dark sky.
8. One night there were more than one hundred thousand stars.
9. There is no more time to take another trip.
10. We met many interesting and nice people.
11. My parents like to go to different places each year.
12. Some day I hope to visit a tropical island with white sand and blue sea.

FRANCIA

PORTUGAL   ESPAÑA
                O Madrid   Barcelona

Islas Baleares

ITALIA

Sevilla

Chapter 21
Adverbs and Adverbial Phrases

Adverbs describe the action expressed by a verb. They explain how, in what way, when, where, or why the action takes place. Adverbs also modify adjectives and other adverbs. They don't change form according to gender and number. Adverbial phrases are groups of words that together function as an adverb.

[1] ADVERBS AND ADVERBIAL PHRASES OF MODE

a. Adverbs of mode (those answering the question *how?* or *in what way?*) are generally formed by adding *-mente* to the feminine singular form of an adjective.

ADJECTIVE	ADVERB
correcta *correct* **fácil** *easy*	**correctamente** *correctly* **fácilmente** *easily*

NOTE:

1. Adjectives that have an accent mark keep the accent mark when they are changed to adverbs.

    rápida   rápidamente

2. The adjectives *bueno* and *malo* form adverbs irregularly.

    bueno *good*   bien *well*
    mal *bad*   mal *badly*

    Es un carro **bueno**,   *It's a good car,*
    pero Pedro conduce **mal**.   *but Pedro drives badly.*

b. Adverbial phrases of mode are usually formed as follows:

de manera + *adjective*
Él habla **de manera extraña**.   *He talks in a strange way.*

de modo + *adjective*
Él habla **de modo extraño**.   *He talks in a strange way.*

EXERCISE A

After Migdalia's first singing recital, people commented on her talent. Complete each comment by writing the appropriate form of the adverb.

EXAMPLE: su profesor de música: correcto
             Ella canta **correctamente**.

1. sus padres: divino

Ella canta _____ .

2. su hermano: malo

Ella canta _____ .

3. sus abuelos: alegre

Ella canta _____ .

4. su novio: dulce

Ella canta _____ .

5. una amiga: suave

Ella canta _____ .

6. otro cantante: bueno

Ella canta _____ .

EXERCISE B

A classmate asks how you do different things. Answer his or her questions using the cue given in parentheses.

EXAMPLE: ¿Cómo completas tus tareas? *(diligente)*
             Yo completo mis tareas **diligentemente**.

1. ¿Cómo almuerzas? *(rápido)*

2. ¿Cómo hablas a tu novio(a)? *(dulce)*

3. ¿Cómo patinas? *(malo)*

4. ¿Cómo caminas a las clases? *(lento)*

5. ¿Cómo saludas a tus amigos? *(cordial)*

6. ¿Cómo comprendes a la maestra de español? *(fácil)*

[2] ADVERBS AND ADVERBIAL PHRASES OF TIME OR FREQUENCY

a. Adverbs of time or frequency

ahora	*now*	entonces	*then*
anoche	*last night*	hoy	*today*
ayer	*yesterday*	luego	*then, next*
¿cuándo?	*when?*	mañana	*tomorrow*

nunca *never*	tarde *late*
pronto *soon*	temprano *early*
siempre *always*	todavía *still, yet*

b. Adverbial phrases of time or frequency

algún día *some day*	muchas veces *often*
a veces *sometimes*	pocas veces *seldom*
esta noche *tonight*	primero *first*
este fin de semana *this weekend*	todos los días *every day*
más tarde *later*	

EXERCISE C

Tell when, or how frequently, you do or are going to do the following things. For each statement, use the suggested adverb or adverbial phrase.

EXAMPLES: bañarse / todos los días.
Yo me baño todos los días.

descansar / mañana
Yo voy a descansar mañana.

1. ir de compras / este fin de semana
2. estudiar para un examen / esta noche
3. llegar a tiempo a la escuela / siempre
4. ser rico / algún día
5. escribir el ejercicio / ahora
6. visitar a los abuelos / pronto
7. recibir malas notas / pocas veces
8. pelear con los padres / nunca

EXERCISE D

Using the expressions given, tell how frequently you do these things.

a veces	nunca	siempre
muchas veces	pocas veces	todas los días

EXAMPLE: lavar los platos
Nunca lavo los platos.

1. preparar la tarea
2. ir al supermercado
3. cocinar
4. arreglar su cuarto

5. pasar la aspiradora
6. lavar el carro
7. trabajar en el jardín

[3] ADVERBS AND ADVERBIAL PHRASES OF PLACE

a. Common adverbs of place (answering the question *where?*)

abajo   *below, downstairs*
¿adónde?   *(to) where?*
allí   *there*
aquí   *here*
arriba   *above, upstairs*

derecho   *straight ahead*
detrás   *behind*
¿dónde?   *where?*
enfrente   *in front of, opposite*

b. Common adverbial phrases of place

a la derecha   *to the right*
a la izquierda   *to the left*
debajo de   *beneath*

delante de   *in front of, ahead of*
detrás de   *behind*
frente a   *facing, in front of*

EXERCISE E

You are helping a new friend become familiar with the downtown area of your city. Use the map below to tell him the location of the buildings listed. Express the location using an adverbial phrase.

EXAMPLE: el banco
El banco **está detrás del cine**.

1. la florería	*5.* el parque
2. la biblioteca	*6.* la escuela
3. el restaurante	*7.* el cine
4. el correo	

MASTERY EXERCISES

EXERCISE F

In each group, select the adverb that is in a different category (mode, time, or place) from the other three.

EXAMPLE:　alegremente, libremente, **temprano**, lentamente

1. ayer, siempre, correctamente, entonces

2. débilmente, ahora, luego, nunca

3. ¿adónde?, dulcemente, bien, rápidamente

4. ¿cuándo?, hoy, nunca, tristemente

5. diligentemente, tarde, sinceramente, perezosamente

6. pronto, aquí, abajo, ¿dónde?

7. allí, arriba, ¿dónde?, fácilmente

8. ¿por qué?, anoche, todavía, mañana

9. felizmente, mal, rápidamente, ¿cuándo?

10. difícilmente, a la derecha, allí, derecho

EXERCISE G

You're talking about your language class. Complete each sentence with the appropriate adverb.

EXAMPLE:　No comprendemos a Jorge cuando habla.
　　　　　Él habla **rápidamente**.

1. Yo hago la tarea sin errores.

   Yo hago la tarea _____ .

2. Yo estudio siete días a la semana.

   Yo estudio _____ .

3. La maestra dice «por favor» y «gracias» a los alumnos.

   Ella habla _____ .

4. Nosotros comprendemos todo lo que dice la profesora.

   Nosotros comprendemos _____ .

5. La maestra tiene una voz bonita.

   Ella canta _____ .

6. A Roberto le gusta hablar.

   Él habla _____ en la clase.

7. Mi amigo no recibe buenas notas.

   Él sale _____ en todos los exámenes.

EXERCISE H

Tell where the objects in the picture below are located. Use adverbial phrases of place in your sentences.

EXAMPLE:

El vaso está al lado de la leche.

1.

El guante de béisbol _____ .

2.

Los gatos _____ .

3.

La niña _____ .

4.

Las papitas _____ .

5.

El automóvil _____ .

EXERCISE I

Express the following in Spanish.

1. The team is going to arrive soon.
2. Ricardo invites his friends often.
3. They always come to his house happily.
4. Now Ricardo has to work rapidly.
5. He cooks well, but he rarely eats the food.
6. He greets his friends cordially at the door.
7. First he opens the soda; then he carefully puts the food on the table.
8. The party turned out *(salir)* perfectly.

Chapter 22
Numbers

[1] CARDINAL NUMBERS

a. 0 to 99

0	cero	13	trece	26	veintiséis (veinte y seis)
1	uno	14	catorce	27	veintisiete (veinte y siete)
2	dos	15	quince	28	veintiocho (veinte y ocho)
3	tres	16	dieciséis (diez y seis)	29	veintinueve (veinte y nueve)
4	cuatro	17	diecisiete (diez y siete)	30	treinta
5	cinco	18	dieciocho (diez y ocho)	31	treinta y uno *(and so on)*
6	seis	19	diecinueve (diez y nueve)	40	cuarenta
7	siete	20	veinte	50	cincuenta
8	ocho	21	veintiuno (veinte y uno)	60	sesenta
9	nueve	22	veintidós (veinte y dos)	70	setenta
10	diez	23	veintitrés (veinte y tres)	80	ochenta
11	once	24	veinticuatro (veinte y cuatro)	90	noventa
12	doce	25	veinticinco (veinte y cinco)	99	noventa y nueve

NOTE:

1. Compound numbers 16 to 99 are connected by *y*.

2. Although numbers 16 to 19 and 21 to 29 may be connected by *y*, they are usually written as one word. Note the spelling changes that occur when these numbers are written as one word.

diez   dieciséis

veinte   veintiuno

3. *Uno* and combinations of *uno* (like *veintiuno* and *treinta y uno*) become *un* before masculine nouns and *una* before feminine nouns.

un libro	*one (a) book*
veintiún asientos	*twenty-one seats*
treinta y un profesores	*thirty-one teachers*
una mesa	*one (a) table*
veintiuna camisas	*twenty-one shirts*
treinta y una sillas	*thirty-one chairs*
veintiún asientos	*twenty-one seats*

EXERCISE A

As you leave a summer camp in Mexico, your new friends give you their telephone numbers. Rewrite them using Spanish words.

EXAMPLE: Silvia 5-47-08-23
cinco - cuarenta y siete - cero ocho - veintitrés

1. Arturo 6-31-74-92

2. Raquel 3-65-22-81

3. Emilio 7-27-00-48

4. Graciela 2-59-11-17

5. Humberto 9-13-36-14

6. Raúl 8-72-12-41

7. Linda 9-97-16-67

8. Pedro 5-33-21-86

EXERCISE B

While touring Spain, you help the tour guide give out the room assignments at the hotel.

EXAMPLE: Enrique y José, 57
Para Enrique y José, el **cincuenta y siete**.

1. Louise y Estela, 38

2. Elisa y Jane, 71

3. Billy y Tomás, 43

4. Javier y Antonio, 15

5. Rita y María, 64

6. Clara y Marcela, 86

7. Felipe y Hugo, 29

EXERCISE C

Use the following map to tell your Spanish-speaking friend the expected high and low temperatures in some major cities of the United States. All temperatures are in degrees Fahrenheit.

EXAMPLE: Los Angeles
La temperatura alta será setenta y seis grados y la baja sesenta y dos grados.

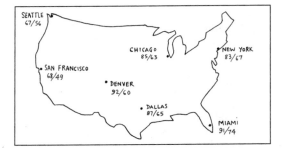

SEATTLE
67/56

SAN FRANCISCO
68/49

CHICAGO
85/63

NEW YORK
83/67

DENVER
92/60

DALLAS
87/65

MIAMI
91/74

1. Miami	*5.* New York
2. Chicago	*6.* Dallas
3. Seattle	*7.* San Francisco
4. Denver	

b. 100 to 1,000,000

100	cien	800	ochocientos (-as)
101	ciento uno (-a)	900	novecientos (-as)
200	doscientos (-as)	1,000	mil
300	trescientos (-as)	2,000	dos mil
400	cuatrocientos (-as)	2,500	dos mil quinientos
500	quinientos (-as)	100,000	cien mil
600	seiscientos (-as)	1,000,000	un millón (de)
700	setecientos (-as)		

NOTE:

1. *Cien* becomes *ciento* when it's followed by another number from one to ninety-nine.

cien libros	*one hundred books*
cien casas	*one hundred houses*
cien mil habitantes	*one hundred thousand inhabitants*
cien millones	*one hundred million*

BUT

cien**to** veinte libros	*one hundred twenty books*

2. Numbers that express hundreds, like *doscientos* and *trescientos,* become *doscientas* and *trescientas* before a feminine noun.

doscientas páginas	*two hundred pages*
trescientas plumas	*three hundred pens*

3. In Spanish, compound numbers higher than a thousand (such as 1,110) are expressed with *mil.* Words like *twelve hundred* have no equivalent in Spanish.

mil doscientos	*twelve hundred*
	(one thousand two hundred)
mil novecientos noventa	*nineteen hundred ninety*
	(one thousand nine hundred ninety)

dos mil quinientos	*twenty-five hundred*
	(two thousand five hundred)

4. No equivalent to the English word *a* or *one* is expressed before *ciento* or *mil*, but the equivalent *un* must be used before *millón*. *Millón* (pl. *millones*) also requires *de* when a noun follows.

ciento diez alumnos	*a (one) hundred ten students*
mil dólares	*a (one) thousand dollars*

BUT

un millón de dólares	*a (one) million dollars*
dos millones de habitantes	*two million inhabitants*

5. In many Spanish-speaking countries, the commas in large numbers change to periods: 1,000 becomes 1.000 and 1,000,000 becomes 1.000.000. The periods in decimal numbers change to commas: 1.10 becomes 1,10.

EXERCISE D

You and a friend are comparing the population of cities around the world. Express the approximate populations of these cities, using Spanish words.

EXAMPLE: Madrid / 3,120,000
tres millones ciento veinte mil habitantes

1. México, D. F. / 8,236,960

2. París / 2,152,423

3. Tokio / 11,000,000

4. Chicago / 2,783,726

5. San Francisco / 723,959

6. Barcelona / 1,623,542

7. Buenos Aires / 2,780,092

8. New Orleans / 496,938

9. Atlanta / 393,929

10. Seattle / 516,259

EXERCISE E

You're using Mexico City as your base for several side trips to other cities. Express in Spanish the approximate distance by car between Mexico City and each of the other cities you plan to visit.

EXAMPLE: Cuernavaca / 82 kilómetros
Cuernavaca está a **ochenta y dos** kilómetros.

1. Acapulco / 305 kilómetros
2. Puebla / 120 kilómetros
3. Veracruz / 424 kilómetros
4. Oaxaca / 516 kilómetros

5. Toluca / 56 kilómetros
6. Guadalajara / 450 kilómetros
7. Querétaro / 257 kilómetros

EXERCISE F

Tell the year in which these family members were born.

EXAMPLE: tu prima favorita
Mi prima favorita **nació en mil novecientos setenta y ocho.**

1. tu padre
2. tu madre
3. tu hermano(a)
4. tu abuelo

5. tu abuela
6. tu tío favorito
7. tú

EXERCISE G

The airlines have just lowered their fares. Tell how much each of these flights will cost one-way (ida) and round-trip (ida y vuelta).

AEROLINEAS INTERNACIONALES
BOLETOS DE IDA
SAN JUAN $139   COSTA RICA $209
CANCÚN $159   BARCELONA $299
BUENOS AIRES $499   CARACAS $299

EXAMPLE: Caracas
ida **doscientos noventa y nueve dólares**
ida y vuelta **quinientos noventa y ocho dólares**

1. Barcelona

   ida _____

   ida y vuelta _____

2. Costa Rica

   ida _____

   ida y vuelta _____

3. San Juan

   ida _____

   ida y vuelta _____

4. Cancún

   ida _____

   ida y vuelta _____

5. Buenos Aires

   ida _____

   ida y vuelta _____

EXERCISE H

Mr. Jiménez is planning his summer vacation and wants to find out the foreign currency exchange rate for various countries. Write down what he finds out in the newspaper.

EXAMPLE: Francia / 5 francos
            Un dólar es igual a cinco francos.

1. Argentina / 1 peso

2. Chile / 430 pesos

3. Colombia / 929 pesos

4. Costa Rica / 152 colones

5. España / 132 pesetas

6. México / 3,115 nuevos pesos

7. Nicaragua / 5 córdobas

8. Paraguay / 1,887 guaraníes

9. República Dominicana / 13 pesos

10. Venezuela / 112 bolívares

EXERCISE I

You're preparing a surprise party for a friend and you're writing the details in Spanish in your diary. Complete the sentences using the correct form of *uno*.

1. Mañana Federico cumple treinta y _____ años.

2. Invitamos a cincuenta y _____ personas.

3. Hay cuarenta y _____ globos.

4. Necesitamos treinta y _____ velas para el pastel.

5. Vamos a necesitar _____ silla más.

6. Podemos comer el pastel con _____ cuchara.

EXERCISE J

You're working at a hotel that is going to be refurbished. Complete the following sentences with *cien* **or** *ciento*.

1. Hay _____ cuartos en el hotel.
2. _____ cincuenta y cinco personas van a pasar la noche en el hotel.
3. Unos cuartos cuestan _____ dólares la noche.
4. Otros cuartos cuestan _____ veinte y cinco dólares.
5. La reparación va a durar _____ días.

[2] ARITHMETIC EXPRESSIONS

The following expressions are used in arithmetic problems in Spanish:

y, más   *plus* (+)
menos   *minus* (−)
por   *(multiplied) by, "times"* (×)
dividido por   *divided by* (÷)
son, es igual a   *equals* (=)

EXERCISE K

Express the following in Spanish.

1. $35 + 70 = 105$
2. $187 + 542 = 729$
3. $691 - 255 = 436$
4. $1{,}323 - 1{,}022 = 301$
5. $1{,}968 + 2{,}741 = 4{,}709$
6. $636 \times 25 = 15{,}900$
7. $338 \div 26 = 13$
8. $700 + 300 = 1{,}000$
9. $500 + 400 = 900$
10. $900 - 350 = 550$
11. $900 + 800 = 1{,}700$
12. $110 + 115 = 225$
13. $743 - 243 = 500$
14. $20{,}000 \div 100 = 200$
15. $800{,}000 + 200{,}000 = 1{,}000{,}000$
16. $1{,}400{,}000 + 600{,}000 = 2{,}000{,}000$
17. $2{,}400 \div 12 = 200$
18. $5{,}000 \div 500 = 10$
19. $930 \times 17 = 15{,}810$
20. $359 \times 26 = 9{,}334$

[3] ORDINAL NUMBERS

1°	primero (-a), primer	1st	*first*
2°	segundo (-a)	2nd	*second*
3°	tercero (-a), tercer	3rd	*third*
4°	cuarto (-a)	4th	*fourth*
5°	quinto (-a)	5th	*fifth*
6°	sexto (-a)	6th	*sixth*
7°	séptimo (-a)	7th	*seventh*
8°	octavo (-a)	8th	*eighth*
9°	noveno (-a)	9th	*ninth*
10°	décimo (-a)	10th	*tenth*

NOTE:

1. **All ordinal numbers agree in gender (*m./f.*) and number (*sing./pl.*) with the nouns to which they refer.**

el séptimo mes	*the seventh month*
la séptima semana	*the seventh week*

2. **The numbers *primero* and *tercero* drop the final -*o* when they come before a masculine singular noun.**

el primer hombre	*the first man*
el tercer mes	*the third month*

    BUT

la primera semana	*the first week*
la tercera vez	*the third time*

3. **If a preposition comes between *primero* or *tercero* and the noun, the full form is used.**

el primero de mayo	*May 1*

4. **Ordinal numbers are generally used to express rank order only from the first to the tenth in a series. Numbers above ten have ordinal forms, too, but they are seldom used. Instead, a cardinal number is placed after the noun, and the word *número* is understood.**

la sexta lección	*the sixth lesson*
Felipe Segundo	*Felipe II (Felipe the Second)*

BUT

la lección catorce	*the fourteenth lesson* or *lesson (number) fourteen*
Alfonso Doce	*Alfonso XII (Alfonso the Twelfth)*

EXERCISE L

You step into a hotel elevator. Tell on which floor each of the following places is located. Use the word *piso* in your response.*

EXAMPLE: El bar **está en el tercer piso**.

1. La piscina _____ .

2. Las tiendas _____ .

3. Las oficinas _____ .

4. La peluquería _____ .

5. El restaurante _____ .

6. El Salón de Banquetes _____ .

7. El Salón Martel _____ .

8. El teatro _____ .

9. La discoteca _____ .

10. Los periódicos _____ .

---

* In most Spanish-speaking countries, the first floor (or ground floor) is called *planta baja (PB);* the second floor, *primer piso;* and so forth.

EXERCISE M

You're helping a younger brother learn the order of the months. Tell what position each month occupies in the calendar year.

EXAMPLE: abril
           el cuarto mes

1. junio

2. septiembre

3. enero

4. diciembre

5. febrero

6. octubre

7. julio

8. marzo

9. agosto

10. mayo

11. noviembre

EXERCISE N

Write the sentences, changing the number in parentheses into a Spanish word.

1. Siéntate en el *(3°)* asiento.

2. Saliste mal en la *(5°)* prueba.

3. Naciste en junio, el *(6°)* mes del año.

4. Acabas de celebrar tu cumpleaños *(15°)*.

5. Vives es un apartamento en el *(1°)* piso.

6. Caminas a la escuela por la Calle *(8°)*.

7. El español es tu *(3°)* clase del día.

8. Estudias el *(2°)* semestre de español.

9. Estamos en la *(10°)* lección.

10. Debes hacer el *(4°)* ejercicio.

[4] FRACTIONS

½ un medio, medio (-a), una mitad de	*(a/one) half, half of*
⅓ un tercio, una tercera parte de	*(a/one) third, the third part of*
¼ un cuarto, una cuarta parte de	*(a/one) fourth, a quarter of*
⅔ dos tercios, las dos terceras partes de	*two-thirds, two-thirds of*

³/₄ tres cuartos, las tres cuartas partes de   *three-fourths, three quarters of*

⁴/₅ cuatro quintos, las cuatro quintas partes de   *four-fifths of*

¹/₁₀ un décimo, la décima parte de   *(a/one) tenth, a tenth of*

NOTE:

1. Except for *medio* and *tercio*, noun fractions are formed with ordinal numbers up through *décimo* (tenth). Thereafter, the ending *-avo* is usually added to the cardinal number to express fractions smaller than a tenth.

    ¹/₁₂ un doceavo, una doceava parte de   *(a/one) twelfth of*

2. Fractions are masculine nouns.

    3 ¹/₃ tres y un tercio   *three and one-third*

    When the fraction precedes the thing divided, it may be used with the feminine noun *parte*, unless a unit of measure is expressed:

    una tercera **parte** (un tercio) del libro   *a third of the book*

    BUT

    un tercio de libra   *a third of a pound*

3. The adjective *medio* (*-a*) means "half," while the noun *la mitad* (*de*) means "half (of)."

    media docena de huevos   *half a dozen eggs*

    la mitad de la clase   *half of the class*

EXERCISE O

Copy the following shopping list, writing out fractions in full.

Lista de compras
½ docena de huevos
½ galón de leche
¼ libra de jamón
¾ libra de queso
½ pan
1½ libra de galletas
½ melón
½ sandía

[5] MULTIPLES

Terms that indicate that one quantity is a multiple of another are used in the same manner as their English equivalents.

una vez *once*	simple *single, simple*
dos veces *twice*	doble *double*
tres veces *three times*	triple *triple*
Me visitó una vez.	*She visited me once.*
Lo leí dos veces.	*I read it twice.*
Escribí el doble de lo que escribiste tú.	*I wrote twice as much as you.*

NOTE:

1. Adverbial phrases expressing the number of times that an event occurs are formed by a cardinal number and the feminine noun *vez* (a time).

   Leí el libro tres veces.   *I read the book three times.*

2. Multiples like *doble, triple* may be either adjectives or nouns.

   Es una máquina de **doble** motor.   *It's a double-motor machine.*

   Este carro cuesta hoy el **doble**.   *This car costs twice as much today.*

EXERCISE P

You overhear your younger sister tell a friend how many times she has done some activities. Tell what she says using the cues in parentheses.

EXAMPLE: ir al parque zoológico *(10)*
                    Fui al parque zoológico **diez veces**.

1. volar en avión *(5)*
2. esquiar *(20)*
3. ver la película «Fantasma» *(2)*
4. jugar al fútbol *(50)*
5. comer al aire libre *(8)*
6. ir a la playa *(100)*
7. preparar la cena *(1)*

M A S T E R Y   E X E R C I S E S

EXERCISE Q

Your parents have remodeled the house to give you a larger room. Write sentences telling how much different things cost.

1.	pintura	$790	*5.*	televisor	$389
2.	ventanas	$1,200	*6.*	cortinas	$56
3.	muebles	$920	*7.*	total	$3,799
4.	alfombra	$444			

EXERCISE R

You are visiting a cousin in Spain. She mentions several tourist attractions and indicates how many times she has visited each one of them. Use the cues in parentheses to express what she says.

EXAMPLE: el Escorial (3)
                     Visité al Escorial tres veces.

1. el Valle de los Caídos *(5)*   *4.* el Palacio Real *(1)*

2. el Museo del Prado *(12)*   *5.* la cuidad de Toledo *(7)*

3. la Plaza Mayor *(20)*   *6.* el Parque del Buen Retiro *(25)*

EXERCISE S

You're writing to a friend about your summer job. Express the following in Spanish.

1. This summer I'm working for the first time.

2. I work 37$^{1}/_{2}$ hours a week.

3. My salary is two hundred and eighty-eight dollars.

4. I have a half-hour for lunch.

5. I work in a large store on Fifth Avenue.

6. There are more than seventy-five employees.

7. One-half of the employees are students.

8. Five hundred people enter the store each day.

9. My first day there I sold fifteen thousand dollars in merchandise.

10. The company earns more than three million dollars a year.
11. Two-thirds of the people use credit cards.
12. The telephone number of the store is 555-9321.
13. The store opened in 1976 on Forty-eighth Street.
14. One-quarter of their business is by telephone.
15. I will work for eleven weeks.
16. I will work 412$\frac{1}{2}$ hours this summer.

Chapter 23
Times and Dates

[1] TIME EXPRESSIONS

a. *¿Qué hora es?* is equivalent to "What time is it?"

b. In expressing time, "It is" is expressed by *Es la* (for one o'clock), and *Son las* for other hours (two o'clock, three o'clock, and so on).

Es la una.	*It's one o'clock.*
Son las dos (tres).	*It's two (three) o'clock.*

c. Time after or past the hour (up to half past) is expressed by the hour + *y*, followed by the number of minutes. "Half past" is expressed by *y media;* "a quarter past" is expressed by *y cuarto.*

Es la una y diez.	*It's ten (minutes) after one. It's 1:10.*
Son las seis **y media.**	*It's half past six. It's 6:30.*
Son las diez **y cuarto.**	*It's a quarter after ten. It's 10:15.*

d. After half past, the time is expressed in terms of the following hour *menos* (minus) the minutes.

Son las dos **menos** veinte.	*It's twenty minutes to two. It's 1:40.*
Son las nueve **menos** cuarto.	*It's a quarter to nine. It's 8:45.*

e. The expression *de la mañana* corresponds to English A.M. (in the morning). *De la tarde* (in the afternoon) and *de la noche* (in the evening) correspond to English P.M. *En punto* means "sharp" or "on the dot."

Son las ocho **de la mañana.**	*It's 8:00 A.M.*
Es la una **de la tarde.**	*It's 1:00 P.M.*
Son las ocho **de la noche en punto.**	*It's 8:00 P.M. sharp.*

NOTE:

1. Instead of *media* and *cuarto,* the number of minutes may be used *(treinta, quince).*

Son las cinco y *treinta.*	*It's five-thirty. It's half past five.*
Es la una y **quince.**	*It's one-fifteen. It's a quarter past one.*

2. It's not uncommon to hear times like 12:45 and 12:50 expressed with *y*.

Son las doce y **cuarenta y cinco**.	*It's twelve-forty-five.*
Son las doce y **cincuenta**.	*It's twelve-fifty.*

f. Common time expressions

¿Qué hora es?	*What time is it?*
¿A qué hora?	*At what time?*
a las dos (tres)	*at two (three) o'clock*
de la mañana	*in the morning, A.M.*
de la tarde	*in the afternoon, P.M.*
de la noche	*at night, P.M.*
Es mediodía.	*It's noon.*
a mediodía	*at noon*
Es medianoche.	*It's midnight.*
a medianoche	*at midnight*
Es tarde.	*It's late.*
Es temprano.	*It's early.*
a tiempo	*on time*
en punto	*exactly, sharp*

EXERCISE A

You're teaching your younger sister to tell time in Spanish. Express the hours indicated on the clocks.

EXAMPLE:

Son las **diez menos cuarto.**

1.

2.

3.

4.

5.

6.

7.

8.

9.

10.

11.

12.

13.

14.

15.   16.

17.   18.

19.   20.

EXERCISE B

Tell at what time in the morning, afternoon, or evening you usually do the following activities.

EXAMPLE: desayunarse
    Me desayuno a las seis y media **de la mañana**.

1. ir a la escuela
2. almorzar
3. preparar la tarea
4. jugar con los amigos
5. salir de la escuela
6. cenar
7. ver su programa favorito de televisión
8. acostarse
9. practicar un deporte
10. bañarse

EXERCISE C

You don't know where the day has gone. Using the notes below, tell at what time you completed each activity.

EXAMPLE: Tú ayudas a tu papá a lavar el carro. Son las ocho y media cuando empiezan. Tardan una hora y media en lavar el carro. ¿Qué hora es?
Son las diez.

1. Tú acompañas a tu mamá al supermercado. Salen de la casa a las diez y cuarto. Regresan a casa ochenta minutos después. ¿Qué hora es?

2. Tu amiga te llama por teléfono a las doce menos cinco. Hablan por quince minutos. ¿A qué hora terminan de hablar?

3. A la una tú arreglas tu cuarto. Necesitas setenta y cinco minutos. ¿Qué hora es?

4. Tienes que sacar un libro de la biblioteca. Sales de tu casa a las tres menos cuarto y vuelves a la casa en dos horas y media. ¿A qué hora vuelves a casa?

5. Después de cenar, estudias para un examen por tres horas y quince minutos. Empiezas a estudiar a las siete y diez. ¿Qué hora es cuando terminas de estudiar?

[2] DATES

a. Days of the week (*Los días de la semana*)

lunes *Monday*	viernes *Friday*
martes *Tuesday*	sábado *Saturday*
miércoles *Wednesday*	domingo *Sunday*
jueves *Thursday*	

NOTE:

1. "On" before a day of the week is expressed by *el* for the singular and *los* for the plural.

el lunes *on Monday*	los lunes *on Mondays*
el viernes *on Friday*	los viernes *on Fridays*
el sábado *on Saturday*	los sábados *on Saturdays*
el domingo *on Sunday*	los domingos *on Sundays*

2. Days of the week whose names end in *-s* do not change their form in the plural.

3. The days of the week are not capitalized in Spanish.

b. Months (*Los meses*)

enero *January*	julio *July*
febrero *February*	agosto *August*
marzo *March*	septiembre *September*
abril *April*	octubre *October*
mayo *May*	noviembre *November*
junio *June*	diciembre *December*

NOTE: Like the days of the week, the months are written with lower-case (small) letters in Spanish.

c. Dates

¿Cuál es la fecha de hoy? ¿A cuántos estamos hoy?	*What is today's date?*
Es el primero de enero. Estamos a primero de enero.	*It's January 1.*
Es el dos de febrero	*It's February 2.*
Es el tres (cuatro) de mayo.	*It's May 3 (4)*
mil ochocientos doce	*1812*
el quince de abril de mil novecientos noventa y seis	*April 15, 1996*

NOTE:

1. Cardinal numbers are used for all dates except *primero* (first).

el **primero** de abril	*April 1*
el tres (cuatro, cinco) de abril	*April 3 (4,5)*

2. The year is expressed in Spanish by thousands and hundreds, not by hundreds alone as in English.

3. The date and month are connected by the preposition *de.* The month and the year are also connected by *de.*

el diez **de** junio **de** mil ochocientos cuarenta	*(on) June 10, 1840*

With dates, *el* corresponds to "on."

EXERCISE D

You're telling an exchange student at your school about important dates in the United States. Give the Spanish equivalent for the dates indicated.

1. February 22

2. December 25

3. February 14

4. January 1

5. October 12

6. July 4

7. November 11

8. April 1

9. October 31

10. February 12

EXERCISE E

You're reading a list of Mexican national holidays. Express these dates in Spanish.

1. May 5

2. September 16

3. November 20

4. May 1

5. February 5

6. March 21

7. January 1

8. December 25

EXERCISE F

Tell the date of birth (including the year) of the following members of your family.

EXAMPLE: tu tía favorita
　　　　　Mi tía favorita **nació** el **dos de agosto** de **mil novecientos sesenta y uno**.

1. tu madre

　 Mi madre _____ .

2. tu padre

　 Mi padre _____ .

3. tu abuelo materno

　 Mi abuelo materno _____ .

4. tu abuela paterna

　 Mi abuela paterna _____ .

5. tu hermano(–a)

Mi hermano(–a) _____ .

6. tu primo(–a) favorito(–a)

Mi primo(–a) favorito(–a) _____ .

7. tú

Yo _____ .

EXERCISE G

Express the following dates in Spanish.

1. March 15, 1271

2. February 2, 1588

3. April 17, 1942

4. May 23, 1848

5. July 4, 1776

6. January 30, 1660

7. July 18, 1395

8. December 13, 1969

9. June 22, 1453

10. March 25, 1124

MASTERY EXERCISES

EXERCISE H

A friend is helping you study for a Spanish test. Answer the questions your friend asks.

1. Si hoy es lunes, ¿qué día es mañana?

2. ¿Cuál es el segundo mes del año?

3. ¿En qué mes celebramos la Navidad?

4. ¿Cuál es el noveno mes del año?

5. Si hoy es jueves, ¿qué día fue ayer?

6. ¿Cuáles son los meses que tienen treinta días?

7. ¿Qué mes tiene veintiocho o veintinueve días?

8. ¿Qué meses tienen treinta y un días?

9. ¿En qué días no hay clases?

10. ¿En qué días vas a la escuela?

11. ¿Cuál es la fecha de hoy?

12. ¿En qué mes celebramos la fiesta nacional de los Estados Unidos?

13. ¿Cuál es el séptimo mes del año?

14. ¿En qué mes celebramos el Año Nuevo?

15. ¿En qué fecha celebras tu cumpleaños?

EXERCISE I

You're telling a friend about your summer plans. Express the following in Spanish.

1. On July 1, my family and I are going to travel by train.

2. The train leaves at 10:30 A.M. sharp.

3. The train always leaves on time.

4. They serve dinner on the train at 6:00 P.M.

5. At 8:00 there is a movie.

6. We leave on Thursday and arrive in Chicago early on Saturday.

7. The party is on Sunday at one o'clock in the afternoon.

8. The party will end at five o'clock in the afternoon.

9. The party is for my grandfather. He was born on July 4, 1924.

10. On Sunday nights my family goes to bed early.

11. We have to wake up at 5:45 A.M. on Monday.

12. We have to be in the train station at 7:00 A.M. because the train leaves at 7:20.

13. We leave on Monday and arrive home on Wednesday.

14. My father has to go to work at midnight on Wednesday.

15. Our trip ends on July 7.

Chapter 24
Interrogatives

[1] INTERROGATIVES

a. Common interrogative expressions

¿qué? *what?*

¿quién (-es)? *who?*

¿a quién (-es)? *whom? to whom?*

¿de quién (-es)? *whose? of whom?*

¿con quién (-es)? *with whom?*

¿cuál (-es)? *which? which one(s)?*

¿cuándo? *when?*

¿cuánto (-a)? *how much?*

¿cuántos (-as)? *how many?*

¿cómo? *how?*

¿por qué? *why?*

¿dónde? *where?*

¿de dónde? *(from) where?*

¿adónde? *(to) where?*

NOTE:

1. All interrogative words have a written accent.

2. In Spanish, questions have an inverted question mark (¿) at the beginning and a standard one (?) at the end.

3. When interrogatives (words such as *¿qué?, ¿cuándo?, ¿dónde?*) are used in a question, the subject-verb order is reversed from the order in statements.

¿Qué hacen ellos?	*What are they doing?*
Ellos bailan.	*They are dancing.*
¿Dónde está María?	*Where is Mary?*
Ella está aquí.	*She is here.*

EXERCISE A

You're talking to a new student in your class for the first time. Write the questions that he has answered.

1. Me llamo Enrique Casas.

2. Yo soy de Colombia.

3. Vivo en la calle Oak.

4. Vivo con mis padres y mis dos hermanos.

5. Llegué a los Estados Unidos el mes pasado.

6. Tengo quince años.

7. Me gustan el tenis y el fútbol.

8. Tengo seis clases.

9. Son el inglés, la historia, la biología, las matemáticas, el español y la educación física.

10. El señor Época es mi profesor de historia.

11. Me gusta más la clase de inglés.

12. Después de las clases voy al parque.

13. Voy al parque porque me gusta remar en el lago.

b. Both *¿qué?* and *¿cuál?* are equivalent to English "what?" and "which?," but the two words are not usually interchangeable in Spanish.

    (1) *¿Qué?* seeks a description, definition, or explanation.

        ¿**Qué** es eso? *What is that?*

    (2) *¿Cuál?* implies a choice or selection.

        ¿**Cuál** perfume prefiere Ud.? *Which perfume do you prefer?*

NOTE: It's common practice in modern Spanish to substitute *¿qué?* for *¿cuál?*.

    ¿**Qué** camisa prefiere José? ⎫
                          ⎬ *Which shirt does José prefer?*
    ¿**Cuál** camisa prefiere José? ⎭

EXERCISE B

Which interrogative word is needed in each question?

1. ¿(Cuál / Qué) es esto?

2. ¿(Cuál / Qué) comes por la mañana?

3. ¿(Cuál / Qué) día es hoy?

4. ¿(Cuál / Cuáles) son los meses del año?

5. ¿(Cuál / Qué) es tu número de teléfono?

6. ¿(Cuál / Cuáles) postres te gustan más?

7. ¿(Cuál / Qué) vas a hacer con el dinero?

8. ¿(Cuál / Qué) haces cuando llueve?

9. ¿(Cuál / Qué) comes en un restaurante mexicano?

10. ¿(Cuál / Qué) libros leíste el año pasado?

EXERCISE C

While Linda is trying to study, her little sister is looking through a book that has many words she doesn't understand. According to the answers given, write the questions Linda's sister asks.

EXAMPLE: Un clavel es una flor.
              ¿Qué es **un clavel**?

1. Un pasaporte es un documento.

2. Una vaca es un animal.

3. Una manzana es una fruta.

4. El oro es un metal.

5. Un diccionario es un libro.

c. *¿Quién (-es)?, ¿a quién (-es)?*, and *¿de quién (-es)?*

    (1) *¿Quién (-es)?* (who?) is used as the subject of the sentence.

    ¿Quién es este alumno?   *Who is this student?*

    ¿Quiénes son estos alumnos?   *Who are these students?*

    (2) *¿A quién (-es)?* (whom?, to whom?) is used as the object of the verb (either direct or indirect object).

    ¿A quién ve Ud.?   *Whom do you see?*

    ¿A quiénes habla Ud.?   *To whom are you speaking?*

(3) ¿De quién (-es) (whose?) is used to express possession.

¿De quién es el libro?	*Whose book is it? (Of whom is the book?)*
¿De quién (-es) son los libros?	*Whose books are they?*
	(Of whom are the books?)

EXERCISE D

Pablo never listens carefully when his friends are talking and always has to ask whom they're speaking about. Write the questions Pablo asks to find out who does the following.

EXAMPLE: Daniel juega al fútbol.
              ¿Quién juega al fútbol?

1. Mis hermanas van a una fiesta.

2. Carlos trabaja en el cine.

3. Nosotros vamos al cine esta noche.

4. Rosa no habla con su hermano.

5. Alberto quiere vender su bicicleta.

6. Yo tengo que estudiar para un examen.

7. Mis tíos llegan mañana.

EXERCISE E

You're with a friend at a party, but you don't know many of the people there. Write what you ask your friend about the other people at the party. They're indicated in parentheses.

EXAMPLE: Marta / hablar *(Gerardo y Hugo)*
              ¿A quiénes habla Marta?

1. Gloria / mirar *(su novio)*

2. Vincent y Sara / ver *(los señores Junco)*

3. Carmen / hablar *(Jorge y Fergus)*

4. tú / saludar *(Pilar)*

5. la señora Junco / servir café *(Jamal y Tony)*

6. Esteban / llamar *(sus padres)*

EXERCISE F

After the party, Mrs. Junco finds that several guests left things at the house. Write what Mrs. Junco asks her daughter, Raquel.

EXAMPLE:

1.

¿**De quién** es la bolsa?

2.

3.

4.

5.

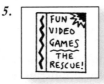

d. *¿Dónde?, ¿adónde?,* and *¿de dónde?*

    (1) *¿Dónde?* (where?) expresses location.

        ¿Dónde está Ana?   *Where's Ana?*

    (2) *¿Adónde?* (to where?) expresses motion to a place.

        ¿Adónde va Ud.?   *Where are you going?*

    (3) *¿De dónde?* (from where?) expresses origin.

        ¿De dónde es Ud.?   *Where are you from?*

EXERCISE G

When Julio's grandmother comes to visit, she wants to know where everyone is. Based on Julio's answers, tell what she asks him.

EXAMPLE: Mi papá está en el jardín.
                 ¿Dónde está tu papá?

1. Mi mamá está en la cocina.

2. Mis hermanas están en el centro.

3. Mis amigos están en el parque.

4. Alfredo está en su dormitorio.

5. El perro está en el sótano.

EXERCISE H

As you go home on the last day of school, a friend asks you about other people's summer plans. Write down his questions.

EXAMPLE: Ricardo

¿**Adónde va** Ricardo durante las vacaciones?

1. Sue y Helen

2. tú

3. la señora Núñez

4. los hermanos Pirelli

5. Álvaro y su familia

EXERCISE I

You invite your cousin to an international fair at your school, where dishes from different countries are being served. Tell what she asks you about each dish.

EXAMPLE: los tacos

¿**De dónde son** los tacos?

1. la paella

2. el asopao

3. los frijoles negros

4. el arroz con pollo

5. la pizza

6. las empanadas

MASTERY EXERCISES

EXERCISE J

A friend is helping you study for a Spanish test. She gives you cards that contain statements. You are to form questions using an interrogative expression in place of the word(s) in boldface.

EXAMPLE: José vive **en Colorado.**

¿**Dónde** vive José?

1. **Pedro** es muy aplicado.

¿ _____ es muy aplicado?

2. El cuaderno es **de Ana**.

   ¿ _____ es el cuaderno?

3. Mis bebidas favoritas son **los jugos y las gaseosas**.

   ¿ _____ son tus bebidas favoritas?

4. Guatemala está **en la América Central**.

   ¿ _____ está Guatemala?

5. Hoy es **el catorce de noviembre**.

   ¿ _____ es la fecha de hoy?

6. El director va **a Italia**.

   ¿ _____ va el director?

7. Un resfriado es **una enfermedad**.

   ¿ _____ es un resfriado?

8. Pienso visitar **a Inglaterra**.

   ¿ _____ país piensas visitar?

9. La señora admira **el vestido de seda**.

   ¿ _____ vestido admira la señora?

10. Hay **cincuenta y dos** semanas en un año.

    ¿ _____ semanas hay en un año?

11. Juana tiene **dos** pares de zapatos.

    ¿ _____ pares de zapatos tiene Juana?

12. Da un paseo **con su hija**.

    ¿ _____ da un paseo?

13. **La bicicleta** vale doscientos dólares.

    ¿ _____ vale doscientos dólares?

14. **Los alumnos** traducen mal.

    ¿ _____ traducen mal?

15. Javier besó **a su abuela**.

    ¿ _____ besó Javier?

16. Almuerzan **porque tienen hambre**.

    ¿ _____ almuerzan?

17. Pablo invitó **a Luisa y Alfredo**.

    ¿ _____ invitó Pablo?

18. Francisco tiene **dolor de muelas**.

    ¿ _____ tiene Francisco?

19. Mi abuelo cenó **a las seis y cuarto**.

¿ _____ cenó tu abuelo?

20. Los alumnos abrieron **las ventanas**.

¿ _____ abrieron las ventanas?

EXERCISE K

An exchange student from Argentina will be staying with your family. Write the questions that you'll ask her when you meet for the first time. From the list below, be sure to use a different interrogative expression in each question.

¿adónde?   ¿cuál(es)?   ¿cuánto?   ¿dónde?   ¿qué?
¿cómo?   ¿cuándo?   ¿de dónde?   ¿por qué? ¿quién(es)?

EXERCISE L

You find a message on your answering machine but you cannot understand certain words in the message. Write the questions that you want to ask as you hear the following message.

1. Habla ******.

2. Son las ****** de la tarde.

3. Estoy en el Hotel ******.

4. Viajo con dos ******.

5. Son muy ******.

6. Ellas se llaman ****** y ******.

7. Vamos a pasar ****** días en esta ciudad.

8. Espero ******.

9. Llámame al número ******.

10. Esta noche vamos al ******.

11. Mis ****** mandan muchos saludos.

EXERCISE M

You and several friends are going to interview a group of Spanish-speaking students who are visiting your school for a month. You will then publish their answers in the school newspaper. Express the following questions in Spanish.

1. What's your name?
2. Where are you from?
3. How old are you?
4. How do you spend your free time?
5. What subjects are you studying in school?
6. Where do you live?
7. How many weeks will you spend at our school?
8. Where are you going next month?
9. What's your favorite sport?
10. Why did you come to the United States?
11. What do you hope to learn here?
12. When will the group return home?
13. Whom do you want to meet?
14. Where does the group want to go?
15. Whose idea was it to come to the United States?
16. What do you like most about the trip?

Chapter 25

Exclamations

Exclamatory words, like interrogative words, have written accents. The most common exclamatory words are:

¡Qué...!   *What . . . ! What a . . . ! How . . . !*

¡Cuánto (-a)...!   *How much . . . !*

¡Cuántos (-as)...!   *How many . . . !*

¡**Qué** libro!	*What a book!*
¡**Qué** grande es!	*How large it is!*
¡**Cuántos** perros tienen!	*How many dogs they have!*
¡**Qué rápido** corre el coche!	*How fast the car runs!*

NOTE:

1. Exclamatory sentences have an inverted exclamation mark (¡) at the beginning and a standard one (!) at the end.

2. If there is an adjective next to a noun, the exclamation is made more intense by placing *tan* or *más* before the adjective.

   ¡Qué niño *tan (más)* inteligente!   *What an intelligent child!*

EXERCISE A

Two friends are raving about their vacation in Puerto Rico. Write what they say.

EXAMPLE: isla / bonita
    ¡**Qué** isla **tan (más)** bonita!

1. vacaciones / fabulosas

2. sol / fuerte

3. piscina / grande

4. clima / agradable

5. deliciosa / ser / la comida

6. playas / hay

7. simpáticos / ser / los puertorriqueños

8. bien / pasar / nosotros / las vacaciones

EXERCISE B

You take your younger brother to the zoo. Write what he exclaims upon seeing the following.

EXAMPLE:

tren / moderno
¡**Qué** tren **más** moderno!

1.

cola / larga

2.

tigre / feroz

3.

globos / bonitos

4.

pájaros / tranquilos

5.

oso / grande

6.

monos / cómicos

7.

pavo real / elegante

8.

serpiente / larga

9.

patos / graciosos

10.

zoológico / interesante

EXERCISE C

You and some friends are returning home from a gathering where you heard about the trip another friend made last summer. Select the correct exclamatory word.

1. ¡(Qué / Cuánto) aburrido! Pasó el verano con su familia.

2. ¡(Qué / Cuánto) viaje más emocionante!

3. ¡(Cuántos / Cuántas) fotos sacó!

4. ¡(Qué / Cuánto) lugares más interesantes visitó!

5. ¡(Cuántos / Cuántas) cosas bonitas compró!

6. ¡(Qué / Cuánto) dinero costó!

7. ¡(Qué / Cuánto) cuentos más divertidos tiene del viaje!

8. ¡(Qué / Cuánto) simpática es su familia!

MASTERY EXERCISES

EXERCISE D

You've just returned from a soccer game. Your friend watched it on television and agrees with your comments. Tell what your friend exclaims when he hears your comments.

EXAMPLE: Era un partido aburrido.
           ¡**Qué** partido **más (tan)** aburrido!

1. Los futbolistas jugaron mal.
2. Necesitan más práctica.
3. El estadio es muy moderno.
4. Mucha gente salió temprano.
5. Perdieron muchos fanáticos.
6. Parecía un partido aficionado.

EXERCISE E

Your friend is going to a Spanish-speaking country and wants to learn some expressions she can use during her trip. Express the following in Spanish.

1. What a beautiful day!
2. What a delicious meal!
3. What a beautiful photo!
4. How great!
5. What a party!
6. What a beautiful house you have!
7. How quickly the days pass!
8. It's so hot!
9. What good friends I have!
10. What a good restaurant!

Chapter 26

Possession

[1] EXPRESSING POSSESSION

a. Possession is normally expressed in Spanish by *de* + the possessor.

el libro de Juan	*John's book*
la casa de los señores Camacho	*the Camachos' house*
los regalos de los niños	*the children's gifts*
el suéter de mi hermana	*my sister's sweater*

b. When the preposition *de* is followed by the definite article *el*, the contraction *del* is formed.

el juguete del niño	*the boy's toy*

c. When followed by a form of *ser*, *¿De quién (-es)...?* is equivalent to the English interrogative "Whose?".

¿De quién es la pelota?	*Whose ball is it?*
¿De quién son los guantes?	*Whose gloves are they?*
¿De quiénes es el coche nuevo?	*Whose new car is it?*
¿De quiénes son las revistas?	*Whose magazines are they?*

EXERCISE A

While visiting your house, Antonio wants to know whom the various things he sees there belong to. Using the cues provided, write Antonio's questions.

EXAMPLE: el televisor
   ¿**De quién es** el televisor?

1. los libros
2. la muñeca
3. los patines
4. los relojes
5. las llaves

6. las camisetas
7. las revistas
8. la calculadora
9. los anteojos
10. el estéreo

EXERCISE B

Using the cues provided, answer the questions Antonio asked you in Exercise A.

EXAMPLE   el televisor / mi papá
           El televisor **es de** mi papá.

1. los libros / María
2. la muñeca / mi hermana
3. los patines / mi primo
4. los relojes / mis padres
5. las llaves / mi abuela
6. las camisetas / mis hermanos
7. las revistas / el vecino
8. la calculadora / mi madre
9. los anteojos / mi abuelo
10. el estéreo / mi mamá

EXERCISE C

While sitting in the dentist's waiting room, Gloria comments on the people she sees there. Tell what she says.

EXAMPLE: las uñas / la señora / largo
            Las uñas **de** la señora **son largas**.

1. el sombrero / el niño / grande
2. los zapatos / la chica / feo
3. la pulsera / la enfermera / bonito
4. la máscara / el dentista / cómico
5. el suéter / el señor / ridículo

[2] POSSESSIVE ADJECTIVES

SINGULAR	PLURAL	MEANING
mi amigo (-a)	mis amigos (-as)	*my*
tu amigo (-a)	tus amigos (-as)	*your* (fam. sing.)
su amigo (-a)	sus amigos (-as)	*his, her, its, their; your* (formal)
nuestro amigo	nuestros amigos	*our*
nuestra amiga	nuestras amigas	
vuestro amigo	vuestros amigos	*your* (fam. pl.)
vuestra amiga	vuestras amigas	

NOTE:

1. Possessive adjectives agree in gender (masculine or feminine) and number (singular or plural) with the person or thing possessed, not with the possessor.

nuestra madre	*our mother*
nuestras madres	*our mothers*
su libro	*his, her, its, their, your (formal), your (pl.) book*
sus libros	*his, her, its, their, your (formal), your (pl.) books*

2. *Nuestro* and *vuestro* have four forms. The other possessive adjectives have two forms.

EXERCISE D

Complete the description that Pedro wrote about a member of his family by selecting the appropriate possessive adjective.

_____ familia y yo vivimos en la ciudad. _____ casa no es muy grande.
  1.   *2.*

Yo comparto _____ dormitorio con uno de _____ hermanos. _____
           3.   *4.*   *5.*

nombre es Enrique. _____ dormitorio es amplio pero tengo que
                  6.

guardar todas _____ cosas en otro cuarto. Enrique tiene muchos juguetes
             7.

pero él tiene la costumbre de dejar _____ cosas en los otros cuartos
                                   8.

de la casa. Enrique nunca usa _____ propia ropa. Le gusta usar _____
                             9.   *10.*

ropa. Usa _____ camisas y _____ suéteres. Aunque Enrique es
         11.   *12.*

_____ hermano menor, _____ talla es la misma. También le
13.   *14.*

gusta molestar a _____ hermanas. Siempre usa _____ cámara para
                15.   *16.*

sacar fotos. Entonces ellas esconden _____ fotos. _____ papás van a
                                    17.   *18.*

darle a Enrique _____ propia cámara para _____ cumpleaños.
               19.   *20.*

EXERCISE E

Roberta and some friends are returning from a camping trip. As they unpack the car, Roberta indicates whom the different things belong to. Use the appropriate possessive adjective to tell what she says.

EXAMPLE: una linterna / de Roberta
Es mi linterna.

1. una cámara / de Alfredo

2. una grabadora / de nosotros

3. unas revistas / de Gregorio

4. una mochila / de Alfredo y Javier

5. los anteojos / de Roberto

6. unas monedas / de Pepe

EXERCISE F

Teresa is guessing who's who in the Jiménez family, but she doesn't know how to read a family tree. Help Teresa figure out the correct family relationships among the following people.

La Familia Jiménez

EXAMPLES: María es la madre de Pepe.
No, María no es la madre de Pepe. **Ella es su abuela.**
OR: **No, María no es** la madre de Pepe. **Ella es la madre de Juan y de Pablo.**

1. Pablo es el padre de María.

2. Blanca es la hermana de Ana.

3. Juan y Paulina son los padres de María y José Antonio.

4. María y José Antonio son los primos de Juanita, Sara y Pedro.

5. Pedro es el hermano de Roberto, Blanca y Pepe.

6. Juanita y Sara son las primas de Pedro.

MASTERY EXERCISES

EXERCISE G

Answer these questions that your parent asks you about some new friends of yours. Use the appropriate possessive adjective in your responses.

1. ¿Cómo se llaman tus amigos nuevos? *(Jorge y Paco)*
2. ¿Cuáles son sus apellidos? *(Nogales, Fuentes)*
3. ¿Dónde está su casa? *(la calle Olmo)*
4. ¿Qué es su padre? *(ingeniero)*
5. ¿Viven cerca de tu tío Daniel? *(sí)*
6. ¿Cuántas personas hay en su familia? *(5)*
7. ¿Son miembros de tu equipo de baloncesto? *(sí)*
8. ¿Salen bien en sus exámenes? *(sí)*
9. ¿Conocen a tus otros amigos? *(sí)*
10. ¿Cuándo vas a su casa? *(mañana)*

EXERCISE H

Anita is talking to a student from Argentina. Express what she says in Spanish.

1. There are many students in our school.
2. My classes are small; your classes are large.
3. Ricardo's teachers arrive on time.
4. He leaves his bicycle in the schoolyard.
5. My friends and I walk to school.
6. Our houses are near the school.
7. Whose photo is that?
8. Is your sister's boyfriend tall?
9. Nilda's brothers are very tall.
10. Can you come to my house after school?
11. You have to meet my parents.
12. When do you celebrate your birthday?
13. Ricardo's birthday is tomorrow.

14. I bought his gift last night.

15. His friends are very nice.

16. Our classes are very interesting today.

17. Patricia's teacher is strict.

18. I like your watch.

19. Do you like my new shoes?

20. I want to be your friend.

Chapter 27

Demonstrative Adjectives

Demonstrative adjectives, like other adjectives, agree with their nouns in gender (masculine or feminine) and number (singular or plural).

	MASCULINE	FEMININE	MEANING
SINGULAR	**este libro**	**esta casa**	*this*
PLURAL	**estos libros**	**estas casas**	*these*

	MASCULINE	FEMININE	MEANING
SINGULAR	**ese libro**	**esa casa**	*that (near you)*
PLURAL	**esos libros**	**esas casas**	*those (near you)*

	MASCULINE	FEMININE	MEANING
SINGULAR	**aquel libro**	**aquella casa**	*that (at a distance)*
PLURAL	**aquellos libros**	**aquellas casas**	*those (at a distance)*

NOTE:

1. *Este (esta, estos, estas)* refers to what is near. *Ese (esa, esos, esas)* refers to what isn't so near. *Aquel (aquella, aquellos, aquellas)*, "that" (those), refers to what is remote from both the speaker and the person addressed.

Esta blusa es negra.	*This blouse is black.*
Mary, dame **esa** blusa que tienes en la mano.	*Mary, give me that blouse that you have in your hand.*
Mary, dame **aquella** blusa.	*Mary, give me that blouse over there.*

2. The adverbs *aquí* (here), *ahí* (there), and *allí* ([over] there) correspond to the demonstrative adjectives *este, ese,* and *aquel.*

   Pon { este libro **aquí.**
   ese cuaderno **ahí.**
   aquel lápiz **allí.** }

   Put { this book here.
   that notebook there.
   that pencil over there. }

EXERCISE A

A week before Mother's Day, Federico accompanies his mother to a department store. He tries to find out what she likes. Tell what he asks her.

EXAMPLE: prendedor
              ¿Te gusta **este** prendedor?

1. aretes
2. pulsera
3. anillos
4. billetera

5. cadenas
6. perfume
7. reloj
8. bolsa

EXERCISE B

Pilar and a friend are visiting a botanical garden. Tell what they say about the plants and flowers they see.

EXAMPLE: árboles / altos
              Esos árboles **son** altos.

1. rosas / delicadas
2. planta / pequeña
3. gladiolas / bonitas
4. orquídeas / exóticas

5. tulipanes / rojos
6. cacto / feo
7. pino / viejo
8. dalia / elegante

EXERCISE C

You and a friend are visiting the observation deck at the tallest building in the city. As you look through the telescope, describe what you see.

EXAMPLE: iglesia / antigua
              Aquella iglesia es antigua.

1. puente / largo
2. barcos / caros
3. estadio / grande
4. calle / corta
5. barrio / interesante

6. estatua / famosa
7. parques / bonitos
8. casas / pequeñas
9. universidad / privada

EXERCISE D

Alice is in a toy store looking for a gift for her brother and sister. She wants to know the price of the things she sees. Tell what she asks.

EXAMPLES: guante de béisbol / aquí
   ¿Cuánto cuesta este guante de béisbol?

   juego electrónico / ahí
   ¿Cuánto cuesta ese juego electrónico?

   muñecas / allí
   ¿Cuánto cuestan aquellas muñecas?

1. bicicletas / allí
2. calculadoras / ahí
3. osito de peluche / aquí
4. pelota / allí
5. discos / ahí
6. grabadora / aquí
7. raqueta de tenis / ahí
8. radio portátil / ahí
9. casa de muñecas / aquí
10. juego de damas / allí

EXERCISE E

Pepe is helping his mother do the shopping. Answer the questions he asks his mother, using the appropriate demonstrative adjective.

EXAMPLE: ¿Prefieres la sandía de ahí?
   Prefiero esa sandía.

1. ¿Te gustan los plátanos de allí?
2. ¿Prefieres los tomates de aquí?
3. ¿Prefieres el melón de allí?
4. ¿Te gustan las manzanas de ahí?
5. ¿Te gusta la piña de aquí?
6. ¿Prefieres las peras de ahí?
7. ¿Quieres las uvas de aquí?
8. ¿Te gusta la fruta de allí?

EXERCISE F

Mr. Molina takes his family on a tour of the city where he went to college. Complete his statements with the appropriate demonstrative adjective.

Yo vivía aquí, en _____ pensión aquí. De _____ ventana en el tercer piso
        1.   2.

veía _____ monumentos que visitamos ayer.   En _____ calle ahí había
        3.   4.

muchos restaurantes buenos y baratos. Tomaba el desayuno en _____ café;
                                                                    5.

almorzaba en _____ restaurante de aquí y cenaba en _____ restaurante
                    6.   7.

que está en la esquina. Compraba el periódico en _____ tienda que está al
                                                        8.

lado de la pensión. Allí había un cine, no existía _____ biblioteca.
                                                        9.

_____ señor que anda ahí vendía los boletos. Vi muchas películas buenas
    10.

en _____ cine. Jugaba fútbol en _____ parque de allí.   En el verano iba a
      11.   12.

nadar en _____ piscina que está dentro del parque. Ahí conocí a _____
            13.   14.

señores que Uds. conocieron ayer. ¡Cómo me divertí en _____ ciudad!
                                                            15.

MASTERY EXERCISES

EXERCISE G

You're in the cafeteria with a friend who's visiting your school. As you point to the different kinds of food, you comment on them. Use a demonstrative adjective to describe five of the items you see.

carne	galletas	papas fritas	postres
ensaladas	helado	pastel	sopa

EXAMPLE: **Este plátano** es delicioso.
           Esas hamburguesas tienen queso.
           Aquel pan es dulce.

EXERCISE H

You and a Spanish-speaking friend are visiting your sister at her college dormitory. You comment on what you see in her room. Express the following in Spanish.

1. This room isn't very large.
2. That poster (near) is interesting.
3. These books are from the library.
4. She uses that bicycle (near) for exercise.
5. Those stories (distant) are amusing.
6. This computer is new.
7. These tourists are lucky.
8. I gave her those flowers (near).
9. She no longer uses this dictionary.
10. Those photos (distant) are of her friends.
11. These magazines are old.
12. This doll is her favorite.
13. Those records (distant) aren't very good.
14. I don't believe this news.
15. That girl (near) is her best friend.

Part four

Word Study

ESPAÑA

Islas Baleares

Islas Canarias

MÉXICO

REPÚBLICA
DOMINICANA
PUERTO RICO

CUBA
HONDURAS
NICARAGUA

GUATEMALA
EL SALVADOR
COSTA RICA
PANAMÁ

VENEZUELA

COLOMBIA

ECUADOR

PERÚ

BOLIVIA

PARAGUAY

CHILE

URUGUAY

ARGENTINA

Chapter 28

Cognates

Many Spanish and English words are related in form (spelling) and meaning because they derive from the same Latin or Greek root. Such pairs of words are called cognates, from *cognatus*, the Latin word for *relative*.

[1] EXACT COGNATES

Spanish words spelled exactly as in English are called exact cognates.

actor	doctor	piano
central	hotel	radio (m. & f.)
color	idea	terrible
chocolate	motor	viola

NOTE: Although the spellings are identical in both languages, the pronunciations are different.

[2] DIRECT COGNATES

Many other cognates can be recognized if we bear in mind certain rules of Spanish spelling and pronunciation.

a. Many Spanish words that end in *-ción* have a corresponding English word that ends in *-tion*.

la pronunciación   *pronunciation*
la combinación   *combination*

EXERCISE A

Write the English words that correspond to the following Spanish words.

1. admiración
2. aviación
3. celebración
4. civilización
5. dirección

6. invitación
7. nación
8. producción
9. repetición
10. sección

b. The Spanish ending -*dad* corresponds to the English ending -*ty*.

la sociedad   *society*
la electricidad   *electricity*

EXERCISE B

Write the English words that correspond to the following Spanish words.

1. autoridad   *6.* necesidad
2. capacidad   *7.* posibilidad
3. curiosidad   *8.* realidad
4. eternidad   *9.* universidad
5. generosidad   *10.* variedad

c. Many Spanish words that end in -*ia*, -*ía*, or -*io* end in *y* in English.

familia   *family*
fotografía   *photography*
vocabulario   *vocabulary*

EXERCISE C

Write the English words (or names) that correspond to the following Spanish words (or names).

1. Antonio   *6.* historia
2. democracia   *7.* María
3. dormitorio   *8.* memoria
4. farmacia   *9.* necesario
5. geografía   *10.* remedio

d. The Spanish ending -*oso* corresponds to the English ending -*ous*.

misterioso   *mysterious*
rigoroso   *rigorous*

EXERCISE D

Write the English words that correspond to the following Spanish words.

1. curioso	**6.** montañoso
2. famoso	**7.** nervioso
3. furioso	**8.** numeroso
4. generoso	**9.** precioso
5. glorioso	**10.** religioso

e. The Spanish adverbial ending -*mente* corresponds to the English adverbial ending -*ly*.

finalmente   *finally*

EXERCISE E

Write the English adverbs that correspond to the following Spanish adverbs.

1. correctamente	**6.** naturalmente
2. diligentemente	**7.** perfectamente
3. exactamente	**8.** rápidamente
4. frecuentemente	**9.** recientemente
5. inmediatamente	**10.** sinceramente

f. In Spanish, there are almost no words beginning with *s* + consonant. Many English words beginning with *s* + consonant have corresponding Spanish words beginning with -*es*.

espacio   *space*

EXERCISE F

Write the English words that correspond to the following Spanish words.

1. escena	**6.** espíritu
2. escriba	**7.** espléndido
3. España	**8.** estudiante
4. especial	**9.** estación
5. espectáculo	**10.** estúpido

[3] INDIRECT COGNATES (PART I)

Many Spanish words are indirectly related in form and meaning to
English words. That is, there is a recognizable similarity in the forms
of the two words, and an indirect connection in meaning. For example: *libro* means "book," and is related in form and meaning to
the English word *library*.

SPANISH WORD	ENGLISH MEANING	ENGLISH COGNATE
agua	*water*	*aquarium*
alto	*high*	*altitude*
aprender	*to learn*	*apprentice*
árbol	*tree*	*arbor*
ascensor	*elevator*	*to ascend, rise*
avión	*airplane*	*aviation*
azul	*blue*	*azure*
bailar	*to dance*	*ballet*
beber	*to drink*	*beverage*
biblioteca	*library*	*bibliography (list of books)*
brazo	*arm*	*bracelet; embrace*
caliente	*hot*	*caloric*
calor	*heat*	*calorie*
cantar	*to sing*	*chant*
carne	*meat*	*carnivore (meat eater)*
carnicería	*butcher shop*	*carnivorous*
carnicero	*butcher*	*carnage (slaughter)*
cien, ciento	*hundred*	*century*
cine	*movies*	*cinema*
comprender	*to understand*	*comprehend*
contra	*against*	*contrary*
correr	*to run*	*current, courier (messenger, runner)*
creer	*to believe*	*credible, creed (belief)*
¿cuánto?	*how much?*	*quantity*
deber	*to owe*	*debt, debtor (ower)*
décimo	*tenth*	*decimal*
día	*day*	*diary*
diente	*tooth*	*dental, dentist*
dormir	*to sleep*	*dormant*
dormitorio	*bedroom*	*dormitory*
duro	*hard*	*endure*

EXERCISE G

For each of the English words given, write the related Spanish word and its meaning in English.

EXAMPLE: chant   **cantar** (to sing)

1. ballet
2. dental
3. beverage
4. century
5. debt
6. apprentice
7 durable
8. aviation

9. quantity
10. comprehend
11. cinema
12. altitude
13. creed
14. dormitory
15. contrary

EXERCISE H

Match the Spanish words in column A with their English indirect cognates in column B.

A	B
1. día	*a.* carnivorous
2. agua	*b.* decimal
3. biblioteca	*c.* bibliography
4. décimo	*d.* diary
5. brazo	*e.* ascend
6. árbol	*f.* bracelet
7. carne	*g.* aquarium
8. azul	*h.* azure
9. ascensor	*i.* arbor
10. calor	*j.* caloric

EXERCISE I

Select the English word that expresses the meaning of the Spanish words given.

1. deber   to drink, to owe, to tell
2. cantar   to count, to sing, to buy

3. duro   tooth, dear, hard

4. comprender   to buy, to understand, to learn

5. ciento   scientist, hundred, central

6. bailar   to dance, to play ball, to believe

7. aprender   to open, to learn, to understand

8. cine   sign, century, movies

9. correr   to believe, to run, to want

10. alto   high, elevator, alter

EXERCISE J

Select the Spanish word that expresses the meaning of the English word given.

1. arm   brazo, amar, armario

2. against   contar, contestar, contra

3. library   libro, libre, biblioteca

4. heat   color, calor, carne

5. airplane   playa, aire, avión

6. how much?   ¿cuánto?, ¿cuándo?, ¿cuál?

7. tree   tres, árbol, alto

8. to drink   creer, bailar, beber

9. to sleep   dormir, decir, morir

10. tooth   día, duro, diente

[4] INDIRECT COGNATES (PART II)

SPANISH WORD	ENGLISH MEANING	ENGLISH COGNATE
edificio	*building*	*edifice (large building)*
enfermedad	*illness*	*infirmity*
enfermo	*sick, ill*	*infirmary*
escribir	*to write*	*scribble, scribe*
fábrica	*factory*	*fabricate (manufacture)*
fácil	*easy*	*facilitate (make easy)*
fácilmente	*easily*	*facile*
feliz	*happy*	*felicity (happiness)*

SPANISH WORD	ENGLISH MEANING	ENGLISH COGNATE
felizmente	*happily*	*felicitous*
flor	*flower*	*florist*
guante	*glove*	*gauntlet*
habitación	*room*	*habitation*
habitante	*inhabitant*	*inhabit*
hierba	*grass*	*herb*
lavar	*to wash*	*lavatory*
leer	*to read*	*legible*
lengua	*language*	*linguist (language specialist)*
libre	*free*	*liberty*
libremente	*freely*	*liberally*
libro	*book*	*library*
luna	*moon*	*lunar*
malo	*bad*	*malefactor (evildoer)*
mano	*hand*	*manually (by hand)*
mayor	*older, greater*	*major, majority*
médico	*doctor*	*medical*
menor	*lesser, younger*	*minor, minority*
menos	*less*	*minus*
mirar	*to look at*	*mirror*
morir	*to die*	*mortal, mortuary*
nuevo	*new*	*novelty*

EXERCISE K

For each English word, write the Spanish cognate and its meaning.

EXAMPLE: linguist **lengua** (language)

1. lunar
2. florist
3. malefactor
4. manual
5. facilitate
6. edifice
7. felicity
8. library
9. herb
10. scribble
11. majority
12. minor
13. mirror
14. medical
15. lavatory

EXERCISE L

Match the Spanish words in column A with their English cognates in column B.

A	B
1. habitación	*a.* liberty
2. menos	*b.* linguist
3. fábrica	*c.* mortal
4. guante	*d.* infirmary
5. leer	*e.* novelty
6. enfermo	*f.* gauntlet
7. libre	*g.* minus
8. nuevo	*h.* inhabit
9. morir	*i.* legible
10. lengua	*j.* fabricate

EXERCISE M

Select the English word that expresses the meaning of the Spanish words given.

1. menos	less, younger, lesser
2. morir	to look at, to die, to show
3. flor	flower, florist, flour
4. malo	mallet, male, bad
5. lavar	to wash, to arrive, to carry
6. habitación	habit, room, to inhabit
7. fácil	easy, factory, flower
8. edificio	office, building, exercise
9. mayor	greater, better, mayor
10. mano	man, manage, hand

EXERCISE N

Select the Spanish word that expresses the meaning of the English words given.

1. younger	mano, menor, menos
2. free	libro, libre, fresco

3. factory   fábrica, flor, fecha
4. happy   feliz, tristemente, bonito
5. grass   hoja, hierba, árbol
6. moon   lunes, moneda, luna
7. new   nuevo, nieve, nueve
8. to look at   ver, mirar, buscar
9. glove   mano, corbata, guante
10. doctor   médico, medio, enfermedad

[5] INDIRECT COGNATES (PART III)

SPANISH WORD	ENGLISH MEANING	ENGLISH COGNATE
patria	*(native) country*	*patriotic*
pedir	*to request*	*petition*
pensar	*to think*	*pensive (thoughtful)*
periódico	*newspaper*	*periodical*
pluma	*pen, feather*	*plume*
pobre	*poor*	*poverty*
precio	*price*	*precious*
primero	*first*	*primary*
pronto	*soon*	*prompt*
revista	*magazine*	*review*
sala	*hall, parlor*	*salon*
sentir	*to feel*	*sentiment*
sol	*sun*	*solar*
sonar	*to sound*	*sonorous (full sounding)*
tarde	*late*	*tardy*
tiempo	*time*	*tempo, temporary*
tierra	*earth, land*	*territory*
todo	*all*	*total*
valer	*to be worth*	*value*
vecino	*neighbor*	*vicinity (neighborhood)*
vender	*to sell*	*vendor*
ventana	*window*	*ventilate*
verdad	*truth*	*verify*
verde	*green*	*verdant (green)*
vida	*life*	*vital, vitality*
vivir	*to live*	*revive, vivid*

EXERCISE O

For each English word, give the Spanish indirect cognate and its meaning.

EXAMPLE: vicinity   **vecino** (neighbor)

1. periodical
2. territory
3. poverty
4. salon
5. primary
6. solar
7. total
8. vivid

9. prompt
10. tempo
11. patriot
12. ventilate
13. plume
14. verdant
15. pensive

EXERCISE P

Match the Spanish words in column A with their English cognates in column B.

A	B
1. valer	a. review
2. vida	b. sonorous
3. precio	c. precious
4. revista	d. value
5. verdad	e. verify
6. pedir	f. sentiment
7. sonar	g. vital
8. tarde	h. tardy
9. sentir	i. vendor
10. vender	j. petition

EXERCISE Q

Select the English word that expresses the meaning of the Spanish words given.

1. periódico   newspaper, period, periodical
2. sala   sale, hall, saloon

3. verde   vertical, divert, green

4. valer   bravery, to be worth, to fly

5. pluma   pen, pencil, plum

6. todo   bull, land, all

7. vecino   time, summer, neighbor

8. patria   country, father, courtyard

9. ventana   window, vent, ventilate

10. tierra   time, earth, terror

EXERCISE R

Select the Spanish word that expresses the meaning of the English words given.

1. sun   sol, hijo, soldado

2. price   costar, precio, valer

3. to request   pedir, perder, poder

4. truth   verdad, verde, viento

5. first   pronto, primero, primo

6. to sell   venir, ver, vender

7. to regret   sentir, sentar, triste

8. poor   pueblo, pobre, pronto

9. late   tiempo, ayer, tarde

10. life   vida, vivir, libre

[6] WORDS FREQUENTLY CONFUSED

In Spanish, there are many pairs of words that are written alike or sound alike, but have different meanings.

a. An accent mark is used to distinguish the following pairs of words:

como	*as, like*	que	*which, that, who*
¿cómo?	*how?*	¿qué?	*what?*
de	*of, from*	se	*himself, herself, yourself, themselves*
dé (Ud.)	*give* (command)	sé	*I know*
el	*the*	si	*if*
él	*he, him*	sí	*yes*

mas	*but*	te	*you, yourself*
más	*more*	té	*tea*
mi	*my*	tu	*your*
mí	*me*	tú	*you*

b. Some words are spelled identically even though they have very different meanings. Their meaning must be determined from the context.

cara	*face*	media	*stocking*
cara (caro)	*expensive*	media (medio)	*half*
como	*as, like*	nada	*nothing, not . . . anything*
como	*I eat*	nada	*you, he, she swims*
entre	*between, among*	(la) parte	*part*
entre	*enter (command)*	parte	*you, he, she departs*
este	*this*	sobre	*on, over*
este	*east*	(el) sobre	*envelope*
mañana	*tomorrow*	tarde	*late*
mañana	*morning*	(la) tarde	*afternoon*
(el) traje	*suit*	vino	*wine*
traje	*I brought*	vino	*you, he, she came*

c. The following groups of words may cause confusion because of their similar spelling and pronunciation.

cantar	*to sing*	llegar	*to arrive*
contar	*to count*	llevar	*to carry, to wear*
¿cuánto?	*how much?*	llorar	*to cry*
¿cuándo?	*when?*	llover	*to rain*
cuento	*story*	música	*music*
cuenta	*account; you, he, she counts*	música (músico)	*musician*
cuarto	*room, fourth*	nueve	*nine*
cuatro	*four*	nuevo	*new*
dólar	*dollar*	pero	*but*
dolor	*ache, pain*	perro	*dog*

falda *skirt*	plata *silver*
falta *mistake, error*	plato *dish, plate*
hermano *brother*	primo *cousin*
hermoso *beautiful*	primero *first*
hambre *hunger*	queso *cheese*
hombre *man*	quiso *you, he, she wanted*
hay *there is, there are*	quince *fifteen*
hoy *today*	quinto *fifth*
inglesa (inglés) *English*	sentarse *to sit down*
iglesia *church*	sentirse *to feel*
libre *free*	veinte *twenty*
libro *book*	viento *wind*
luna *moon*	viaje *trip*
lunes *Monday*	viejo *old, old man*

EXERCISE S

Select the word in parentheses that correctly completes each sentence.

1. ¿Expresas bien (tu / tú) idea?
2. ¿Expresas (tu / tú) bien la idea?
3. (Si / Sí), señor, soy norteamericana.
4. Su (pero / perro) es muy (hermano / hermoso).
5. ¿Cómo (se / sé) llama Ud.?
6. Colón es el (hambre / hombre) (que / qué) descubrió el Nuevo Mundo.
7. Su (primo / primero) habla demasiado.
8. ¿(Como / Cómo) están Uds.?
9. ¿Quién inventó (el / él) teléfono?
10. (De / Dé) Ud. el examen al maestro.
11. No vi (la luna / el lunes) anoche.
12. No (te / té) reconozco con la máscara.
13. El vapor (llega / lleva) el martes próximo.
14. Vamos al restaurante. Tengo (hambre / hombre).
15. Esa invitación es para (mi / mí).

EXERCISE T

Select the Spanish word that expresses the meaning of the English words given.

1. fifth   quince, quinientos, quinto
2. skirt   fábrica, falda, falta
3. brother   hermano, hermoso, hierro
4. ache   cabeza, dólar, dolor
5. stocking   media, medio, mientras
6. today   hay, hoja, hoy
7. trip   viaje, viejo, vieja
8. how much?   ¿cómo?, ¿cuándo?, ¿cuánto?
9. music   museo, música, músico
10. silver   plata, plato, plaza
11. cheese   queso, quise, quiso
12. to rain   llenar, llorar, llover
13. new   nieve, nueve, nuevo
14. twenty   veinte, ventana, viento
15. four   cuadro, cuarto, cuatro

M A S T E R Y   E X E R C I S E S

EXERCISE U

Complete the crossword puzzle by filling in the Spanish cognates of the words given.

ACROSS		
1. herb	16. decimal	28. novelty
4. prompt	18. salon	29. poverty
5. lunar	21. contrary	30. quantity
9. remedy	22. plume	31. geography
10. memory	24. tardy	32. library
12. solar	26. tempo	
15. carnivorous	27. mortal	

DOWN		
2. invitation	**8.** diary	**17.** facilitate
3. religious	**11.** spectacle	**19.** inhabit
4. patriotic	**13.** bracelet	**20.** liberty
6. furious	**14.** verify	**23.** medical
7. perfectly	**16.** endure	**25.** infirmary

EXERCISE V

Write two meanings for each of the following words.

1. nada

2. tarde

3. mañana

4. cara

5. parte

6. sobre

7. como

8. vino

9. media

10. este

Chapter 29
Synonyms and Antonyms

[1] SYNONYMS

Synonyms are two or more words or expressions with the same meaning.

SYNONYMS	ENGLISH MEANINGS
a menudo, frecuentemente, muchas veces	*often, frequently*
a veces, algunas veces	*at times, sometimes*
al fin, finalmente	*finally, at last*
la alcoba, el dormitorio	*bedroom*
alegre, contento, feliz	*merry, happy*
algunos, unos, varios	*some, several*
la alumna, la estudiante	*pupil, student (f.)*
el alumno, el estudiante	*pupil, student (m.)*
la amiga, la compañera	*friend, companion (f.)*
el amigo, el compañero	*friend, companion (m.)*
andar, caminar, ir a pie	*to walk*
aplicado, diligente	*diligent, studious*
el automóvil, el carro, el coche	*automobile, car*
bonito, lindo	*pretty*
la camarera, la mesera, la moza	*waitress*
el camarero, el mesero, el mozo	*waiter*
el catarro, el resfriado	*cold (illness)*
comenzar, empezar	*to begin*
completar, terminar	*to complete, to finish*
comprender, entender	*to understand*
contestar, responder	*to answer*
el cuarto, la habitación	*room*
el cuento, la historia	*story*
la chica, la niña	*child (f.)*
el chico, el niño	*child (m.)*
delante de, en frente de	*in front of, opposite*

de nuevo, otra vez	*again*
desear, querer	*to wish; to want*
el doctor, el médico	*doctor (m.)*
la doctora, la médico	*doctor (f.)*
encontrar, hallar	*to find*
entonces, luego	*then*
el error, la falta	*error, mistake*
la esposa, la mujer	*wife*
el esposo, el marido	*husband*
el examen, la prueba	*test, examination*
la maestra, la profesora	*teacher (f.)*
el maestro, el profesor	*teacher (m.)*
la montaña, el monte	*mountain*
la nación, el país	*nation, country*
partir, salir	*to leave, to depart*
poseer, tener	*to own, to have*
regresar, volver	*to return*

EXERCISE A

Select the synonym of the words given.

1. amigo — dueño, compañero, hombre
2. delante de — alguna vez, sobre, enfrente de
3. cuarto — habitación, casa, jardín
4. unos — muchos, varios, pocos
5. estudiante — maestro, amigo, alumno
6. bonito — lindo, simpático, joven
7. examen — nota, prueba, trabajo
8. país — ciudad, nación, estado
9. niño — chico, esposo, hermano
10. desear — respetar, gastar, querer
11. poseer — conservar, tener, recordar
12. entonces — pronto, primero, luego
13. alegre — generoso, contento, triste

14. historia   cuento, noticia, propina

15. no hay de qué   por favor, gracias, de nada

EXERCISE B

Match the words in column A with their synonyms in column B.

A	B
1. andar	**a.** terminar
2. empezar	**b.** maestro
3. salir	**c.** aplicado
4. encontrar	**d.** ir a pie
5. diligente	**e.** falta
6. profesor	**f.** alcoba
7. error	**g.** automóvil
8. completar	**h.** comenzar
9. coche	**i.** partir
10. dormitorio	**j.** hallar

EXERCISE C

Retell Hector's story by replacing the words in parentheses with their synonyms.

No voy al doctor *(a menudo)* _____ . Nunca *(quiero)* _____ ir al doctor.
                                    1.   2.

Pero la semana pasada tenía *(un catarro)* _____ muy fuerte. Llamé al doctor
                                            3.

para hacer una cita. Mi mamá tenía *(el automóvil)* _____ y tuve que
                                                     4.

(caminar) _____ a su oficina. Había *(varias)* _____ personas en su
            5.   6.

consultorio. El doctor *(empezó)* _____ a examinarme la boca. Me dio una
                                  7.

receta. Le di las gracias y él respondió: *(No hay de qué)* _____ .
                                                            8.

(Volví) _____ a casa a las cinco. Ahora estoy *(contento)* _____
          9.   10.

porque no tengo catarro.

EXERCISE D

Complete the crossword puzzle with the synonym of the words given.

ACROSS		
1. estudiante	**10.** responder	**20.** país
3. error	**12.** finalmente	**21.** frecuentemente
5. dormitorio	**13.** desear	**22.** no hay de qué
7. montaña	**15.** niño	
9. andar	**17.** maestro	

DOWN		
2. algunos	**9.** automóvil	**17.** examen
4. completar	**10.** historia	**18.** de nuevo
5. contento	**11.** comprender	**19.** regresar
6. compañero	**14.** mujer	
8. mozo	**16.** poseer	

[2] ANTONYMS (PART I)

An antonym is a word or expression opposite in meaning to another word.

WORD / EXPRESSION	ANTONYM
a menudo, frecuentemente *frequently*	pocas veces *rarely*
abajo *down, downstairs*	arriba *up, upstairs*
abrir *to open*	cerrar *to close*
abuelo *grandfather*	nieto *grandson*
ahora *now*	después *later*
alegre, feliz *happy*	triste *sad*
algo *something*	nada *nothing*
alguien *someone*	nadie *no one*
alguno *some*	ninguno *none*
allí *there*	aquí *here*
alto *high*	bajo *low*
amigo *friend*	enemigo *enemy*
ancho *wide*	estrecho *narrow*
antes de *before*	después de *after*
aplicado, diligente *diligent*	perezoso *lazy*
ayer *yesterday*	mañana *tomorrow*
barato *cheap*	caro *expensive, dear*
bien *well*	mal *badly*
blanco *white*	negro *black*
bueno *good*	malo *bad*
caliente *hot, warm*	frío *cold*
cerca de *near*	lejos de *far from*
comprar *to buy*	vender *to sell*
con *with*	sin *without*
corto *short*	largo *long*
dar *to give*	tomar *to take*
debajo de *under, beneath*	sobre *upon, over*
delante de *in front of*	detrás de *in back of*
derecho *right*	izquierdo *left*
despacio *slowly*	rápidamente *quickly*
día *day*	noche *night*

EXERCISE E

Select the antonym of the word or expression given.

1. ancho   derecho, bastante, estrecho
2. enemigo   amigo, primo, dueño
3. arriba   hacia, abajo, detrás de
4. mal   demasiado, mucho, bien
5. blanco   plata, negro, alto
6. vender   comprar, valer, prestar
7. despacio   poco a poco, espacio, rápidamente
8. nada   alguno, algo, corto
9. bajo   alto, vacío, grande
10. abrir   cenar, celebrar, cerrar
11. frío   nieve, caliente, sur
12. caro   rico, barato, mucho
13. alguien   unos, muchos, nadie
14. más tarde   ahora, pocas veces, al fin
15. feliz   contento, gordo, triste

EXERCISE F

Match the word in column A with its antonym in column B.

A	B
1. frecuentemente	*a.* nieto
2. diligente	*b.* dar
3. tomar	*c.* corto
4. derecho	*d.* perezoso
5. alguno	*e.* mañana
6. largo	*f.* debajo de
7. sobre	*g.* pocas veces
8. abuelo	*h.* ninguno
9. ayer	*i.* día
10. noche	*j.* izquierdo

EXERCISE G

Sam and his brother have returned from visiting a friend's new home. His brother always contradicts what Sam says. Tell what his brother says by using an appropriate antonym in each sentence.

EXAMPLE: Ricky es nuestro amigo.
Ricky es nuestro **enemigo**.

1. Hay una piscina detrás de la casa.
2. El agua de la piscina está fría.
3. Su hermana está muy contenta.
4. Antes de salir de la casa tomamos un café.
5. Arturo es una persona diligente.
6. Le gusta salir con sus amigos.
7. Viven cerca de la universidad.
8. Nadie estaba en la piscina.
9. Viven en la parte alta de la ciudad.
10. La casa es de color blanco.

EXERCISE H

Answer your parents' questions using the antonym in parentheses.

1. ¿Deseas comer ahora? *(después)*
2. ¿Compras las plumas baratas? *(caras)*
3. ¿Te gusta comer pescado a menudo? *(pocas veces)*
4. ¿Estudias antes de cenar? *(después de)*
5. ¿Vas a vender limonada? *(comprar)*

[3] ANTONYMS (PART II)

WORD / EXPRESSION	ANTONYM
empezar *to begin*	terminar *to end, to finish*
entrar *to enter*	salir (de) *to leave*
este *east*	oeste *west*

fácil *easy*	difícil *difficult, hard*
feo *ugly*	hermoso *beautiful*
feo *ugly*	bonito, lindo *pretty*
fuerte *strong*	débil *weak*
gordo *chubby, fat*	flaco *thin*
grande *large, big*	pequeño *small, little*
hombre *man*	mujer *woman*
invierno *winter*	verano *summer*
levantarse *to stand up*	sentarse *to sit down*
lleno *full*	vacío *empty*
más *more*	menos *less*
mayor *greater, older*	menor *lesser, younger*
mediodía *noon*	medianoche *midnight*
moreno *brunette*	rubio *blond*
mucho *much*	poco *little*
no *no*	sí *yes*
norte *north*	sur *south*
nunca *never*	siempre *always*
olvidar *to forget*	recordar *to remember*
perder *to lose*	encontrar, hallar *to find*
perder *to lose*	ganar *to win*
pobre *poor*	rico *rich*
ponerse *to put on*	quitarse *to take off*
pregunta *question*	respuesta *answer*
preguntar *to ask*	contestar, responder *to answer*
presente *present*	ausente *absent*
presente *present*	pasado *past*
ruido *noise*	silencio *silence*
subir *to go up*	bajar *to go down*
tarde *late*	temprano *early*
viejo *old*	joven *young*
viejo *old*	nuevo *new*
vivir *to live*	morir *to die*

EXERCISE I

Select the antonym of the words given.

1. empezar   lograr, comenzar, terminar
2. mediodía   media, medianoche, remedio
3. mayor   numeroso, menor, medio
4. viejo   nuevo, noveno, nueve
5. encontrar   perder, inventar, desaparecer
6. olvidar   recordar, reconocer, referir
7. moreno   pardo, rubio, rosado
8. norte   sur, este, oeste
9. fuerte   duro, nervioso, débil
10. pregunta   contestar, responder, respuesta
11. más   menor, poco, menos
12. vivir   existir, morir, romper
13. subir   sentir, bajar, poseer
14. nunca   siempre, nadie, algo
15. entrar   sacar, llenar, salir

EXERCISE J

Match the words in column A with their antonyms in column B.

A	B
1. este	*a.* silencio
2. levantarse	*b.* mujer
3. no	*c.* poco
4. ponerse	*d.* vacío
5. mucho	*e.* viejo
6. hombre	*f.* contestar
7. joven	*g.* oeste
8. preguntar	*h.* sí
9. ruido	*i.* quitarse
10. lleno	*j.* sentarse

EXERCISE K

Laura's grandfather always mixes up his stories. Correct the following one by replacing the words in parentheses with their antonyms.

Ayer vimos una escena *(fea)* _____. *(Enfrente de)* _____ las dos casas

　　　　　　　　　　　　　　　1.　　　　　　　　　　　　2.

hay un espacio *(pequeño)* _____. La niña que vive *(aquí)* _____

　　　　　　　　　　　　　　3.　　　　　　　　　　　　　　4.

estaba muy *(contenta)* _____. Ella *(compraba)* _____ limonada

　　　　　　　　　　　5.　　　　　　　　　　　6.

porque hacía *(frío)* _____. Una mujer muy *(alta)* _____ y *(flaca)*

　　　　　　　　7.　　　　　　　　　　　　　　8.

_____ llegó. Quería *(vender)* _____ una limonada porque era *(cara)*

　9.　　　　　　　　　　　10.

_____. Tenía *(poco)* _____ dinero y bebió toda la limonada. Ahora

11.　　　　　　　　12.

todas las botellas están *(llenas)* _____ y todo el mundo está *(triste)* _____ .

　　　　　　　　　　　　　　　13.　　　　　　　　　　　　　　　14.

EXERCISE L

Adrián's brother never listens to what he says and usually answers his questions foolishly. Answer Adrian's questions negatively, using an antonym for the words in boldface.

EXAMPLE:　¿Es **difícil** la geografía?

　　　　　　No, la geografía es **fácil**.

1. ¿Es **bonita** tu amiga?
2. ¿Hay mucha nieve en el **invierno**?
3. ¿Hace calor en el **sur**?
4. ¿Hace sol a **mediodía**?
5. ¿Tienen muchos juguetes los niños **ricos**?
6. ¿Son **grandes** los elefantes?
7. ¿Sacas tú **buenas** notas en las clases?
8. ¿Te gusta el **silencio**?
9. ¿Llegas **temprano** a la escuela?
10. ¿Siempre **encuentras** las llaves?

EXERCISE M

Complete the crossword puzzle with the antonym of the words given.

ACROSS

2. comprar
3. nada
4. delante de
5. a menudo
9. alguno
10. caliente

11. ayer
13. alto
14. allí
16. alegre
18. con
19. abuelo

21. enemigo
22. diligente
23. corto
24. sobre

DOWN

1. lejos de
3. abajo
6. después
7. abrir

8. caro
9. alguien
12. día
15. derecho

17. ancho
20. blanco

M A S T E R Y   E X E R C I S E S

EXERCISE N

Match the words in column A with their synonyms in column B and their antonyms in column C.

A (synonym)	B (antonym)	C
1. alegre	*a.* comenzar	*A.* preguntar
2. delante de	*b.* unos	*B.* terminar
3. bonito	*c.* diligente	*C.* triste
4. amigo	*d.* lindo	*D.* feo
5. empezar	*e.* hallar	*E.* ningunos
6. a menudo	*f.* feliz	*F.* detrás de
7. responder	*g.* contestar	*G.* enemigo
8. algunos	*h.* enfrente de	*H.* perezoso
9. aplicado	*i.* frecuentemente	*I.* perder
10. encontrar	*j.* compañero	*J.* pocas veces

EXERCISE O

Describe the pictures using the following words.

ancho	invierno	mediodía	quitarse
bajar	lleno	menor	rubio
débil	más	menos	subir
estrecho	mayor	moreno	vacío
fuerte	medianoche	ponerse	verano

1.

2.

3.

4.

5.

6.

7.

8.

9.

10.

11.

12.

13.

14.

15. **16.**

17. **18.**

19. **20.**

Chapter 30
Topical (Thematic) Vocabulary

[1] PERSONAL IDENTIFICATION

a. Características físicas

alto, -a *tall*	joven *young*
bajo, -a *short*	lindo, -a *pretty*
bonito, -a *pretty*	moreno, -a *dark-haired, dark-skinned*
delgado, -a *thin*	pelirrojo, -a *redheaded*
feo, -a *ugly*	rubio, -a *fair, blond*
gordo, -a *fat*	trigueño, -a *dark-skinned*
guapo -a *handsome*	viejo, -a *old*

b. Características de la personalidad

aburrido, -a *boring*	independiente *independent*
agradable *pleasant, nice, likable*	inteligente *intelligent*
amable *courteous, kind*	interesante *interesting*
antipático, -a *unpleasant, not nice*	irresponsable *irresponsible*
bueno, -a *good*	malo, -a *bad*
cariñoso, -a *affectionate*	paciente *patient*
desagradable *unpleasant*	popular *popular*
divertido, -a *fun, amusing*	responsable *responsible*
egoísta *selfish*	simpático, -a *friendly, nice, likable*
generoso, -a *generous*	tacaño, -a *stingy*
impaciente *impatient*	tonto, -a *dumb; stupid*

c. Otras palabras

el apellido *last name*	el lugar de nacimiento *place of birth*
el cumpleaños *birthday*	la nacionalidad *nationality*
la dirección *address*	el nombre *name*
la edad *age*	el número de teléfono *telephone number*
la fecha de nacimiento *date of birth*	

EXERCISE A

Select the word in each group that is in a different category from the other three.

1. gordo, desagradable, lindo, alto
2. generoso, divertido, cariñoso, bajo
3. paciente, bueno, pelirrojo, independiente
4. tacaño, moreno, rubio, pelirrojo
5. edad, simpático, cumpleaños, fecha de nacimiento
6. egoísta, joven, bueno, popular
7. apellido, tacaño, lugar de nacimiento, dirección
8. aburrido, desagradable, guapo, irresponsable
9. delgado, tonto, viejo, moreno
10. impaciente, responsable, malo, rubio

EXERCISE B

How would you describe yourself? First, make a list of the adjectives that describe your appearance; and then, make a list of five adjectives that describe your personality.

EXERCISE C

Your new pen pal would like to know more about you. She asks you to write a description of yourself in a minimum of five sentences.

EXERCISE D

You have to exchange a gift you bought but you can't find the salesperson who helped you. In a minimum of five sentences, describe him (her) to the store manager.

EXERCISE E

Mrs. García is talking about Luis and Ricky, her twin grandsons. Their personalities are complete opposites. List at least five adjectives that she would use to describe each boy.

EXERCISE F

Complete the crossword puzzle with the appropriate Spanish words for the clues given in English.

ACROSS		DOWN	
1. patient	**19.** handsome	**1.** redheaded	**12.** amusing
5. selfish	**20.** age	**2.** good	**13.** thin
7. interesting	**22.** friendly	**3.** ugly	**14.** old
10. name	**25.** bad	**4.** generous	**15.** independent
11. fat	**26.** blonde	**6.** courteous,	**21.** address
16. intelligent	**27.** pretty	kind	**23.** boring
17. dumb	**28.** last name	**8.** tall	**24.** affectionate
18. young	**29.** dark hair	**9.** stingy	

[2] HOUSE AND HOME

a. La casa

la alcoba   *bedroom* ☑

el apartamento   *apartment*

el ascensor   *elevator*

el balcón   *balcony*

el (cuarto de) baño   *bathroom*

la casa   *house, home*

la casa particular   *private house*

la cocina   *kitchen*

el comedor   *dining room*

el cuarto   *room*

el desván   *attic*

el dormitorio   *bedroom*

la escalera   *stairs, staircase*

el estudio   *study, den*

el garaje   *garage*

la habitación   *room*

el jardín   *garden*

el pasillo   *corridor, hall*

el patio   *courtyard*

la piscina   *swimming pool*

el piso   *floor, story, apartment*

la sala   *parlor, living room*

la sala de estar   *family room*

el sótano   *cellar, basement*

el suelo   *floor, ground*

la terraza   *terrace*

b. Los muebles

la alfombra   *rug, carpet*

el armario   *closet*

la cama   *bed*

la cómoda   *bureau, dresser*

la cortina   *curtain*

el escritorio   *desk*

la lámpara   *lamp*

la mesa   *table*

los muebles   *furniture*

la silla   *chair*

el sillón   *armchair*

el sofá   *sofa*

EXERCISE G

In each group, select the word that is *not* thematically in the same category as the other three.

1. comedor, alcoba, sótano, libro

2. dormitorio, habitación, coche, sala

3. sótano, cama, armario, silla

4. mesa, patio, sofá, cómoda

5. escalera, ascensor, alfombra, piso

6. pasillo, estudio, desván, lámpara

7. terraza, sala, cortina, patio

8. armario, mesa, cómoda, garaje

9. alfombra, apartamento, casa particular, piso

10. garaje, estudio, cama, patio

EXERCISE H

Match the activities in column A with the appropriate room in column B.

A	B
1. dormir	**a.** baño
2. preparar la comida	**b.** garaje
3. plantar flores	**c.** alcoba
4. lavarse la cara	**d.** sala
5. nadar	**e.** pasillo
6. estacionar el carro	**f.** cocina
7. estudiar y hacer la tarea	**g.** piscina
8. subir de un piso a otro	**h.** jardín
9. ir de un cuarto a otro	**i.** estudio
10. ver la televisión	**j.** escalera

EXERCISE I

You're planning your dream house. Using the plan below, what are the different rooms shown in the floor plan.

EXERCISE J

Your family is moving to a larger house and you will no longer have to share your room with a sibling. Prepare a list of the furniture and accessories you would like to have in your room.

EXERCISE K

A friend is telling you about her house. If the statement is true, write *Sí*; if it's false, correct it by replacing the word(s) in boldface.

1. Puse una alfombra en **la mesa**.

2. Solamente **una familia** vive en una casa particular.

3. **El suelo** es el cuarto más grande del apartamento.

4. La lámpara y la mesa son **muebles**.

5. Mi madre prepara las comidas en **la escalera**.

6. Mi papá estaciona el carro en **la sala**.

7. Ponemos las cortinas en **las camas**.

8. Mi abuelo se sienta en **la cómoda** para leer el periódico.

9. Guardo la ropa en **el balcón**.

10. Uso **el desván** para ir de un piso a otro.

[3] FAMILY LIFE

la abuela *grandmother*	el hijo *son*
el abuelo *grandfather*	los hijos *children, sons and daughters*
los abuelos *grandparents*	la madrastra *stepmother*
el cuñado *brother-in-law*	la madre *mother*
la cuñada *sister-in-law*	la madrina *godmother*
la esposa *wife*	la mamá *mom, mother*
el esposo *husband*	la nieta *granddaugher*
la familia *family*	el nieto *grandson*
la hermana *sister*	la niña *girl*
el hermano *brother*	el niño *boy*
los hermanos *brothers, brothers and sisters*	la nuera *daughter-in-law*
la hija *daughter*	el padrastro *stepfather*
	el padre *father*

los padres   *parents*   el suegro   *father-in-law*
los papás   *parents*   la suegra   *mother-in-law*
el pariente   *relative*   la tía   *aunt*
la prima   *cousin*   el tío   *uncle*
el primo   *cousin*   los tíos   *uncles, aunts and uncles*
la sobrina   *niece*   el yerno   *son-in-law*
el sobrino   *nephew*

EXERCISE L

If the statement is true, write *Sí*; if it's false, correct it by replacing the words in boldface.

1. El hijo de mi tío es **mi hermano**.

2. La madre de mi madre es **mi abuela**.

3. La hermana de mi papá es **mi prima**.

4. El yerno de mi abuelo es **mi sobrino**.

5. Yo soy **el hijo** de mi abuelo.

6. Mis abuelos son los suegros de **mis hermanos**.

7. **Mi sobrino** es el hijo de mis padres.

8. Mi madre **es la nuera** de mi padre.

9. **Mis nietos** son los sobrinos de mis papás.

10. Mi padrastro es **el hermano** de mi madre.

EXERCISE M

Match the words in columns A and B logically, following the example.

EXAMPLE: padre   **hija**

A	B
1. abuelos	*a.* padres
2. sobrina	*b.* suegra
3. yerno	*c.* cuñado
4. niño	*d.* nietos
5. primos	*e.* tío
6. hijos	*f.* madre
7. cuñada	*g.* primas

EXERCISE N

Identify the family relationship in each statement.

EXAMPLE: La hija de mi padre es mi **hermana**.

1. Los padres de mis tíos son mis _____ .
2. El hermano de mi madre es mi _____ .
3. Los hijos de mis tíos son los _____ de mis padres.
4. El hermano de mi papá es el _____ de mi mamá.
5. Mi padre es el _____ del padre de mi madre.
6. Mis abuelos maternales son los _____ de mi padre.
7. Yo soy el _____ de los hijos de mis tíos.

[4] COMMUNITY/NEIGHBORHOOD

a. Areas

el barrio   *neighborhood*

el campo   *country*

el centro   *downtown*

la ciudad   *city*

el pueblo   *town*

el suburbio   *suburbs*

el vecindario   *neighborhood*

b. Los edificios

el aeropuerto   *airport*

el banco   *bank*

la biblioteca   *library*

el café   *coffee shop*

la casa   *house*

la catedral   *cathedral*

el centro comunal   *community center*

el cine   *movies, movie theater*

el correo   *post office*

el edificio   *building*

la escuela   *school*

la estación   *(train) station*

el estadio   *stadium*

el hospital   *hospital*

el hotel   *hotel*

la iglesia   *church*

el museo   *museum*

el palacio   *palace*

el parque   *park*

la piscina   *swimming pool*

el puente   *bridge*

el restaurante   *restaurant*

el teatro   *theater*

la terminal de autobuses   *bus terminal*

el templo   *temple*

la universidad   *university*

c. Las tiendas

el almacén *department store*	el mercado *market*
la bodega *grocery store*	la panadería *bakery*
la carnicería *butcher*	la pastelería *pastry shop*
la farmacia *drugstore, pharmacy*	el supermercado *supermarket*
la ferretería *hardware store*	la tienda *store, shop*
la florería *flower shop*	la tienda de ropa *clothing store*
la frutería *fruit store*	la tintorería *dry cleaners*
la lavandería *laundry*	la zapatería *shoe store*

EXERCISE O

In each group, select the word that is *not* related to the other three.

1. familia, templo, iglesia, catedral
2. carnicería, bodega, panadería, templo
3. universidad, escuela, fiesta, biblioteca
4. lámpara, estación, terminal, aeropuerto
5. parque, estadio, piscina, esquina
6. almacén, zapatería, hospital, tienda de ropa
7. carnicería, puente, panadería, frutería
8. cine, museo, teatro, lavandería
9. café, edificio, museo, palacio
10. casa, centro, palacio, hotel

EXERCISE P

Match each activity in column A with the location where it takes place in column B.

A	B
1. comer	*a.* el cine
2. estudiar	*b.* el hotel
3. comprar estampillas	*c.* la piscina
4. ver una película	*d.* el restaurante
5. curar a los enfermos	*e.* la estación
6. nadar	*f.* la biblioteca
7. caminar	*g.* el banco

A (Con'd)	B (Con'd)
8. buscar un libro	**h.** el correo
9. rezar	**i.** el estadio
10. ver un partido	**j.** el museo
11. tomar el tren	**k.** la escuela
12. ver una obra de arte	**l.** el café
13. buscar a un turista	**m.** la iglesia
14. tomar el autobús	**n.** el aeropuerto
15. tomar un café	**o.** el hospital
16. cambiar dinero	**p.** el parque
17. viajar en avión	**q.** la terminal

EXERCISE Q

You're running some errands in town. Indicate the stores you'll visit to buy the following items.

1. rosas, claveles y geranios
2. refrescos, leche, queso
3. jamón, biftec, pollo
4. una camisa blanca, una corbata
5. manzanas, peras, uvas
6. aspirinas, algodón, curitas
7. zapatos, pantuflas
8. un pastel de cumpleaños

EXERCISE R

Read the passage below and determine which store the person should go to.

1. Ramón va a pasar el fin de semana en las montañas con unos amigos. Tiene que comprar un suéter grueso porque va a hacer mucho frío allí. ¿Adónde debe ir Ramón?

2. Vamos a tener invitados a cenar el sábado por la noche. Mi mamá prepara una lista de las cosas que necesita para preparar la cena. ¿Adónde debe ir mi mamá?

3. Susana y Alicia van a pasar las vacaciones en Puerto Rico. Su avión sale a las tres de la tarde. ¿Adónde deben ir las chicas?

4. Pablo está enfermo. El médico le da una receta para una medicina. ¿Adónde debe ir Pablo?

5. Mi prima se casa mañana. La ceremonia de la boda es a las doce. ¿Adónde debo ir?

EXERCISE S

You and your family are driving through Mexico in a van. You arrive at a small town around lunchtime. Tell which places the members of your family want to visit in the town.

EXAMPLE: Mi padre **quiere visitar el museo**.

1. Mi madre _____ .

2. Mi hermano _____ .

3. Mi hermana _____ .

4. Mis padres _____ .

5. Mi abuela _____ .

6. Yo _____ .

[5] PHYSICAL ENVIRONMENT

a. La geografía

el cayo *key (Key West)*	el golfo *gulf*
el continente *continent*	la isla *island*
la cordillera *mountain range*	el país *country, nation*
el estado *state*	la península *peninsula*

b. La naturaleza

el aire *air*	el lago *lake*
el árbol *tree*	la luna *moon*
el bosque *forest*	la lluvia *rain*
el campo *country*	el mar *sea*
el cielo *sky*	la montaña *mountain*
el clavel *carnation*	el mundo *world*
la estrella *star*	la naturaleza *nature*
la flor *flower*	la nieve *snow*
la hierba *grass*	la nube *cloud*
la hoja *leaf*	la planta *plant*
el jardín *garden*	la playa *beach, seashore*

el río   *river*

la rosa   *rose*

el sol   *sun*

la tierra   *earth, land*

la violeta   *violet*

c. Las estaciones y el tiempo

el calor   *heat, warmth*

la estación   *season*

el fresco   *coolness*

el frío   *cold*

el grado   *degree*

el invierno   *winter*

la lluvia   *rain*

la nieve   *snow*

el otoño   *autumn*

la primavera   *spring*

el sol   *sun*

la temperatura   *temperature*

el tiempo   *weather*

el verano   *summer*

el viento   *wind*

hace (calor, fresco, frío, sol, viento)
   it's (hot, cool, cold, sunny, windy)

llover   *to rain*

nevar   *to snow*

d. Los meses

enero   *January*

febrero   *February*

marzo   *March*

abril   *April*

mayo   *May*

junio   *June*

julio   *July*

agosto   *August*

septiembre   *September*

octubre   *October*

noviembre   *November*

diciembre   *December*

e. Los días

el domingo   *Sunday*

el lunes   *Monday*

el martes   *Tuesday*

el miércoles   *Wednesday*

el jueves   *Thursday*

el viernes   *Friday*

el sábado   *Saturday*

EXERCISE T

In each group, select the word that is *not* related to the other three.

1. mundo, cielo, aire, mercado

2. clavel, lluvia, rosa, violeta

3. tienda, bosque, montaña, campo

4. nieve, viento, estado, lluvia

5. playa, ciudad, estado, país

6. árbol, planta, hoja, cielo

7. primavera, estrella, otoño, invierno

8. estación, abril, noviembre, enero

9. verano, miércoles, sábado, viernes

10. calor, luna, frío, viento

11. tierra, lago, río, mar

12. cielo, estrella, sol, pueblo

13. hierba, flor, mundo, planta

14. día, mes, estación, fresco

15. tiempo, frío, lluvia, tierra

EXERCISE U

If the statement is true, write *Sí*; if it's false, correct it by replacing the word(s) in boldface.

1. Después de abril viene el mes de **mayo**.

2. Hace calor en **el invierno**.

3. Cuando **hace sol** uso un paraguas.

4. El sábado y el domingo son **el fin de semana**.

5. Las rosas y las violetas son **árboles**.

6. Durante la noche vemos **el sol** en el cielo.

7. El verano y el otoño son **meses**.

8. El Misisipí es **un lago**.

9. California es **un país**.

10. Puerto Rico es **una ciudad**.

11. Hay edificios altos en **el campo**.

12. Vemos muchas estrellas en **el bosque**.

13. Nadamos en **el suburbio**.

14. Un árbol tiene muchas **nubes**.

15. En el parque hay **un lago**.

EXERCISE V

You're talking about your hometown to your host family in Venezuela. Describe or explain how the following things are where you live.

1. una estación del año

2. tu ciudad o pueblo

3. el mes de febrero

4. los suburbios

5. el cielo en una noche de verano

[6] MEALS / FOOD / BEVERAGES

a. Las comidas

el almuerzo *lunch*	almorzar *to have (eat) lunch*
la cena *supper, dinner*	cenar *to have (eat) supper*
la comida *meal, food*	desayunar *to have (eat) breakfast*
el desayuno *breakfast*	

b. La comida / la bebida

el agua *water*	la naranja *orange*
el alimento *food*	el pan *bread*
el (la) azúcar *sugar*	la papa, la patata *potato*
el café *coffee*	el pastel *pie, pastry*
la carne *meat*	la pera *pear*
la cereza *cherry*	el pescado *fish*
el chocolate *chocolate*	la pimienta *pepper* (spice)
la ensalada *salad*	el pimiento *pepper* (vegetable)
la fruta *fruit*	el pollo *chicken*
la gaseosa *soda, pop*	el postre *dessert*
el helado *ice cream*	el refresco *refreshment, soda*
el huevo *egg*	la sal *salt*
la leche *milk*	la sopa *soup*
la legumbre *vegetable*	el té *tea*
el limón *lemon*	el vino *wine*
la mantequilla *butter*	beber *to drink*
la manzana *apple*	comer *to eat*

EXERCISE W

In each group, select the word that is *not* related to the other three.

1. fruta, manzana, cereza, puente
2. naranja, azul, ensalada, pera
3. vino, hoja, café, agua
4. queso, pan, huevo, burro
5. almuerzo, cena, chocolate, desayuno
6. sopa, azúcar, pimienta, sal
7. comer, almorzar, caminar, beber
8. pollo, refresco, carne, pescado
9. leche, mantequilla, queso, limón
10. legumbre, postre, helado, pastel
11. té, pescado, chocolate, café
12. cereza, pera, helado, naranja

EXERCISE X

Answer your friend's questions about your eating preferences.

1. ¿Cuál es tu comida favorita?
2. ¿Qué desayunas por la mañana?
3. ¿A qué hora comes el almuerzo?
4. ¿Cuál prefieres, el pollo o el pescado?
5. ¿Qué frutas te gustan?
6. ¿Qué tomas con la cena?
7. ¿Cuál es tu postre preferido?
8. ¿Qué comes mientras ves la televisión?
9. ¿Cuándo comes helado?
10. ¿Por qué comes?

EXERCISE Y

You and some friends are planning a barbecue. List the foods and beverages that you have to buy when you go to the supermarket.

[7] HEALTH AND WELL-BEING

a. El cuerpo

la boca	*mouth*	la lengua	*tongue*
el brazo	*arm*	la mano	*hand*
la cabeza	*head*	la muela	*molar (tooth)*
la cara	*face*	la nariz	*nose*
el cuerpo	*body*	el ojo	*eye*
el dedo	*finger, toe*	la oreja	*ear*
el diente	*tooth*	el pelo	*hair*
el estómago	*stomach*	el pie	*foot*
la garganta	*throat*	la pierna	*leg*
el labio	*lip*		

b. Medicina y salud

bien	*well*	la medicina	*medicine*
el dentista	*dentist*	el médico	*doctor*
el doctor	*doctor*	el paciente	*patient*
el dolor	*ache, pain*	la receta	*prescription*
la enfermedad	*illness*	el resfriado	*cold (illness)*
la enfermera	*nurse*	la salud	*health*
enfermo, -a	*ill, sick*	doler	*to ache*
el hospital	*hospital*	tener dolor de	*to ache*

EXERCISE Z

In each group, select the word that is *not* related to the other three.

1. labio, muela, pelo, ascensor
2. médico, cortina, enfermera, hospital
3. sopa, pie, dedo, pierna
4. ojos, postre, nariz, orejas
5. dedo, mano, estómago, brazo
6. comida, medicina, receta, dolor
7. doctor, profesor, dentista, enfermera
8. salud, bien, enfermo, frío

EXERCISE AA

If the statement is true, write *Sí*; **if it's false, correct it by replacing the word(s) in boldface.**

1. Tengo cinco **dientes** en cada mano.
2. Si estoy **enfermo(-a)** mi madre llama al doctor.
3. Llevo zapatos en **los pies**.
4. Comemos con **la nariz**.
5. Usamos **los ojos** para oír.
6. Comemos con **los brazos**.
7. Una enfermera trabaja en **una tienda**.
8. Tomamos **postre** cuando estamos enfermos.
9. El resfriado es una clase de **receta**.
10. Usamos **la lengua** para hablar.

EXERCISE BB

Tell what's wrong with these people. Use *doler* **or** *tener dolor de* **in your responses.**

EXAMPLE: Marta no puede oler las flores.
Le duele la nariz.

1. Roberto no puede comer porque no puede masticar la comida.
2. Mi abuelo tiene dificultad al caminar.
3. José no puede escribir el examen.
4. Graciela no puede hablar.
5. No tengo apetito y no quiero comer nada.
6. Lola no quiere ver la televisión ni leer una revista.

[8] EDUCATION

a. La escuela

la alumna *pupil (f.)*	el bolígrafo *ballpoint pen*
el alumno *pupil (m.)*	el borrador *eraser (chalkboard)*
la asignatura *subject*	la cafetería *cafeteria*
el autobús escolar *school bus*	la clase *class*
la bandera *flag*	el colegio *school, college*

el cuaderno   *notebook*
el diccionario   *dictionary*
el dictado   *dictation*
el error   *mistake, error*
la escuela (primaria, secundaria)
school (elementary, secondary/high school)
el (la) estudiante   *student*
el examen   *examination, test*
la falta   *mistake, error*
la frase   *sentence*
la goma   *eraser*
el horario   *schedule, program*
el lápiz   *pencil*
la lección   *lesson*
el libro   *book*
el maestro (la maestra)   *teacher*
el marcador   *felt-tip pen*
la materia   *subject*
la mochila   *backpack*
la nota   *mark, grade*
la página   *page*
la palabra   *word*
el papel   *paper*
el párrafo   *paragraph*

la pizarra   *chalkboard*
la pluma   *pen*
el profesor   *teacher (m.)*
la profesora   *teacher (f.)*
la prueba   *examination, test*
el pupitre   *(pupil's) desk*
la regla   *rule, ruler*
las sala de clase   *classroom*
la tarea   *assignment*
la tiza   *chalk*
la universidad   *college, university*
el vocabulario   *vocabulary*
aprender   *to learn*
contestar   *to answer*
enseñar   *to teach*
escribir   *to write*
escuchar   *to listen (to)*
estudiar   *to study*
explicar   *to explain*
hacer la tarea   *to do homework*
leer   *to read*
preguntar   *to ask*
responder   *to answer*
salir bien (mal)   *to pass (fail)*

b. Las materias

el álgebra   *algebra*
el arte   *art*
las artes industriales   *shop*
la biología   *biology*
las ciencias   *sciences*
el coro   *choir*
el dibujo   *drawing*
la economía doméstica   *home economics*
la educación física   *physical education*
el español   *Spanish*
la física   *physics*

el francés   *French*
la geografía   *geography*
la geometría   *geometry*
la historia   *history*
la informática   *computer science*
el inglés   *English*
la música   *music*
la pintura   *painting*
la química   *chemistry*
el recreo   *recess*

EXERCISE CC

In each group, select the word that is *not* related to the other three.

1. párrafo, dictado, menú, página
2. aprender, enseñar, nadar, escuchar
3. escuela, papel, lección, leche
4. pizarra, clase, cabeza, pupitre
5. manzana, bolígrafo, lápiz, tiza
6. prueba, tarea, examen, salud
7. receta, dibujo, coro, física
8. asignatura, clase, materia, dolor
9. borrador, tiza, cuaderno, pizarra
10. deporte, química, biología, ciencia

EXERCISE DD

Match the words in column A with their respective synonyms or related words in column B.

A	B
1. falta	*a.* maestro
2. escuela	*b.* coro
3. profesor	*c.* pizarra
4. asignatura	*d.* prueba
5. contestar	*e.* error
6. examen	*f.* estudiante
7. alumno	*g.* responder
8. música	*h.* materia
9. biología	*i.* colegio
10. tiza	*j.* ciencia

EXERCISE EE

Using the following drawings, make a list of the school supplies you have to buy for the new school year.

EXERCISE FF

Answer these questions that a new student from Argentina asks you.

1. ¿Cuántas materias estudias este año?

2. ¿Qué lengua aprendes?

3. ¿Qué clase de ciencia tienes?

4. ¿Tomas una clase de informática?

5. ¿Cómo son los exámenes de la clase de matemáticas?

6. ¿Cúal es tu asignatura favorita?

7. ¿Te gusta tu horario este año?

[9] EARNING A LIVING

a. Las profesiones y los oficios

la abogada, el abogado *lawyer*

el actor *actor*

la actriz *actress*

el agricultor, la agricultora *farmer*

el / la artista *artist, entertainer*

la barbera, el barbero *barber*

el / la bombero *firefighter*

la carnicera, el carnicero *butcher*

el / la chófer (chofer) *chauffeur*

la científica, el científico *scientist*

el / la comerciante
  businessperson, entrepreneur

la criada *maid*

el criado *butler*

el / la dentista *dentist*

el director, la directora *director*

el doctor, la doctora   *doctor*

la dueña, el dueño   *owner, boss*

la enfermera, el enfermero   *nurse*

el escritor, la escritora   *writer*

la farmacéutica, el farmacéutico
   pharmacist

el / la gerente   *manager*

el hombre / la mujer de negocios
   businessperson

la ingeniera, el ingeniero   *engineer*

la jefa, el jefe   *supervisor, boss*

la maestra, el maestro   *teacher*

la médica, el médico   *doctor*

el oficio   *occupation*

la panadera, el panadero   *baker*

el / la periodista   *journalist*

el / la piloto   *pilot*

el policía / la (mujer) policía
   police officer

el profesor, la profesora
   teacher, professor

el programador / la programadora de
   computadoras   *computer programmer*

la sastra, el sastre   *tailor*

la secretaria, el secretario   *secretary*

el / la soldado   *soldier*

la taquígrafa, el taquígrafo   *stenographer*

la veterinaria, el veterinario   *veterinarian*

la zapatera, el zapatero   *shoemaker*

estar desempleado   *to be unemployed*

ganarse la vida   *to earn a living*

trabajar   *to work*

b. Los lugares de trabajo

la barbería   *barber shop*

el consultorio   *doctor's office*

la corte   *court*

la escuela   *school*

la fábrica   *factory*

el hospital   *hospital*

el laboratorio   *laboratory*

la oficina   *office*

la peluquería   *hair salon*

el salón de belleza   *beauty salon*

la tienda   *store*

la universidad   *university, college*

EXERCISE GG

Identify the profession that is associated with the following drawings.

1.

2.

3.

4.

5.

6.

7.

8.

9.

10.

11.

12.

13.

14.

15.

EXERCISE HH

Use the clues below to identify the professions described.

1. Preparo la medicina que el doctor ordena en una receta.
2. Defiendo la patria cuando hay una guerra.
3. Protejo a las personas. Llevo uniforme.
4. Preparo a los jóvenes para el futuro. Me gustan los exámenes.
5. Ayudo a los médicos y cuido a los enfermos.
6. Hago experimentos. Trabajo en un laboratorio.
7. Corto el pelo a los hombres y a las mujeres.
8. Trabajo en las películas. Trato de divertir al público.
9. Me gusta la vida del campo. Cultivo la tierra y tengo animales como las vacas y los pollos.
10. Escribo las noticias todos los días. Las personas compran mi producto diariamente.
11. Trato de mejorar la vida con edificios nuevos y puentes.
12. Ayudo a las personas cuando tienen dolor de muelas.
13. Trabajo en una oficina donde contesto el teléfono y escribo cartas a máquina.
14. Reparo la ropa de las personas. Me gusta coser.
15. Me fascina volar y siempre llevo a muchas personas de una ciudad a otra.

[*10*] LEISURE

el ajedrez *chess*	la grabadora *tape recorder*
el béisbol *baseball*	el instrumento *instrument*
el billar *pool*	la música *music*
el campeón *champion*	el partido *game, match*
la canción *song*	el pasatiempo *pastime, hobby*
el cine *movies*	la película *film, movie*
la cinta *cassette tape*	el programa *program*
el concierto *concert*	el / la radio *radio*
el disco *record*	el teatro *theater*
el disco compacto *CD*	la televisión *television*
las diversiones *amusements*	el tenis *tennis*
el equipo *team*	el tocadiscos *record player*
el fútbol *soccer*	las vacaciones *vacation*

andar en bicicleta *to ride a bicycle*	jugar *to play (a game, sport)*
bailar *to dance*	levantar pesas *to lift weights*
cantar *to sing*	mirar televisión *to watch television*
coleccionar monedas (estampillas, muñecas, insectos) *to collect coins (stamps, dolls, insects)*	nadar *to swim*
	patinar *to skate*
correr *to run*	practicar el judo *to practice judo*
dar un paseo *to take a walk*	sacar fotos *to take pictures*
escuchar *to listen (to)*	salir con los amigos *to go out with friends*
esquiar *to ski*	
hacer gimnasia *to do gymnastics*	ser fanático de *to be a fan of*
hacer yoga *to practice yoga*	tocar *to play* (music)
ir de compras *to go shopping*	viajar *to travel*

EXERCISE II

In each group, select the word that is *not* related to the other three.

1. leer, disco, tocadiscos, música

2. bailar, cantar, patinar, trabajar

3. película, juego, cine, actriz

4. música, equipo, fútbol, partido

5. esquiar, estudiar, nadar, correr

6. concierto, televisión, escuela, teatro

7. programa, béisbol, tenis, fútbol

8. hacer yoga, levantar pesas, ir de compras, hacer gimnasia

EXERCISE JJ

Identify the pastime that each of these people enjoys most.

1. A Rogelio le gusta conocer otros países y ciudades. Le fascina visitar los museos.

2. Luis siempre me pide los sobres de las cartas que recibo de mi amigo de correspondencia. También le gusta ver las tarjetas postales que recibo de mis amigos cuando visitan otros países.

3. Sarita y Gladys quieren ser bailarinas. Practican mucho y hacen ejercicios especiales.

4. Jorge quiere tener músculos grandes. Es socio de un gimnasio donde hace este ejercicio todos los días.

5. A Enrique le gustan mucho los juegos de mesa. Practica con mucha frecuencia y es el campeón del equipo de la escuela. Prefiere el juego más difícil y exigente.

6. A Sofía le gusta gastar dinero. Compra regalos bonitos para todo el mundo.

7. A Beto le gusta la zoología. Le fascina caminar en el parque y en el bosque. A su hermana no le gustan las cosas que Beto colecciona en sus paseos.

[*11*] PUBLIC AND PRIVATE SERVICES

autoridad de aqueductos
  water utilities company

el correo   *mail, post office*

la electricidad   *electricity*

hablar por teléfono
  to speak on the telephone

hacer una llamada   *to make a call*

llamar   *to call*

la estampilla   *stamp*

el gas   *gas company*

el teléfono   *telephone*

marcar un número   *to dial a number*

pagar el agua (el gas)
  to pay the water (the gas) bill

EXERCISE KK

Complete each statement with the appropriate words.

1. Para mandar una carta tengo que comprar _____ . Las compro en el _____ .

2. Durante el verano visité un pueblo muy primitivo. Las casas no tienen _____ y tienen que usar el _____ del río.

3. Mi tío vive en Buenos Aires. Cada domingo nos _____ por teléfono. Es una llamada de _____ . Él no puede _____ ; tiene que hablar con la operadora primero.

4. No distribuyen _____ en la calle en que vivo hasta las dos de la tarde. Mis padres reciben mucho _____ : cartas, tarjetas postales, revistas y cuentas.

[*12*] SHOPPING

a. Las tiendas

el almacén   *department store, warehouse*
la bodega   *grocery store*
la carnicería   *butcher shop*
el centro comercial   *mall*
la farmacia   *pharmacy, drugstore*
la florería   *florist shop*
la lavandería   *laundry*
la librería   *bookstore*
el mercado   *market*
la mueblería   *furniture store*

la panadería   *bakery*
la papelería   *stationery store*
la pastelería   *pastry shop*
la peluquería   *barbershop, hair salon*
el salón de belleza   *beauty shop*
el supermercado   *supermarket*
la tienda   *store*
la tienda de ropa   *clothing store*
la zapatería   *shoe store*

b. Palabras relacionadas

barato, -a   *cheap, inexpensive*
la caja   *cashier*
caro, -a   *expensive*
el cheque   *check*
el / la dependiente   *salesperson*
el efectivo   *cash*
en especial   *on sale*
la etiqueta   *tag* ahorrar   *to save*
la ganga   *sale, bargain*

grande (mediano, pequeño)
  large (medium, small)
el precio   *price*
la queja   *complaint*
rebajado, -a   *reduced*
la talla   *(clothing) size*
el tamaño   *(package) size*
la tarjeta de crédito   *credit card*

ahorrar *to save*	quedarle bien *to look well on*
comprar *to buy*	regatear *to bargain*
devolver *to return* (an item)	vender *to sell*
pagar con cheque / tarjeta de crédito	¿Cuánto vale (cuesta)?
to pay with check / credit card	*How much does it cost?*
pagar en efectivo *to pay cash*	¿En qué puedo servirle?
probarse *to try (on)*	*How may I help you?*

EXERCISE LL

Match the words in column A with their related words in column B.

A	**B**
1. carnicería	*a.* diccionario
2. farmacia	*b.* ropa limpia
3. mueblería	*c.* calcetines
4. librería	*d.* cortar el pelo
5. florería	*e.* sandalias
6. lavandería	*f.* refrescos
7. papelería	*g.* biftec
8. salón de belleza	*h.* muchos departamentos
9. pastelería	*i.* pan
10. tienda de ropa	*j.* sofá
11. bodega	*k.* tiendas
12. centro comercial	*l.* claveles
13. panadería	*m.* postre
14. zapatería	*n.* tarjetas
15. almacén	*o.* receta

EXERCISE MM

Complete each statement with the appropriate word or expression.

1. En una tienda la persona que atiende al cliente es _____ .

2. No tengo ni dinero ni un cheque; voy a pagar con _____ .

3. Busco un suéter, _____ grande.

4. Leo el precio del artículo en _____ .

5. Estos zapatos cuestan mucho; quiero algo más _____ .

6. Este pantalón está _____ , ahora cuesta solamente veinte dólares.

7. Pago por las compras en _____ .

8. No me gusta este artículo. Quiero hablar con el gerente porque lo tengo que _____ .

9. En esta tienda tenemos que pagar el precio indicado; no podemos _____ .

10. El perfume viene en dos _____ : pequeño o grande.

11. No me gusta el suéter. Voy a _____ el suéter a la tienda.

12. Debes _____ el suéter antes de salir de la tienda.

[*13*] TRAVEL

a. Medios de transporte

el autobús *bus*

el automóvil *car, automobile*

el avión *airplane*

el barco *boat*

la bicicleta *bicycle*

el coche, el auto *car, automobile*

el ferrocarril *railroad*

la motocicleta *motorcycle*

el tren *train*

el vapor *steamship*

b. Palabras relacionadas

el aeropuerto *airport*

el asiento *seat*

el baúl *trunk*

el billete *ticket*

el boleto *ticket*

el camino *road, way*

la entrada *entrance*

la estación *station*

el este *east*

la fila *row*

la maleta *suitcase*

el mapa *map*

el norte *north*

el oeste *west*

la parada *bus stop*

el pasillo *aisle*

el plano (de la ciudad) *(city) map*

la puerta *gate, door*

la salida *exit*

el sur *south*

el viaje *trip, voyage*

el vuelo *flight*

caminar *to walk*

hacer la maleta *to pack*

regresar *to return*

salir *to leave, depart*

viajar *to travel*

volver *to return*

EXERCISE NN

In each group, select the word that is *not* related to the other three.

1. avión, sala de clase, bicicleta, coche
2. vapor, ferrocarril, viajar, teatro
3. libro, maleta, baúl, viaje
4. este, pregunta, norte, oeste
5. aeropuerto, calle, parada, estación
6. comer, billete, puerta, boleto
7. tren, vuelo, estación, ferrocarril
8. mapa, calle, plano, número de teléfono
9. asiento, fila, pasillo, baúl
10. vapor, mar, barco, camino

EXERCISE OO

Match the words in column A with their related words in column B.

	A		B
1.	asiento	*a.*	salir
2.	maleta	*b.*	aeropuerto
3.	avión	*c.*	barco
4.	parada	*d.*	puerta
5.	tren	*e.*	fila
6.	regresar	*f.*	autobús
7.	mapa	*g.*	plano
8.	entrada	*h.*	coche
9.	automóvil	*i.*	baúl
10.	vapor	*j.*	ferrocarril

EXERCISE PP

Complete each of the sentences with the appropriate word or expression.

1. Ponemos la ropa en _____ .
2. El Canadá está al _____ de México.

3. México está al _____ de los Estados Unidos.

4. El avión llega al _____ .

5. En el avión me siento en la _____ 31, _____ C.

6. Para subir al avión tengo que mostrar el _____ .

7. Una bicicleta con un motor es una _____ .

8. En la ciudad uso un _____ para encontrar la calle que busco.

9. Antes de viajar, escojo la ropa para _____ .

10. Tomo el autobús en la _____ .

[*14*] ENTERTAINMENT

el actor *actor*	el horario *schedule*
la actriz *actress*	el locutor *announcer*
el / la artista *artist, entertainer, performer*	la noticia *news item*
el billete *ticket*	las noticias *news*
el boleto *ticket*	el noticiero *news broadcast*
el cine *movies*	la obra *(theater) work, play*
el concierto *concert*	la película *film*
el estadio *stadium*	la taquilla *box office*
el estreno *opening (of a performance), showing*	el teatro *theater*
la función *performance, showing*	hacer cola *to wait in line*

EXERCISE QQ

Match the words in column A to their related words in column B.

A	B
1. el boleto	*a.* el artista
2. la película	*b.* el horario
3. la obra	*c.* el locutor
4. la taquilla	*d.* el cine
5. la función	*e.* el teatro
6. el concierto	*f.* los deportes
7. el estadio	*g.* hacer cola
8. el noticiero	*h.* la taquilla

EXERCISE RR

Complete this story with the appropriate word or expression in the list below. Note that the words or expressions are arranged in alphabetical order, not in order of appearance.

billetes	esperar	hacer cola	película
boletos	estadio	horario	taquilla
cine	estreno	locutor	
concierto	función	música	

Sergio invita a Blanca a acompañarle a un _____ de su grupo favorito. Tiene

1.

dos _____ para el _____ pero no sabe _____ . Tiene que recoger los

2. 3. 4.

_____ en la _____ del _____ . Cuando Sergio y Blanca llegan allí hay

5. 6. 7.

mucha gente y tienen que _____ . Mientras ellos _____ , escuchan _____

8. 9. 10.

en un radio portátil. El _____ anuncia que el avión en que llegaba el grupo

11.

favorito de Sergio no va a llegar a tiempo y que van a cancelar la _____ .

12.

Sergio está enojado y triste pero decide ir con Blanca a ver una _____ de

13.

ciencia ficción en el _____ .

14.

MASTERY EXERCISES

EXERCISE SS

Ramón's little brother, Pepito, is learning many new words. Write *Sí*, if the sentence is true. If it's false, correct it by replacing the words in boldface with the correct ones.

EXAMPLE: Los médicos trabajan en **una carnicería**.

Los médicos trabajan en **un hospital**.

OR: Los médicos trabajan en **un consultorio**.

1. **Hago las maletas** antes de viajar.
2. Hay muchos libros en **una florería**.
3. Compramos pan en **la mueblería**.

 4. El secretario trabaja en **una oficina**.

 5. La química y la historia son **asignaturas**.

 6. Tengo los ojos y **las piernas** en la cara.

 7. Para **escribir**, uso una pluma o un lápiz.

 8. Mi padre cocina en **la sala**.

 9. Cuando hace **calor** llevamos abrigo, guantes y botas.

 10. La cereza y la pera son **legumbres**.

EXERCISE TT

You're going on a vocabulary game-show, where you must read each definition and write its corresponding word or words.

EXAMPLE: libro donde se explican las palabras de una lengua **un diccionario**

 1. persona de pelo negro

 2. el cuarto donde duermo

 3. yo soy su nieta

 4. lugar donde se sale a comer

 5. tienda donde se venden flores

 6. sinónimo de montaña

 7. estación en que hace mucho frío en Norteamérica

 8. mes entre septiembre y noviembre

 9. día antes del sábado

 10. fruta amarilla que no es dulce

 11. parte del cuerpo donde llevo un sombrero

 12. lengua que hablan en Perú

 13. persona que estudia

 14. lugar donde van los enfermos

 15. el deporte más popular de Hispanoamérica

 16. medio de transporte necesario para ir de México a Argentina

 17. artista de cine

 18. tienda donde compro libros

 19. objeto para escribir en la pizarra

 20. palabras que tengo que aprender

Part five

Spanish and Spanish-American Civilizations

ESPAÑA
Islas Baleares

Islas Canarias

MÉXICO

REPÚBLICA
DOMINICANA
PUERTO RICO

CUBA
HONDURAS

GUATEMALA
EL SALVADOR
COSTA RICA
PANAMÁ

NICARAGUA

VENEZUELA

COLOMBIA

ECUADOR

PERÚ

BOLIVIA

PARAGUAY

CHILE

URUGUAY

ARGENTINA

Chapter 31
Spanish Influence in the United States

FIRST SPANISH EXPLORERS

1. **Cristóbal Colón** (Christopher Columbus) is believed to be the Genoese navigator Cristoforo Colombo, who became an explorer for Spain and the first European to reach the New World (1492). He made four voyages, touching on various parts of what is now Spanish America.

2. **Hernán Cortés** conquered Mexico (1519–1521), defeating the Aztecs and their king, Moctezuma.

3. **Francisco Pizarro** conquered Peru (1532–1535), defeating the Incas and their king, Atahualpa. Pizarro founded the city of Lima in 1535.

4. **Juan Ponce de León** was the first Spanish governor of Puerto Rico and the first European to explore what is now Florida (1513) in his search for the Fountain of Youth. He arrived on an Easter Sunday (Domingo de Pascua Florida), therefore naming it Florida.

5. **Álvar Núñez Cabeza de Vaca** shipwrecked on the Texas coast in 1528. He was captured by Native Americans, whom he served as a slave and medicine man. He later escaped and wandered for six years, exploring parts of Texas, Kansas, and New Mexico. After traveling thousands of miles, Cabeza de Vaca finally reached Mexico in 1536. His reports from the Pueblo Indians led to the myth of the "Seven Cities of Cibola."

6. **Francisco Vásquez de Coronado** was the first Spaniard to explore what are now New Mexico and Arizona (1540, including the Grand Canyon) in his search for the supposedly rich and prosperous "Seven Cities of Cibola."

7. **Hernando de Soto** explored much of Georgia, the Carolinas, Tennessee, Alabama, and Oklahoma. He was the first European explorer to reach the Mississippi River (1541), where he was later buried.

8. **Juan Rodríguez Cabrillo** explored the coast of California in 1542.

9. **Vasco Núñez de Balboa** was the first European explorer to reach the Pacific Ocean (1513).

EARLY SPANISH SETTLEMENTS

1. **St. Augustine** (Florida) is the oldest city in the United States. It was established by the Spaniards in 1565.

2. **Santa Fe** (New Mexico) is the oldest capital city in the United States. It was established in 1609.

3. **Spanish missions** were established by priests in the southwestern part of the United States.

   a. **Fray Junípero Serra** was the most famous of the Spanish missionaries. He and his followers established a chain of twenty-one missions from San Diego to San Francisco (1769–1823) along the **Camino Real** (royal road), which is today called Coast Highway 101.

317

b. The most famous California missions are **San Juan Capistrano** and **Santa Barbara,** which is called the "Queen of the California Missions."

GEOGRAPHIC NAMES OF SPANISH ORIGIN

1. **States:** California, Colorado, Florida, Montana, Nevada.
2. **Cities:** El Paso, Las Vegas, Los Angeles, Sacramento, Santa Fe, San Francisco.
3. **Rivers:** Brazos (Texas); Colorado (Colorado, Utah, Arizona), Río Grande (New Mexico, Texas).
4. **Mountains:** San Juan (Colorado); Sierra Nevada (California).

SPANISH INFLUENCE IN ARCHITECTURE

1. Many modern American homes and buildings, especially in the southwest, show the influence of the old adobe ranch houses and mission buildings constructed by the Spaniards.
2. **Characteristics of Spanish Architecture**
   a. **Patio** (inner courtyard). An attractive spot for family relaxation, frequently with flowers, shade trees, and an ornamental fountain.
   b. **Reja** (iron grating on windows). Used for security and decoration. In Spanish-speaking countries, it has been a traditional meeting place for sweethearts, with the young lady behind the **reja** and her suitor outside, on the other side of the reja.
   c. **Balcón** (balcony). Used for displaying flags during celebrations, watching processions and

parades, and sunning flowering plants.
   d. **Tejas** (roof tiles). Made of baked clay, red in color.
   e. **Arcada** (arcade). A covered passageway along a row of columns in front of commercial buildings. Provides protection from the weather (rain or hot sun) for patrons and strollers.

SPANISH INFLUENCE ON ECONOMIC LIFE

1. **Cattle Raising**
   a. Spaniards brought the first cows, horses, goats, pigs, and sheep to the New World.
   b. From the Spanish cowboy, the American cowboy copied his dress, equipment, vocabulary, and ranching techniques.
2. **Mining**
   Spaniards developed the first gold and silver mines in the New World. Their methods and success influenced the mining industry in America.

SPANISH INFLUENCE ON LANGUAGE

1. Spanish explorers, missionaries, and settlers in North America contributed many Spanish words to our language. Some of these words are identical in English and Spanish. Others have been slightly changed.
2. **Common English Words of Spanish Origin**
   a. **Ranch life:** bronco, chaps **(chaparreras),** cinch **(cincha),** corral, lariat **(la reata),** lasso **(lazo),** mustang **(mesteño),** ranch **(rancho),** rodeo, stampede **(estampida).**

b. Foods: avocado **(aguacate)**, banana, barbecue **(barbacoa)**, chili **(chile)**, potato **(patata)**, tomato **(tomate)**, vanilla **(vainilla)**.

c. Beverages: sherry **(Jerez)**.

d. Clothing: bolero, brocade **(brocado)**, mantilla, poncho, sombrero.

e. Animals and insects: alligator **(lagarto)**, burro, chinchilla, cockroach **(cucaracha)**, coyote, llama, mosquito.

f. Types of people: cannibal **(caníbal)**, comrade **(camarada)**, desperado **(desesperado)**, padre, peon **(peón)**, renegade **(renegado)**, vigilante.

g. Nature: arroyo, canyon **(cañón)**, cordillera, lagoon **(laguna)**, mesa, sierra, tornado.

h. Shipping and commerce: armada, canoe **(canoa)**, cargo **(carga)**, contraband **(contrabando)**, embargo, flotilla, galleon **(galeón)**.

i. Buildings and streets: adobe, alameda, hacienda, patio, plaza.

j. Miscellaneous words: bonanza, cigar **(cigarro)**, fiesta, filibuster **(filibustero)**, guerrilla, siesta.

POPULAR MEXICAN FOODS

1. **Tortilla**—a flat, thin cornmeal pancake.
2. **Enchilada**—a rolled tortilla filled with chopped meat or chicken and served with hot chili sauce.
3. **Tamal**—seasoned ground meat or chicken rolled in cornmeal dough, wrapped in corn husks, and steamed.
4. **Chile con carne**—red pepper, chopped meat, and hot chili sauce.
5. **Taco**—a crisp tortilla folded over and filled with seasoned chopped meat or chicken, lettuce, and tomatoes.

POPULAR SPANISH-AMERICAN DANCES

1. **Tango** (Argentina).
2. **Rumba** (Cuba).
3. **Mambo** (Cuba).
4. **Cha-cha-chá** (Cuba).
5. **Merengue** (Dominican Republic).

EXERCISE A

If the statement is true, write *Sí;* if it's false, correct it by replacing the word(s) in boldface.

1. Fray Junípero Serra and his followers established **twenty-seven** missions in California.

2. There are many houses of Spanish-style architecture in the **northwestern** United States.

3. The **American** cowboy copied a great deal from the Spanish cowboy.

4. The Spaniards used **adobe** for building.

5. The **Spaniards** established the cattle-raising industry in the New World.

6. The words *rodeo* and *corral* are related to Spanish **city** life.

7. The oldest city in the United States is **San Diego.**

8. In **New Mexico** there are numerous cities that have Spanish names.

9. The **rejas** of Spanish houses have flowers and trees.

10. A **tamal** is a crisp tortilla filled with meat or beans.

EXERCISE B

Match the expressions in column A with their corresponding definitions in column B.

A	B
1. tango	a. tortilla with chopped meat and chili sauce
2. De Soto	b. roofing material
3. Camino Real	c. inner courtyard
4. Santa Fe	d. covered passageway
5. Las Vegas	e. city in Nevada
6. arcada	f. capital city in New Mexico
7. enchilada	g. Spanish word related to *alligator*
8. lagarto	h. Argentine dance
9. patio	i. road connecting the Spanish missions
10. tejas	j. explorer of the Mississippi River
11. Ponce de León	k. founder of California missions
12. Fray Junípero Serra	l. explorer of Florida

EXERCISE C

Complete the following statements.

1. A mountain range in California with a Spanish name is _____ .

2. A popular dance of the Dominican Republic is the _____ .

3. Two states with Spanish names are _____ and _____ .

4. The river that separates the United States from Mexico is the _____ .

5. A popular Cuban dance is the _____ .

6. An American city with a Spanish name is _____ .

7. One of the animals that the Spaniards brought to the New World is the _____ .

8. The San Juan Mountains are in the state of _____ .

9. A city in Texas with a Spanish name is _____ .

10. The oldest city in the United States is _____ .

EXERCISE D

In each group of words, select the word that isn't related to the other three.

EXAMPLE: rumba, tango, estampida, mambo   **estampida**

1. burro, chinchilla, llama, banana

2. bronco, flotilla, mesteño, rodeo

3. bolero, tornado, arroyo, mesa

4. brocado, tortilla, barbacoa, vainilla

5. sombrero, desesperado, poncho, mantilla

6. patio, hacienda, lazo, alameda

7. taco, tamal, enchilada, bonanza

8. camarada, tomate, patata, chile

9. peón, padre, renegado, embargo

10. armada, contrabando, canoa, sierra

EXERCISE E

Select the words in parenthesis that correctly complete each of the following sentences.

1. (Francisco Pizarro / Juan Ponce de León / Cristóbal Colón) was the first governor of Puerto Rico.

2. (Álvar Núñez Cabeza de Vaca / Hernán Cortés / Hernando de Soto) was the first European explorer to reach the Mississippi River.

3. (Atahualpa / Moctezuma / Cíbola) was the Aztec king conquered by Hernán Cortés.

4. (Fray Junípero Serra / Atahualpa / Juan Rodríguez Cabrillo) was a famous Spanish missionary.

5. (Santa Fe / Santa Barbara / San Francisco) is the oldest capital city in the United States.

6. (San Juan Capistrano / El Paso / St. Augustine) is a famous Spanish mission.

7. The (*tamal / rumba / cincha*) is a popular Spanish-American dance.

8. The tango is a popular dance from (Mexico / Cuba / Argentina).

Chapter 32
Geography of Spain

LOCATION OF SPAIN

Located in the southwestern part of Europe, Spain occupies eighty percent of the Iberian peninsula, which it shares with Portugal.

SIZE AND POPULATION

Spain has an area of about 200,000 square miles (four times the size of New York State), and a population of about 40,000,000 inhabitants.

MOUNTAINS

1. The Pyrenees **(los Pirineos),** in the northeast, separate Spain from France.
2. Cantabrian Mountains **(la Cordillera Cantábrica)** in the northwest.
3. Guadarrama Mountains **(la Sierra de Guadarrama),** near Madrid.
4. **Sierra Nevada** and **Sierra Morena,** in the south.

RIVERS

1. **El Ebro,** in the northeast, flows into the Mediterranean Sea.
2. **El Tajo,** in the central region, is the longest river. It runs by the city of Toledo.
3. **El Guadalquivir** in the south, is the deepest and most navigable river in Spain. It runs by the cities of Seville **(Sevilla)** and Cordova **(Córdoba).**

OVERSEAS POSSESSIONS

1. The Balearic Islands **(Islas Baleares)** are located in the Mediterranean Sea.

They are a popular resort area. **Mallorca** is the largest island in the group.
2. The Canary Islands **(Islas Canarias)** are located in the Atlantic Ocean, off the northwestern coast of Africa.
3. **Ceuta** and **Melilla** are two port cities in Morocco, Africa.

IMPORTANT PRODUCTS

1. Spain is both an industrial and an agricultural country.
2. The **principal agricultural** products are **olives, oranges, grapes, wheat, lemons,** and **cork.**
   a. Spain occupies third place in **wine** production in Europe.
   b. The wines of Jerez (sherry), **Rioja,** and **Málaga** are world-famous.
   c. Spain is one of the world's leading producers of **olive oil.**
3. **Mineral resources** are **coal, iron, mercury, lead,** and **copper.**

REGIONS OF SPAIN

Spain is divided into fifteen regions.

Cantabria, in the north
Galicia, in the northwest
Asturias, in the north, east of Galicia
Basque Country **(País Vasco),** in the north, bordering the Pyrenees
Navarre **(Navarra),** in the north
Aragon **(Aragón),** in the northeast, east of Navarra
Catalonia **(Cataluña),** in the northeastern corner

Rioja (**La Rioja**), south of Navarra
Castile and Leon (**Castilla y León**), in
the north central part of the peninsula
Castile–La Mancha (**Castilla–La Mancha**), in the center
Madrid, in the center, north of
Castile–La Mancha
Valencia, in the east
Extremadura, in the west, between
Portugal and Castile–La Mancha
Andalusia (**Andalucía**), in the south

LANGUAGES

1. Spanish (**español**, or **castellano**) is the principal language spoken in Spain.
2. Galician (**gallego**) is spoken in Galicia.
3. Basque (**vascuence**) is spoken in the Basque Country.
4. **Catalán** is spoken in Catalonia.

EXERCISE A

Match the words in column A to their related words in column B.

A	B
1. Asturias	*a.* Balearic Islands
2. Spanish	*b.* Atlantic Ocean
3. Sierra Morena	*c.* Spain's longest river
4. Galician	*d.* region in the northeast
5. Tajo	*e.* wine
6. Guadalquivir	*f.* language spoken in the northwest
7. Jerez	*g.* most navigable river
8. Canary Islands	*h.* mountains
9. Catalonia	*i.* region in the north
10. Mallorca	*j.* principal language of Spain

EXERCISE B

If the statement is true, write *Sí*, if it's false, correct it by replacing the word(s) in boldface.

1. The Pyrenees separate Spain from **Portugal.**
2. The Mediterranean Sea is situated **west** of Spain.
3. Spain and Portugal form the **Iberian** Peninsula.
4. Some Spanish **wines** are world-famous.
5. Spain has a population of about **60,000,000.**
6. Mallorca is one of the **Canary** Islands.
7. The Cantabrian Mountains are in the **south** of Spain.

8. The most navigable river in Spain is the **Tajo.**
9. **Málaga** is an important wine producing country.
10. The principal language of Spain is **Basque.**

EXERCISE C

Select the word or expression that correctly completes each sentence.

1. The (Guadarrama / Pyrenee / Cantabrian) Mountains separate Spain from France.
2. (Apples/ Oranges / Machines) are an important product of Spain.
3. Spain is located in the (southwestern / northeastern / central) part of Europe.
4. Spain has two ports that are situated in (South America / Africa / Mexico).
5. A popular resort area of Spain is (the Balearic Islands / the Canary Islands / Extremadura).
6. The (Tajo / Ebro / Guadalquivir) River passes by Toledo.
7. (Murcia / Aragon / Leon) is in the northwestern part of Spain.
8. An important mineral resource of Spain is (gold / tin / mercury).
9. Spain has an area of (40,000,000 / 200,000 / 1,300) square miles.
10. The (Pyrenee / Guadarrama / Cantabrian) Mountains are near Madrid.

EXERCISE D

Complete the following statements.

1. The _____ is the longest river of Spain.
2. The _____ are islands in the Mediterranean Sea that belong to Spain.
3. _____ is a region of central Spain.
4. Spain is the one of the world's leading producers of _____ .
5. _____ is a region that covers most of southern Spain.
6. The Cantabrian Mountains are in the _____ part of Spain.
7. Spain consists of _____ regions.
8. The Sierra Nevada is a mountain range in the _____ part of Spain.
9. The regional language of Catalonia is _____ .
10. A Spanish river that flows into the Mediterranean Sea is _____ .

Chapter 33
History of Spain

EARLY INHABITANTS

1. The Iberians **(los iberos)** and the Celts **(los celtas)**, the earliest inhabitants of Spain, united to form the Celtiberians **(los celtíberos)**.

2. The Phoenicians **(los fenicios)** and the Greeks **(los griegos)** established colonies and trading posts in Spain from about the eleventh to the eighth century B.C.

3. The Carthaginians **(los cartagineses)** invaded Spain in the third century B.C.

4. The Romans **(los romanos)**:
   a. defeated the Carthaginians (about 200 B.C.).
   b. ruled Spain for six centuries (until about A.D. 400).
   c. built bridges, aqueducts, and roads.
   d. introduced their language, Latin, from which present-day Spanish is derived.

5. The Visigoths **(los visigodos)** were a Germanic tribe that defeated the Romans and invaded Spain (A.D. 409).

6. The Moors **(los moros)** invaded Spain, defeating the Visigoths in A.D. 711. They ruled large areas of Spain for about seven centuries, and were finally driven out of Spain in 1492. The Moors:
   a. made great contributions in the fields of philosophy, medicine, mathematics, and astronomy.
   b. developed commerce and agriculture and devised an irrigation system by means of a waterwheel called **noria**.
   c. introduced many Arabic words into the Spanish language, mostly those beginning with **al-** (**algodón, alcalde, álgebra**, and many others).

HEROES OF THE RECONQUEST

1. **Don Pelayo** was the first leader in the Reconquest of Spain from the Moors. He defeated them in the **Battle of Covadonga** (A.D. 718).

2. **El Cid (Rodrigo Díaz de Vivar)**, is Spain's national hero. He continued the struggle against the Moors and captured Valencia from them in 1094.

IMPORTANT RULERS

1. **Fernando** and **Isabel**, known as **los Reyes Católicos** (the Catholic Rulers), completed the Reconquest by driving the Moors from Granada, the last remaining Spanish region under Moorish control (1492). They also financed Columbus's four expeditionary voyages.

2. **Carlos V** (1516–1556), grandson of Fernando and Isabel, was one of the most powerful Spanish kings. During his reign, Spain ruled most of Europe and the New World.

3. **Felipe II**, son of Carlos V. His "Invincible Armada" was defeated in an attempt to invade England in 1588.

NINETEENTH AND TWENTIETH CENTURIES

1. **The War of Independence** (1808–1814) started with a rebellion of

the people against French rule under Napoleon.

2. **The Spanish-American War** (1898) between the United States and Spain resulted in the latter's defeat. Spain agreed to give up Cuba, Puerto Rico, the Philippines, and Guam.

3. **The Civil War** (1936–1939) was won by General Francisco Franco and his supporters, who overthrew the republic and set up a dictatorship. At Franco's death (1975), Spain became a constitutional monarchy.

4. In 1975, **Prince Juan Carlos de Borbón** was proclaimed King. In 1982, **Felipe González Márquez** became Prime Minister. Spain joined the European Common Market in 1985.

EXERCISE A

Match the words in column A with their related words in column B.

A	B
1. Pelayo	*a.* early inhabitants of Spain
2. waterwheel	*b.* dictator
3. A.D. 711	*c.* Catholic Rulers
4. el Cid	*d.* Moorish defeat at Granada
5. Felipe II	*e.* Rodrigo Díaz de Vivar
6. 1808	*f.* Invincible Armada
7. 1492	*g.* brought to Spain by the Moors
8. Celtiberians	*h.* War of Independence
9. Franco	*i.* Moorish invasion
10. Fernando and Isabel	*j.* Covadonga

EXERCISE B

If the statement is true, write Sí; if it's false, correct it by replacing the word(s) in boldface.

1. The Spanish "Invincible" Armada, at war with England, was defeated in **1588**.
2. The Moors governed Spain for **two** centuries.
3. The **Celtiberians** established trading posts in Spain.
4. The **Visigoths** invaded Spain in A.D. 711.
5. Carlos V was the father of **Felipe II.**
6. El Cid captured **Valencia** from the Moors.
7. The **Carthaginians** built bridges and aqueducts in Spain.

8. Fernando and Isabel completed the Reconquest from the **Moors.**

9. The **Moors** developed philosophy and the sciences.

10. The **Phoenicians** conquered the Carthaginians.

EXERCISE C

Select the word or expression that correctly completes each sentence.

1. The first leader in the Reconquest of Spain was (Franco / Pelayo / el Cid).

2. The Spanish–American War took place in (1898 / 1936 / 1516).

3. Felipe II was the son of (Fernando and Isabel / el Cid / Carlos V).

4. The Spanish language is derived from (Portuguese / Latin / Basque).

5. The Moors were driven out of Spain in (1588 / 1808 / 1492).

6. The Romans ruled Spain for (two / six / eight) centuries.

7. Many Spanish words that begin with **al-** are of (Greek / Arabic / Portuguese) origin.

8. Prince Juan Carlos de Borbón was proclaimed King in (1898 / 1975 / 1982).

9. Columbus's voyages were financed by (Carlos V / Fernando and Isabel / Felipe II).

10. Spain's national hero is (don Pelayo / el Cid / Franco).

EXERCISE D

a. When did . . .

1. the Moors invade Spain?

2. don Pelayo win at Covadonga?

3. Fernando and Isabel recapture Granada?

4. the Spaniards rebel against Napoleon?

5. England defeat the "Invincible Armada"?

b. Who . . .

6. captured Valencia from the Moors?

7. financed Columbus's voyages?

8. was the father of Felipe II?

9. built the Alhambra?

10. overthrew the Spanish republic in 1939?

Chapter 34
Important and Interesting Places in Spain

1. Madrid is Spain's capital and largest city (population: approximately 4,500,000). In Madrid and its vicinity there are many interesting places to visit, among which are:
   a. **el Prado,** a world-famous art museum.
   b. the Royal Palace **(el Palacio Real),** one of the most luxurious palaces in Europe, built in the eighteenth century. The Spanish royal family lived there until King Alfonso XIII was forced to leave the country. The palace is now a museum.
   c. **la Puerta del Sol,** the central plaza of Madrid. Streets originate from it in all directions, to all parts of the city.
   d. **el Escorial,** a huge building combining a palace, art museum, monastery, library, and burial place for Spanish kings. It was built between 1563 and 1584 by order of Felipe II.
   e. the Valley of the Fallen **(el Valle de los Caídos),** an enormous monument in memory of the soldiers who died in the Spanish Civil War (1936–1939).

2. **Barcelona,** the principal city of **Catalonia** and the second largest city in Spain (population about 4,000,000). Spain's main industrial city, it has been an important seaport for more than two thousand years. It contains unique works by master architect **Gaudí.** Many Spanish books are printed in Barcelona.

3. Seville **(Sevilla),** in Andalusia **(Andalucía),** located on the bank of the Guadalquivir River. Seville is one of Spain's most picturesque cities for its gypsies and flamenco dancing.
   a. the Cathedral of Seville **(la Catedral de Sevilla),** the largest in Spain, and one of the largest in the world. Some historians believe it contains the tomb of Columbus.
   b. **la Giralda,** the tower of the Cathedral of Seville, an admirable example of Moorish architecture.

4. **Valencia,** located in a rich agricultural region on the Mediterranean coast called the "garden of Spain," is a leading export center for oranges and rice.

5. **Granada,** a picturesque city in the south; the last Moorish possession in Spain, recaptured by the Christians in 1492. The famous Moorish palace, the **Alhambra,** attracts visitors from everywhere.

6. **Toledo,** a famous medieval city on the **Tajo River** (near Madrid). It is important in metalworking, especially fine steel and exquisite jewelry. Toledo was the home of the famous painter **El Greco,** and contains many of his works.

7. Salamanca, site of the **University of Salamanca,** the oldest in Spain, and among the oldest and best universities of Europe. It was established in the thirteenth century.

8. Cordova **(Córdoba)**, on the **Guadalquivir River.** During the tenth and eleventh centuries it was the Moorish capital of Spain and one of the most important cultural centers of Europe. The city's main tourist attraction is the Mosque **(la Mezquita**—a Muslim place of worship), built in the eighth century and converted into a Roman Catholic cathedral in 1238.

9. **Burgos,** home of **el Cid,** Spain's national hero. **The Cathedral of Burgos,** one of the finest in Europe, contains his tomb.

10. **Bilbao,** a seaport in the north, where some of Spain's most important mines and steelyards are located.

11. **Segovia,** an ancient city in central Spain. A Roman aqueduct known as the Bridge **(el Puente),** built under the Roman Emperor Trajan (A.D. 53–117), is still in use today.

· EXERCISE A

If the statement is true, write *Sí;* if it's false, correct it by replacing the word(s) in boldface.

1. Barcelona is an important seaport on the **Atlantic Ocean.**
2. The Royal Palace is in **Segovia.**
3. The largest cathedral in Spain is located in **Seville.**
4. Valencia and Bilbao are important **regions** of Spain.
5. The Escorial was built by order of **Carlos V.**
6. **Madrid** is located on the Guadalquivir River.
7. **Granada** was the last Moorish possession in Spain.
8. Toledo was the home of **El Greco.**
9. Cordova was an important cultural center in the **nineteenth** century.
10. The aqueduct of Segovia is an important **Moorish** monument.

EXERCISE B

Select the word or expression that correctly completes each sentence.

1. A burial place for kings is located in the (Cathedral of Burgos / Valley of the Fallen / Escorial).
2. The Alhambra is located in (Granada / Bilbao / Salamanca).
3. An important mining area of Spain is located near (Segovia / Madrid / Bilbao).
4. The Valley of the Fallen is near (Barcelona / Madrid / Burgos).
5. Cordova is famous for its (castle / mosque / university).
6. The oldest university in Spain is located in (Toledo / Madrid / Salamanca).

7. The second largest city of Spain is (Sevilla / Barcelona / Madrid).
8. Valencia is famous for its (minerals / wines / oranges).
9. The (Prado / Giralda / Alhambra) is a famous art museum in Madrid.
10. The population of Madrid is about (2,000,000 / 4,500,000 / 37,000,000).

EXERCISE C

Match the words in column A with their related words in column B.

A	B
1. Mosque	*a.* Madrid
2. Valencia	*b.* Alhambra
3. la Giralda	*c.* the "garden of Spain"
4. Granada	*d.* tower in Seville
5. Puerta del Sol	*e.* Burgos
6. el Cid	*f.* Muslim temple
7. Toledo	*g.* steel-manufacturing center
8. books	*h.* university
9. Salamanca	*i.* medieval city
10. Bilbao	*j.* Barcelona

EXERCISE D

Complete the following statements.

1. The cities of Seville and Cordova are located on the _____ River.
2. _____ is Spain's most picturesque city.
3. _____ is a monument to the soldiers who died in the Spanish Civil War.
4. The central plaza of Madrid is called _____ .
5. _____ was one of the most important cultural centers of Europe during the tenth century.
6. Many Spanish kings are buried in _____ .
7. _____ is the capital of Spain.
8. A very important industrial city of Spain is _____ .
9. Toledo is located on the _____ River.
10. Granada was recaptured from the Moors in the year _____ .

Chapter 35
People and Customs of Spain

NAMES

1. **Family Names**

   a. Spaniards have at least two family names (the father's family name followed by the mother's).

   > **Pedro Ortega Gómez**

   This name would be filed under **Ortega** because the father's name is considered more important.

   b. When a woman marries, she keeps her family name and takes on her husband's preceded by **de.** Thus, **Pedro's** wife, whose maiden name was **Elena López Suárez,** would be:

   > **Elena López de Ortega**

   NOTE: The mother's family names of both **Pedro** and **Elena** are omitted.

2. Saint's Day **(el Día del Santo).** Most people in Spain (and in the rest of the Spanish-speaking countries) have as their given name, the name of a saint. They generally celebrate their saint's day instead of, or in addition to, their birthday.

CUSTOMS

1. **La tertulia** is an informal social gathering for meeting and chatting with friends. It often extends well past midnight.
2. **La siesta** is an afternoon nap or rest following the noon meal. Many stores are closed at this time.
3. The lottery **(la lotería)** is a government-controlled game whose earnings are used to finance many services, such as public assistance for orphans or widows.

RELIGIOUS HOLIDAYS

1. Christmas **(Navidad)** is one of the most important religious holidays in Spain. Christmas trees are not used. Instead, each home has its nativity scene **(nacimiento),** clay figures representing the scene of the birth of Christ. On Christmas Eve **(Nochebuena)** people attend a midnight mass **(Misa del Gallo).** Children receive gifts on January 6, the Day of the Three Wise Men **(Día de los Reyes Magos).** The **Reyes Magos** play the same role in Spanish life as Santa Claus.
2. Easter **(Pascua Florida)** is celebrated throughout Spain and Spanish America. Holy Week **(Semana Santa)** is observed the week before, with solemn ceremonies. The Holy Week celebration in Seville is world-famous.
3. Carnival **(Carnaval)** is a celebration that occurs during the last three days before Lent.
4. All Souls' Day **(Día de los Muertos)** is observed solemnly on November 2. People visit the graves of dead relatives and friends.

NATIONAL HOLIDAYS

1. **May 2** commemorates the uprising of the Spaniards against French rule (1808). It is Spain's national holiday.
2. **October 12** corresponds to Co-

lumbus Day. It is called **El Día de la Hispanidad** or **El Día de la Raza.**

TYPICAL FOODS AND BEVERAGES

1. **Arroz con pollo,** yellow rice with chicken, popular in Spain and Spanish America.
2. **Paella,** yellow rice with chicken and seafood.
3. **Cocido,** beef stew that is popular among farmers and laborers.
4. **Chocolate,** thick hot cocoa, usually served at breakfast with **churros,** a kind of cruller.
5. **Horchata,** cold drink made with crushed toasted almonds or sesame seeds, water, and sugar.

REGIONAL DANCES

1. **Andalusia: bolero, fandango, flamenco.** Generally accompanied by a guitar.
2. **Aragon: jota.**
3. **Catalonia: sardana.**

PICTURESQUE CHARACTERS

1. **The tuna** is a group of strolling musicians, usually university students, who play romantic and lively music. This is a tradition that exists since the sixteenth century.
2. The Gypsies **(los gitanos)** are found mostly in the south, especially around Seville and Granada. It is believed that they came from northern India. Their language is called *Romani.*

EXERCISE A

Match the words in column A with their related words in column B.

A	B
1. Saint's Day	*a.* Aragon
2. Carnival	*b.* afternoon nap
3. flamenco	*c.* beverage
4. Holy Week	*d.* birthday celebration
5. siesta	*e.* Lent
6. jota	*f.* Santa Claus
7. Three Wise Men	*g.* midnight mass
8. tertulia	*h.* Easter
9. horchata	*i.* Andalucia
10. Christmas	*j.* social gathering

EXERCISE B

Select the word or expression that correctly completes each statement.

   1. A popular Spanish dish is (sardana / paella / tertulia).

2. Spaniards usually have (horchata / tea / chocolate) at breakfast.

3. The lottery is managed (by the church / privately / by the government).

4. Instead of Christmas trees, Spaniards usually have a (basket / bull / nativity scene) set up in the house.

5. The jota is a Spanish (dance / musical instrument / dish).

6. The Spanish national holiday is (May 2 / October 12 / November 2).

7. A gathering for the purpose of talking is a (nacimiento / tertulia / cocido).

8. The city of (Seville / Valencia / Granada) is famous for its Holy Week celebration.

9. Spanish children receive their Christmas gifts on (December 16 / December 25 / January 6).

10. Spaniards visit the cemeteries on (their saint's day / All Soul's Day / Christmas Day).

EXERCISE C

Complete the following sentences.

1. The *fandango* is a regional dance of _____ .

2. Juan López Serrano marries Dolores Moreno Ortega. The wife's full name is now _____ .

3. Juan and Dolores have a son, Carlos, whose full name is _____ .

4. Christmas eve is called _____ in Spain.

5. A group of university students who sing in the streets is called a _____ .

6. A typical dish of Spain is _____ .

7. A _____ is a Nativity scene.

8. The uprising against the French took place on _____ , 1808.

9. A regional dance of Catalonia is the _____ .

10. _____ is celebrated on October 12.

EXERCISE D

Define each of the following.

1. arroz con pollo

2. dos de mayo

3. Reyes Magos

4. cocido
5. nacimiento
6. Día de la Raza
7. tertulia
8. misa del gallo
9. Nochebuena
10. gitano
11. Día del Santo
12. siesta
13. churros
14. la tuna
15. horchata

Chapter 36
Spanish Literature, Science, and the Arts

WRITERS

1. **Middle Ages**
   a. **Juan Ruiz,** known as **Arcipreste de Hita** (1283–1351), *El libro de buen amor.*
   b. **Fernando de Rojas** (?–1541), *La Celestina* (or *Comedia de Calisto y Melibea)* 1499.
   c. Anonymous, *Lazarillo de Tormes* (1554).
2. **Golden Age (Siglo de Oro [1560–1680])**
   a. **Miguel de Cervantes** (1547–1616), one of Spain's greatest novelists, wrote the world-famous novel *El ingenioso hidalgo don Quijote de la Mancha.*
   b. **Lope de Vega** (1562–1635), one of Spain's leading dramatists, wrote hundreds of plays.
   c. **Pedro Calderón de la Barca** (1600–1681), the last great figure of the Golden Age, wrote the famous play *La vida es sueño (Life Is a Dream).*
3. **Nineteenth and Twentieth Centuries**
   a. **Benito Pérez Galdós** (1843–1920), another great Spanish novelist, among the most famous of the nineteenth century. He wrote *Marianela.*
   b. **Vicente Blasco Ibáñez** (1867–1928), famous novelist who wrote *The Four Horsemen of the Apocalypse (Los cuatro jinetes del Apocalipsis)* and *Blood and Sand (Sangre y arena).* He also wrote many novels about Valencia, of which the most famous is *La barraca.*
   c. **Jacinto Benavente** (1866–1954), famous dramatist, winner of the Nobel Prize for Literature in 1922.
   d. **Juan Ramón Jiménez** (1881–1958), famous poet, winner of the Nobel Prize for Literature in 1956.
   e. **Federico García Lorca** (1898–1936), famous poet and dramatist whose works deal with folkloric and traditional themes. His plays *Bodas de sangre* and *La casa de Bernarda Alba* continue to be presented in the theater. He died tragically during the Spanish Civil War.
   f. **Vicente Aleixandre** (1898–1984), renowned essayist and poet, winner of the Nobel Prize for Literature in 1977.
   g. **Camilio José Cela** (1916–   ), famous novelist of contemporary Spain, winner of the Nobel Prize for Literature in 1989.
   h. **Carmen Laforet** (1921–   ), famous contemporary novelist whose novel *Nada* deals with life in Spain immediately after the Civil War.
   i. **Ana María Matute** (1926–   ), famous contemporary novelist whose works have received numerous national prizes.

SCIENTISTS

1. **Santiago Ramón y Cajal** (1852–1934), winner of the Nobel Prize for Medicine in 1906, for his stud-

ies on the structure of the nervous system.

2. **Juan de la Cierva** (1895–1936), aeronautical engineer who invented the autogyro, the forerunner of the helicopter, in 1923.

3. **Severo Ochoa** (1905–   ), winner of the Nobel Prize for Medicine (1959) for his studies on heredity.

PAINTERS

1. **Doménico Theotocopulos**, known as **El Greco** (1541–1614), sixteenth century Greek painter who settled in Toledo, where many of his works can still be found. Most of his paintings deal with religious themes.

2. **Diego Velázquez** (1599–1660), considered by many to be one of Spain's greatest painters. He was court painter to Felipe IV (seventeenth century). His most famous work is *Las meninas.*

3. **Francisco Goya** (1746–1828), among the greatest Spanish painters of the eighteenth and nineteenth centuries. His work attacks the social and political decay of the period.

4. **Pablo Picasso** (1881–1973), one of the outstanding painters of the twentieth century, and the founder of cubism, a style of painting in which figures are deconstructed into geometric forms.

5. **Joan Miró** (1893–1983), one of the greatest painters of abstract art of the twentieth century.

6. **Salvador Dalí** (1904–1989), an outstanding twentieth-century painter of surrealist art.

COMPOSERS AND MUSICIANS

1. **Isaac Albéniz** (1860–1909), composer of music for the piano.

2. **Manuel de Falla** (1876–1946), one of Spain's greatest composers and foremost representatives of modern Spanish music.

3. **José Iturbi** (1896–1980), famous pianist, composer, and conductor.

4. **Andrés Segovia** (1893–1987), among the most famous guitarists, gave many concerts all over the world.

5. **Pablo Casals** (1876–1973), cellist of international fame.

6. **Plácido Domingo** (1941–   ), **José Carreras** (1947–   ), **Monserrat Caballé** (1933–   ) are opera singers of international fame.

7. **Julio Iglesias** (1943–   ), famous singer of popular music.

EXERCISE A

If the statement is true, write *Sí*; if it's false, correct it by replacing the word(s) in boldface.

1. Andrés Segovia was a world-famous **pianist.**

2. Pablo Casals was one of Spain's greatest **composers.**

3. **Blasco Ibáñez** wrote *The Four Horsemen of the Apocalypse.*

4. Lope de Vega was one of Spain's leading **poets.**

5. **Ramón y Cajal** invented the autogyro.

6. **Cervantes** was one of the greatest Spanish novelists.

7. José Carreras is a famous **painter.**

8. **Velázquez** was the founder of cubism.

9. **Carmen Laforet** wrote plays about Spanish folklore.

10. **Dalí** won a Nobel Prize for Literature.

EXERCISE B

Match the names in column A with their related words in column B.

A	B
1. Plácido Domingo	*a.* twentieth-century dramatist
2. Calderón	*b.* religious paintings
3. Ramón y Cajal	*c. Las meninas*
4. Albéniz	*d. El ingenioso hidalgo don Quijote de la Mancha*
5. Jacinto Benavente	*e.* Golden Age dramatist
6. Blasco Ibáñez	*f.* studies of the nervous system
7. El Greco	*g.* tenor
8. Miguel de Cervantes	*h.* novels about Valencia
9. Diego Velázquez	*i.* cubism
10. Pablo Picasso	*j.* composer

EXERCISE C

Select the word or expression that correctly completes each statement.

1. The Golden Age occurred during the (eighteenth and nineteenth / nineteenth and twentieth / sixteenth and seventeenth) centuries.

2. One of the most famous Spanish composers is (Pablo Picasso / Manuel de Falla / Pablo Casals).

3. A Spanish novelist who won the Nobel Prize was (Ana María Matute / Camilo José Cela / Federico García Lorca).

4. The last great dramatist of the Golden Age was (Velázquez / Calderón / Cervantes).

5. The autogyro was invented by (Juan de la Cierva / Severo Ochoa / Juan Miró).

6. Juan Ramón Jiménez was a famous (poet / musician / painter).

7. (Lope de Vega / Plácido Domingo / Andrés Segovia) was a great Spanish guitarist.

8. One of the greatest painters of eighteenth-century Spain was (Francisco Goya / Diego Velázquez / Salvador Dalí).

9. One of the greatest novelists of Spain was (Miguel de Cervantes / José Carreras / Vicente Aleixandre).

10. Severo Ochoa received a Nobel Prize in the field of (literature / medicine / economics).

EXERCISE D

Complete the following statements.

1. A sixteenth-century painter who lived in Toledo was _____ .

2. An author who wrote about Spain after the Civil War is _____ .

3. _____ was a famous pianist and orchestra leader.

4. *Sangre y arena* was written by _____ .

5. _____ was court painter to Felipe IV.

6. _____ is the author of *La vida es sueño*.

7. _____ was among the most famous novelists of the nineteenth century.

8. _____ won the Nobel Prize for Literature in 1977.

9. _____ earned his fame as a painter of abstract art.

10. _____ is a famous Spanish soprano.

EXERCISE E

a. Who wrote . . .

1. *El ingenioso hidalgo don Quijote de la Mancha?*

2. *La Casa de Bernarda Alba?*

3. *Nada?*

4. about Valencia?

5. hundreds of plays?

b. Who was . . .

6. Joan Miró?

7. one of Spain's greatest composers?

8. Santiago Ramón y Cajal?

9. the father of cubism?

10. Francisco Goya?

Chapter 37
Geography of Spanish America

COUNTRIES AND THEIR CAPITALS

1. In North America

Mexico (capital: **Federal District of Mexico**) is directly south of the United States of America, bordering the states of Texas, New Mexico, Arizona, and California; our nearest Spanish–American neighbor. Land of the **Aztecs** and the **Mayas,** two of the most advanced Native-American civilizations.

2. In Central America

a. **Costa Rica** (capital: **San José**) is one of the most progressive countries in Central America. It has good environmental laws and no army.

b. **El Salvador** (capital: **San Salvador**) is the smallest country in Central America.

c. **Guatemala** (capital: **Guatemala City**) is the main producer of *chicle,* used in the manufacture of chewing gum. Guatemala was the center of the old Mayan empire.

d. **Honduras** (capital: **Tegucigalpa**) has important mineral and timber resources. Exports mainly bananas and coffee.

e. **Nicaragua** (capital: **Managua**) is the largest country in Central America. Exports cotton and textiles, coffee and sugarcane.

f. **Panama** (capital: **Panama City**) is an isthmus joining Central and South America. The Panama Canal is located there.

3. In the Caribbean (Antilles)

a. **Cuba** (capital: **Havana**) is the largest island of the Caribbean.

b. **Dominican Republic** (capital: **Santo Domingo**), together with French-speaking Haiti, forms the island of Hispaniola.

c. **Puerto Rico** (capital: **San Juan**) is a commonwealth of the United States. The smallest of the Greater Antilles, it's also called **Borinquen,** its native name.

4. In South America

a. **Argentina** (capital: **Buenos Aires**) is the largest Spanish-speaking country in South America.

b. **Bolivia** (two capitals: **La Paz** and **Sucre**) is the only country in South America without an outlet to the sea. Although Sucre is the official capital, La Paz is the actual seat of government.

c. **Colombia** (capital: **Bogotá**) is the only South American country with seacoasts on both the Atlantic and Pacific Oceans.

d. **Chile** (capital: **Santiago**) is the longest and narrowest country in South America.

e. **Ecuador** (capital: **Quito**) is crossed north to south by two parallel ranges of very high volcanic peaks, part of the Andes Mountains. The **Galápagos Islands** belong to Ecuador.

f. **Paraguay** (capital: **Asunción**) has a large Native-American population. Paraguay produces soybeans and packed meats; also

produces **yerba mate,** a popular tea used widely in Argentina.

g. Peru (capital: Lima) The land of the Incas, a Native-American civilization that flourished centuries before the arrival of Europeans in America.

h. Uruguay (capital: Montevideo) is the smallest Spanish-speaking country in South America.

i. Venezuela (capital: Caracas) is the richest oil-producing country in South America; is also the birthplace of Simón Bolívar, "The Liberator."

NOTE: Some countries are not mentioned here because their cultural heritage is not Spanish but French (Haiti, Martinique, Guadeloupe, French Guiana); English (Belize, Jamaica, Trinidad and Tobago, Guyana), Portuguese (Brazil); or Dutch (Surinam).

GEOGRAPHIC FEATURES

1. Mountain Ranges

a. The **Andes** extend the entire length of South America along the west coast. There are many high peaks; the highest, **Aconcagua,** has an altitude of nearly 23,000 feet (more than four miles), and it is the highest peak in the Western Hemisphere. There are many other peaks nearly as high.

b. The **Sierra Madre** (Mexico) consists of two parallel mountain chains, the **Sierra Madre Oriental** (Eastern) and the **Sierra Madre Occidental** (Western), with a great plateau between them.

2. Principal Rivers

a. The **Orinoco** (Venezuela) is the longest single river in Spanish America. (The **Amazon River,** which is more than twice as long, is in Brazil.)

b. The **Río de la Plata** (between Uruguay and Argentina) has the capitals of both countries, Argentina and Uruguay, on its banks.

c. The **Paraná–Paraguay** System is formed by the Paraná and Paraguay Rivers. It connects with the **Río de la Plata,** to form the chief water outlet from the interior regions to the sea.

d. The **Magdalena** (Colombia) crosses the whole country from south to north; it is an important means of transportation.

3. Climate

a. **Argentina, Uruguay, Paraguay,** and **Chile** are in the South Temperate Zone. Northern Mexico is in the North Temperate Zone. Southern Mexico and the rest of Spanish America lie in the tropics (Torrid Zone).

b. Most cities located in the tropics, except the ones at high altitudes, are very warm.

ANIMAL LIFE

1. Birds

a. The **condor** is a carrion-eating bird from the Andes; probably the largest among flying birds.

b. The **quetzal** is a brilliantly colored bird of Central America. It is the national emblem of Guatemala, and gives name to its monetary unit.

2. **Wool-Bearing Animals**
   a. **Alpaca, guanaco, llama, vicuña** (in the Andes).
   b. **Sheep** (mainly in Argentina and Uruguay).
3. **Beasts of Burden**
   a. The **burro** is the most common beast of burden in Spanish America.
   b. The **llama** is the main beast of burden of the Andean countries (Peru, Ecuador, Bolivia).

IMPORTANT PRODUCTS

1. Some of the products that Spanish America gives to the world are potatoes, corn, tomatoes, chocolate, vanilla, pineapples, peanuts, pecans, and cashew nuts.

2.
AGRICULTURAL PRODUCTS	MAIN PRODUCERS
apples and peaches	Chile
bananas	most Central-American countries
beef	Argentina, Uruguay
cacao bean (used in manufacturing chocolate)	Ecuador, Venezuela
coffee	Colombia, Venezuela
sugar	Cuba, Dominican Republic
corozo nuts (used in manufacturing buttons)	Ecuador
tobacco	Cuba
wheat	Argentina, Uruguay

3.
MINING AND CHEMICAL INDUSTRIES	MAIN PRODUCERS
copper	Chile, Peru
emeralds	Colombia
nitrates (used for fertilizer)	Chile
petroleum	Venezuela, Mexico
platinum	Colombia
silver	Mexico, Peru
tin	Bolivia

EXERCISE A

If the statement is true, write *Sí;* if it's false, correct it by replacing the word(s) in boldface.

1. Two important products of Venezuela are **petroleum** and **coffee**.

2. Lima is the capital of **Argentina**.

3. **Santiago** is the capital of Colombia.

4. Costa Rica and Honduras produce many **bananas**.

5. The Parana River flows into the **Pacific Ocean**.

6. Spanish is the language of **six** countries in South America.

7. **Montevideo** is the capital of Venezuela.

8. The condor lives in the **Andes**.

9. Mexico and Peru produce **emeralds**.

10. There are **six** countries in Central America.

EXERCISE B

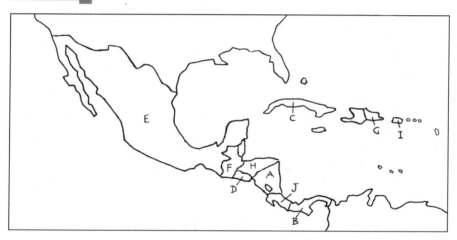

In the map above, identify each of the following countries.

1. Panama

2. Puerto Rico

3. Costa Rica

4. Honduras

5. El Salvador

6. Guatemala

7. Mexico

8. Cuba

9. Nicaragua

10. Dominican Republic

EXERCISE C

In the map above, identify each of the following countries.

1. Bolivia

2. Argentina

3. Chile

4. Ecuador

5. Uruguay

6. Colombia

7. Peru

8. Paraguay

9. Venezuela

EXERCISE D

Match the words in column A with their corresponding definitions in column B.

A	B
1. Sierra Madre	*a.* river in Colombia
2. corozo nuts	*b.* capital of Nicaragua
3. yerba mate	*c.* used to manufacture chocolate
4. Aconcagua	*d.* fabric borne by the alpaca
5. tin	*e.* mountains in Mexico
6. Magdalena	*f.* highest peak in the Western Hemisphere
7. Managua	*g.* used to manufacture buttons
8. cacao	*h.* bird of the Andes
9. wool	*i.* element found in Bolivia
10. condor	*j.* popular tea from Paraguay

EXERCISE E

Write the word that is needed to complete each statement.

1. The longest river in Venezuela is the _____ .
2. The Andes are situated in _____ .
3. The quetzal is found mainly in _____ .
4. The main beast of burden in the Andes is the _____ .
5. In Chile, Argentina, and Uruguay it is cold in the months of _____ .
6. The capital of Costa Rica is _____ .
7. The only country in South America without an outlet to the ocean is _____ .
8. The country crossed north to south by two parallel ranges of peaks is _____ .
9. The richest oil-producing country of South America is _____ .
10. The ingredient used to manufacture chocolate is _____ .

Chapter 38
Famous Names in Spanish America

NATIONAL HEROES OF SPANISH AMERICA

1. **Simón Bolívar** (1783–1830) was one of the main figures in the struggle for South American independence from Spain. Called **El Libertador** (the Liberator), he won independence for the northern part of South America. **Bolivia** was named in his honor.

2. **José de San Martín** (1778–1850) was an Argentinian general who won independence for the southern part of South America, including Argentina and Chile.

3. **Bernardo O'Higgins** (1778–1842) was a Chilean general who helped San Martín in the liberation of Chile. O'Higgins became the first president of Chile.

4. **Antonio José de Sucre** (1795–1830) defeated the Spanish army in the battle of Ayacucho (Peru), the last battle for South American Independence (1824).

5. **Miguel Hidalgo** (1753–1811) was a Mexican priest and patriot who began the struggle for Mexican independence (1810).

6. **Benito Juárez** (1806–1872) fought against Archduke Maximilian, Emperor of Mexico. Juárez was later called the "Abraham Lincoln of Mexico."

7. **José Martí** (1853–1895) was a famous Cuban poet and patriot who died fighting for Cuban independence from Spain.

WRITERS

1. **Andrés Bello** (1781–1865) was a Chilean poet, critic, and a leading intellectual of Spanish America. He wrote *Gramática de la lengua castellana.*

2. **Domingo Faustino Sarmiento** (1811–1888) was an Argentinian educator and statesman, known as the "Schoolmaster President." He wrote *Facundo,* which deals with the life of a **gaucho** (Argentinian cowboy) leader.

3. **Ricardo Palma** (1833–1919) wrote *Tradiciones peruanas,* a collection of stories about Peru during colonial times.

4. **Rubén Darío** (1867–1916) was born in Nicaragua. One of the greatest poets of Spanish America, he helped create a new poetic style called "modernism."

5. **Mariano Azuela** (1873–1952) was a Mexican novelist who wrote *Los de abajo,* a novel about the Mexican Revolution of 1910–1920.

6. **Gabriela Mistral** (1889–1957) was a Chilean poet who won the Nobel Prize for Literature in 1945.

7. **Rómulo Gallegos** (1884–1969) was a Venezuelan novelist and statesman who wrote *Doña Bárbara,* a novel about life on the plains of Venezuela.

8. **Miguel Ángel Asturias** (1899–1974) was a Guatemalan novelist whose books describe the suffer-

ing caused by the local dictator and by the big "Yanqui" companies. He received the Nobel Prize for Literature in 1967.

9. **Pablo Neruda** (1904–1973) was a Chilean poet and diplomat who received the Nobel Prize for Literature in 1971.

10. **Gabriel García Márquez** (1928–) is a Colombian novelist who wrote *Cien años de soledad,* the history of an imaginary town in Colombia. He received the Nobel Prize for Literature in 1982.

11. **Octavio Paz** (1914–) is a Mexican poet and essayist who received the Nobel Prize for Literature in 1990.

PAINTERS

1. **Diego Rivera, José Clemente Orozco,** and **David Alfaro Siqueiros** are the three most important painters of Mexico. All three specialized in mural painting, and all treated political and social topics.

2. **Cesáreo Bernaldo de Quirós,** of Argentina, painted scenes of gaucho life.

COMPOSERS AND MUSICIANS

1. **Carlos Chávez** was a famous Mexican composer and orchestra conductor.

2. **Claudio Arrau** was a famous Chilean pianist.

EXERCISE A

Identify each of the following names by selecting the corresponding letter.

a. patriot   b. writer   c. painter   d. composer-musician

1. Mariano Azuela

2. Andrés Bello

3. Rubén Darío

4. Rómulo Gallegos

5. Antonio José de Sucre

6. Benito Juárez

7. Gabriela Mistral

8. Octavio Paz

9. Diego Rivera

10. Bernardo O'Higgins

11. Carlos Chávez

12. Claudio Arrau

13. Cesáreo Bernaldo de Quirós

14. Miguel Ángel Asturias

15. José Clemente Orozco

EXERCISE B

Match the names in column A with their related words in column B.

A	B
1. Juárez	*a.* novelist
2. Sarmiento	*b.* great Spanish-American poet

A (Con'd)	B (Con'd)
3. San Martín	**c.** *Tradiciones peruanas*
4. Martí	**d.** Schoolmaster President
5. García Márquez	**e.** murals
6. Darío	**f.** Mexican patriot
7. Orozco	**g.** painter
8. Palma	**h.** Argentina's independence
9. Bolívar	**i.** Cuban patriot
10. Rivera	**j.** "the Liberator"

EXERCISE C

Select the name, title, or word that correctly completes each statement.

1. (Siqueiros / Neruda / Martí) was the second writer to win a Nobel Prize for Chile.
2. (Juárez / Hidalgo / San Martín) was called the "Abraham Lincoln of Mexico."
3. One of the greatest Spanish-American poets was (Ricardo Palma / Rubén Darío / Rómulo Gallegos).
4. (*Doña Bárbara* / *Facundo* / *Los de abajo*) is a novel about the Mexican Revolution.
5. (Claudio Arrau / Bernardo O'Higgins / Gabriela Mistral) was a famous Chilean pianist.
6. Diego Rivera was a famous (musician / novelist / painter).
7. The last battle in the struggle for South American independence took place at (Lima / Ayacucho / Mexico).
8. (Gabriela Mistral / Jose Martí / Andrés Bello) won the Nobel Prize for Literature.
9. The first president of Chile was (Sucre / O'Higgins / Azuela).
10. Sarmiento wrote (*Facundo* / *Cien años de soledad* / *Tradiciones peruanas*).

EXERCISE D

a. Write a name that would fit each definition.

1. Mexican painter
2. Argentine educator

3. Spanish-American novelist
4. Spanish-American poet
5. country named for Bolívar
6. Mexican composer
7. a Mexican Nobel Prize winner
8. a Colombian Nobel Prize winner

b. Tell who wrote the following titles.

9. *Facundo*
10. *Doña Bárbara*
11. *Cien años de soledad*
12. *Tradiciones peruanas*
13. *Los de abajo*
14. *Gramática de la lengua castellana*

EXERCISE E

Complete the following statements.

1. One of Nicaragua's most famous poets is _____ .
2. San Martín won independence for Chile and _____ .
3. The Mexican movement for independence from Spain was begun by _____ .
4. Bernaldo de Quirós painted scenes of the life of the _____ .
5. The Spanish army was defeated by Sucre at the battle of _____ .
6. José Clemente Orozco was a Mexican _____ .
7. José Martí was killed in the war for the independence of _____ .
8. The Chilean general who helped San Martín win independence for Chile is _____ .

Chapter 39

Places of Interest in Spanish America

INTERESTING PLACES IN MEXICO

1. The Federal District of Mexico (**Distrito Federal de México**) is the capital of Mexico. It was the original capital of the Aztec empire (**Tenochtitlán**). Today it is a large and modern city, the largest Spanish–speaking city in the world.

   a. The Metropolitan Cathedral (**Catedral Metropolitana**) is the largest and oldest cathedral on the North American continent.

   b. The Sun Stone (**La Piedra del Sol**) is an ancient stone inscribed with the Aztec calendar. It is found at one of the most beautiful museums in the world, the Museum of Anthropology (**Museo Antropológico**).

   c. **Chapultepec** is a large, beautiful park with an impressive castle.

   d. The Palace of Fine Arts (**Palacio de Bellas Artes**) contains a beautiful theater and art museum.

   e. **Ciudad Universitaria** is the site of the National University, the oldest university of the North American continent.

   f. **Popocatépetl** and **Ixtaccíhuatl** are picturesque volcanoes overlooking the Federal District of Mexico.

   g. **Xochimilco** is a town near the Federal District famous for its floating gardens.

2. **Taxco** is one of Mexico's most picturesque cities. The Spanish colonial atmosphere is still preserved. Taxco is famous for its silver.

3. **Cozumel** and **Cancún** are fashionable seaside resorts, which are in the region of Mayan temples, such as **Chichén-Itzá, Uxmal,** and **Palenque.**

INTERESTING PLACES IN CENTRAL AND SOUTH AMERICA

1. **Monteverde** (Costa Rica), rain forest.

2. **Tikal** (Guatemala), Mayan ruins.

3. **Buenos Aires** (Argentina), one of the most beautiful capitals in the world.

4. **Lima** (Peru) is the capital and main industrial and cultural center of Peru. The University of San Marcos, the oldest university in South America, is located here.

5. **Cuzco** (Peru) is the ancient capital of the Incas. Nearby are the famous Inca ruins of Machu-Picchu.

6. **Bogotá** is the capital and most important cultural center of Colombia. It has many excellent examples of colonial architecture.

7. **Quito** is the capital and principal textile center of Ecuador. It is located almost at the equator, but it has a pleasant climate due to its high altitude (nearly 10,000 feet).

8. **Lake Titicaca** is located in the Andes Mountains between Bolivia and Peru. It is the highest navigable lake in the world.

9. The Iguazú Falls (**Las Cataratas del Iguazú**) are spectacular waterfalls located between Argentina

and Brazil; they are higher than the Niagara Falls.

10. Christ of the Andes (**El Cristo de los Andes**) is a giant statue of Christ located in the Andes Mountains, on the border between Chile and Argentina. It was erected to commemorate the peaceful settlement of a boundary dispute.

EXERCISE A

Match each of the tourist attractions in column A with its description in column B.

A	B
1. Monteverde	*a.* floating gardens
2. Tenochtitlán	*b.* seaside resort
3. Cristo de los Andes	*c.* Mayan ruins in Guatemala
4. Popocatépetl	*d.* statue
5. Cuzco	*e.* rain forest
6. Iguazú	*f.* original Aztec capital
7. Xochimilco	*g.* lake
8. Cancún	*h.* volcano in Mexico
9. Titicaca	*i.* Inca capital
10. Tikal	*j.* waterfall

EXERCISE B

If the statement is true, write *Sí*; if it's false, correct it by replacing the word(s) in boldface.

1. The **Piedra del Sol** is a famous theater in Mexico.
2. The city of **Quito** is located near the equator.
3. The University of San Marcos is located in **Bolivia.**
4. Bogotá is the capital of **Colombia.**
5. Taxco is a picturesque city in **Argentina.**
6. **Chichén-Itzá** is a famous beach in Mexico.
7. **Iguazú Falls** are located between Bolivia and Peru.
8. The largest Spanish-speaking city in the world is **Buenos Aires.**
9. The oldest university in North America is located in **Peru.**
10. The ruins of Machu-Picchu are located near **Cuzco.**

EXERCISE C

Complete the following statements.

1. The volcanoes *Popocatépetl* and *Ixtaccíhuatl* are located near _____ .
2. The highest navigable lake in the world is _____ .
3. The oldest university in South America is located in _____ .
4. *El Cristo de los Andes* commemorates the settlement of a dispute between Argentina and _____ .
5. The famous rain forest in Costa Rica is _____ .
6. The oldest university in Mexico is _____ .
7. Quito has a pleasant climate because of its _____ .
8. Between Brazil and Argentina there is a waterfall called _____ .
9. Cozumel is a seaside resort in _____ .
10. Cuzco was the ancient capital of the _____ .

EXERCISE D

Identify the country where each of the following is located.

1. Palacio de Bellas Artes
2. Cuzco
3. Cataratas del Iguazú
4. Bogotá
5. Cancún
6. Titicaca
7. Buenos Aires
8. Piedra del Sol
9. Tikal
10. Lima

Chapter 40
People and Customs of Spanish America

PEOPLE OF SPANISH AMERICA

Most Spanish-American countries have several different racial groups. The four principal groups are:

1. **Whites,** descendants of Spanish settlers and other European immigrants (from Italy, Germany, England, Ireland, and the Slavic countries).
2. **Native Americans,** found in great numbers in many Spanish-American countries, especially in Mexico, Central America, Ecuador, Bolivia, Paraguay, and Peru. Most are descendants of the Aztecs, the Mayas, and the Incas.
3. **Blacks,** descendants of Africans who were brought to Spanish America for heavy labor. They are most numerous in the Caribbean.
4. **Mestizos** (people of mixed European and Native-American ancestry), the largest racial group in many Spanish-American countries.
5. **Mulattos** (people of mixed European and African ancestry), most numerous in the Caribbean.

NATIONAL HOLIDAYS

1. **October 12 (El Día de la Raza),** corresponds to Columbus Day and is celebrated throughout the Spanish-speaking world.
2. **September 16,** the Mexican national holiday that commemorates the beginning of the rebellion against Spain (1810).
3. **May 5,** commemorates the Mexican freedom struggle against France and Maximilian, the emperor of Mexico.

RELIGIOUS HOLIDAYS

1. Christmas **(Navidad)** is one of the most important religious holidays in Spanish America.
2. **Las Posadas** (December 16-24) is a Mexican celebration that takes place during the nine days before Christmas. Children break piñatas (colorful figures containing candy, fruit, and toys).
3. Carnival **(Carnaval)** is a celebration that takes place before Lent.
4. Easter **(Pascua Florida)** is celebrated throughout Spanish America.
5. All Souls' Day **(El Día de los Muertos)** is celebrated on November 2 and is observed solemnly throughout the Spanish-speaking world. It is also known as **El Día de los Difuntos.**

PICTURESQUE TYPES

1. **El charro,** the typical Mexican cowboy.
2. **La china poblana,** the female companion of the charro.
3. **El mariachi,** a group of Mexican street singers.
4. **El gaucho,** the cowboy of the Argentine **pampas** (plains).

CLOTHING

In the cities, people generally dress as we do in the United States. However, one often sees traditional dress, especially during holiday celebrations.

1. **El sarape** is a bright colored Mexican blanket (serape). It is worn by men and women, slung

over the shoulders.

2. **El poncho** is a cape worn by the Mexicans, gauchos, and other Spanish Americans, as protection from the cold and the rain.

3. **El rebozo** is a shawl worn by Mexican women.

4. **El sombrero de jipijapa** (Panama hat) is a high-quality straw hat made in Ecuador, not in Panama.

SPORTS AND SPECTACLES

1. Soccer (**el fútbol**) is a very popular game in most Spanish-speaking countries.

2. **Jai-alai** is a game that originated in the Basque country of Spain. This sport is popular in Spain, Mexico, Venezuela, Cuba, as well as Connecticut and Florida. Jai-alai is somewhat similar to handball.

a. El frontón is a three-walled court on which jai-alai is played.

b. La cesta is a curved basket strapped to the player's wrist, in which the ball is caught and thrown against the wall.

3. Bullfights (**las corridas de toros**) are prohibited in some Spanish-American countries, but they are still popular in Mexico, Peru, Colombia, and Venezuela.

EXERCISE A

Match the words in column A with their related words in column B.

A	B
1. charro	a. jai-alai
2. Día de los Muertos	b. Lent
3. Las Posadas	c. candy
4. gaucho	d. Argentina
5. fútbol	e. Christmas
6. frontón	f. china poblana
7. sarape	g. soccer
8. Carnaval	h. Columbus Day
9. piñata	i. November 2
10. Día de la Raza	j. blanket

EXERCISE B

If the statement is true, write *Sí;* if it's false, correct it by replacing the word(s) in boldface.

1. The **incas** were the dominant Native American culture in Mexico.

2. **El Día de los Muertos** is celebrated in Mexico.

3. The cowboy of Argentina is the **charro.**

4. The gauchos wear **ponchos** as protection from the rain.

5. Panama hats are made in **Panama.**

6. **El Día de la Raza** is celebrated in Spanish America and Spain.

7. **Jai-alai** originated in the Basque country in Spain.

8. Bullfights are popular in **Mexico.**

9. *Las Posadas* occur immediately **after** Christmas.

10. A **corrida** is a Mexican blanket.

EXERCISE C

Select the word or expression that correctly completes each sentence.

1. Mexican women wear a shawl called a *(rebozo / poncho / cesta).*

2. In (Argentina / Bolivia / Uruguay) most of the inhabitants are Indians.

3. A three-walled court is used for (bullfighting / jai-alai / soccer).

4. One of the most important religious holidays in Spanish America is *(Navidad / Día de los Muertos / Carnaval).*

5. The Mexican street singers are called *(charros / gauchos / mariachis).*

6. The Mexican national holiday is (November 2 / October 12 / September 16).

7. A person of mixed Native American and European ancestry is called a *(china poblana / mestizo / sarape).*

8. On May 5, Mexicans commemorate the rebellion against (Maximilian / Bolívar / Martí).

9. *El Día de la Raza* corresponds to (All Soul's Day / Easter / Columbus Day).

10. On November 2, Spanish Americans celebrate (Christmas / All Soul's Day / Easter).

EXERCISE D

Define each of the following.

1. mestizos

2. Día de la Raza

3. cesta

4. sarape

5. frontón

6. mariachi

7. gauchos

8. piñata

9. china poblana

10. poncho

Part six

Comprehensive Testing:
Speaking, Listening, Reading, Writing

ESPAÑA

Islas Baleares

Islas Canarias

MÉXICO

REPÚBLICA
DOMINICANA
PUERTO RICO

CUBA
HONDURAS
NICARAGUA

GUATEMALA
EL SALVADOR
COSTA RICA
PANAMÁ

VENEZUELA

COLOMBIA

ECUADOR

PERÚ

BOLIVIA
PARAGUAY

CHILE

URUGUAY

ARGENTINA

1. SPEAKING: ORAL COMMUNICATION TASKS

Read the information provided for each situation and prepare a spoken response within the context of the situation. Each task prescribes a simulated conversation and requires four utterances on your part. An utterance is a spoken statement that is comprehensible and appropriate and leads to accomplishing the stated task. Assume that in each situation you are dealing with a person who speaks Spanish.

2. LISTENING COMPREHENSION

a. MULTIPLE CHOICE (ENGLISH)

For each question, you will hear some background information in English. Then you will hear a passage in Spanish *twice,* followed by a question in English. Listen carefully. After you have heard the questions, read the question and the four suggested answers in your book. Choose the best suggested answer based on the information you heard.

1. What did the teacher announce?
   1 Classes will be canceled tomorrow.
   2 A special program will be held in the auditorium.
   3 Students will be dismissed at one o'clock.
   4 All classes have been lengthened to forty minutes.

2. What does the announcer advise the people to do?
   1. Stay at home.
   2. Go to emergency shelters.
   3 Prepare for a hurricane.
   4 Shut off all electrical appliances.

3. How is your friend going to spend the afternoon?
   1 Watching television.
   2 Reading a book.
   3 Playing soccer.
   4 Copying his assignment.

4. Why is Felipe not at home?
   1 He had an accident.
   2 He went to the store.
   3 He went to the emergency room.
   4 He went to the hospital.

5. What does the doctor tell you to do?

   1 Return to school.

   2 Take some medicine.

   3 Take your temperature.

   4 Make an appointment in two days.

b. MULTIPLE CHOICE (SPANISH)

For each question, you will hear some background information in English. Then you will hear a passage in Spanish *twice,* followed by a question in Spanish. Listen carefully. After you have heard the question, read the question and the four suggested answers in your book. Choose the best suggested answer based on the information you heard.

1. ¿Qué actividad le gusta más a tu amigo?

   1 Ir al centro.

   2 Ir al cine.

   3 Practicar un deporte.

   4 Leer un libro.

2. ¿Por qué te pide perdón tu amiga?

   1 No le gustó tu regalo.

   2 Salió con otros amigos.

   3 Volvió a casa muy tarde.

   4 No devolvió tu llamada.

3. ¿Qué debes hacer ahora?

   1 Limpiar la sala.

   2 Descansar en tu cuarto.

   3 Arreglar tu cuarto.

   4 Pasar la aspiradora.

4. ¿Qué anuncian en el aeropuerto?

   1 Que el avión tiene un problema mecánico.

   2 Que los pasajeros deben bajarse del avión ahora.

   3 Que los pasajeros deben volver al hotel.

   4 Que el avión no puede salir porque hace mal tiempo.

5. ¿Por qué no quiere ver esa película tu amigo?

   1 Tiene mucha violencia.

2 Prefiere los deportes.

3 No tiene ningún dinero.

4 Es una película corta.

c. MULTIPLE CHOICE (VISUAL)

For each question, you will hear some background information in English. Then you will hear a passage in Spanish *twice*, followed by a question in English. Listen carefully. After you have heard the question, read the question and look at the four pictures in your book. Based on the information you heard, choose the picture that best answers the question.

1. Who is Manuel?

1   2   3   4

2. Where does Gabriela want to go?

1   2   3   4

3. What hobby does he prefer?

1   2   3   4

4. What food does your friend like?

| 1 | 2 | 3 | 4 |

5. What is your friend planning to do during her vacation?

| 1 | 2 | 3 | 4 |

6. Where does your friend's mother work?

| 1 | 2 | 3 | 4 |

7. What activity does the doctor restrict?

| 1 | 2 | 3 | 4 |

8. What did your friend lose?

| 1 | 2 | 3 | 4 |

9. What piece of furniture are you going to buy?

| 1 | 2 | 3 | 4 |

10. What does your friend want to buy?

| 1 | 2 | 3 | 4 |

3. READING COMPREHENSION

a. MULTIPLE CHOICE (ENGLISH)

This activity consists of questions or incomplete statements in English, each based on a reading selection in Spanish. Choose the expression that best answers the question or completes the statement. Base your choice on the content of the reading selection.

1. What is Dr. Elizondo's specialty?

    1 Allergies.
    2 Hearing.
    3 Vision.
    4 Bones.

2. What is the advantage of this option?

    1 It can be done in the winter.
    2 The students receive a free horse.
    3 There is a minimal fee for the equipment that is needed.
    4 It's an intensive program.

EL GATO CON BOTAS

*El espectáculo para niños creado por
Hugo Midón se ha repuesto en cartelera y
constituye una buena opción para llevar
a los chicos en las vacaciones de invierno.*

*Paseo La Plaza, Calle Corrientes #1600, Buenos Aires
(Funciones a las 5:00 y a las 6:45)*

3. What is "El gato con botas"?

1 A shoe store.

2 A pet shop.

3 A television program.

4 A show.

CANAL 13
10:00   **Noticias de América**   *Informativo con Juan Carlos Pereira.*
11:00   **Sin Vergüenza**   *Entretenimientos, con la participación del público en la calle; con Andrea Martín.*
12:00   **Almorzando con Mirtha Carter**   *Interés general, con entrevistas a invitados.*
1:30   **El Desprecio**   *Telenovela venezolana-mexicana, con Maricarmen López y Flavio Guzmán.*
2:30   **Visiones**   *Magazine de actualidad con Belén Ríos y Sergio Méndez. Colaboran: Catalina Lago (en espectáculos) y Virginia Rivera (en deportes).*

4. On which program does the host interview guests?

1 Noticias de América.

3 Visiones.

4 Sin Vergüenza.

2 Almorzando con Mirtha Carter.

$

LA TASA PARA GANAR ESTÁ EN EL PLAZO FIJO DEL

BANCO COMERCIAL DE VENEZUELA

Obtenga desde un **47%** hasta un **55%** de interés colocando su dinero a 30 días. Con una inversión mínima de 250 mil bolívares adquiera su certificado, *¡su más firme aliado!*

$

5. This advertisement offers you help in

1 buying stocks.

2 investing your money.

3 avoiding high interest rates.

4 investing in industry.

b. MULTIPLE CHOICE (SPANISH)

This activity consists of questions or incomplete statements in Spanish, each based on a reading selection in Spanish. Choose the expression that best answers the question or completes the statement. Base your choice on the content of the reading selection.

VACACIONES DIFERENTES EN EL CAMPAMENTO VACACIONAL RANITA

Para niños entre 8 y 12 años. Situado en Sanare, Falcón, con una extensión de 400 hectáreas, donde sus niños podrán disfrutar el contacto directo con la Naturaleza. Actividades diversas, tales como:

- paseos a caballo
- elaboración de quesos
- cuidado de animales
- paseos diurnos y nocturnos
- juegos de campo
- gimkana
- deportes varios y mucho más

PRIMER GRUPO: del 25 de junio al 10 de julio
SEGUNDO GRUPO: del 15 de julio al 30 de agosto

Para más información, llame a los teléfonos:
08.27.62.14   08.27.62.37   08.27.68.93

1. ¿Qué es lo atractivo de este campamento?

1 Ofrece una variedad de actividades.

2 Los niños puenden vivir en casa mientras asisten al campamento.

3 Es un programa largo y entretenido.

4 Los niños no van a estar al aire libre, en compañía de los animales.

¡OFERTA POR TIEMPO LIMITADO!
¿Eres ambicioso?

Nosotros te damos el mejor entrenamiento en ventas y la mejor comisión. No importa tu experiencia. Tenemos el mejor producto y el sistema de ventas más seguro.
Llama al siguiente número para solicitar una entrevista.
09.86.86.51

2. ¿Qué ofrece este anuncio?

1 Un trabajo.

2 Una venta.

3 Productos buenos.

4 Sistemas modernos.

CONOCE A GENTE INTERESANTE EN

LA LÍNEA LOCA

CHISMES   DEPORTES   FARÁNDULA   ROMANCE

¡Ahora puedes hablar con gente divertida e interesante en nuestra línea de conversación continua! Llama a cualquier hora a los teléfonos:

31.01.60.09   31.01.67.10   31.01.60.50

(Una llamada a LA LÍNEA LOCA cuesta lo mismo que una llamada a los Estados Unidos, aproximadamente 126 bolívares por minuto. La tarifa está sujeta a cambios.)

3. Esta información les interesa a personas que quieren

1 visitar a los Estados Unidos.

2 hacer amistades por teléfono.

3 conversar en otro idioma.

4 recibir llamadas de otros países.

TALLER MUSICAL VACACIONAL
Para niños de 6 a 12 años

¡FABULOSA INICIACIÓN MUSICAL en un ambiente ameno y divertido! Tres semanas, desde el lunes 19 de julio.

**Caurimare, Calle B-2, No. 97
Teléfono: 04.86.62.34**

4. Este anuncio es para los niños que

1 cantan bien.

2 tocan instrumentos musicales.

3 quieren aprender música.

4 participan en una orquesta.

GRAN VENTA ESPECIAL

*FALDAS desde **$30**   *BLAZERS desde **$95**
*CAMISAS desde **$45**   *TRAJES DE SEDA desde **$150**

y durante esta semana. . . ¡REGALOS!
1 FALDA Y 1 CAMISA (ó 1 BLAZER), con compras de **$200** o más.

TIENDA MARÍA LISA
PASEO ALCORTA
Local 2046, Segundo Nivel
Salguero 3172, Distrito Federal
Se Aceptan Tarjetas de Crédito

5. ¿Qué debe hacer el cliente para recibir un regalo?

1 Recomendar a otros clientes.

2 Usar su tarjeta de crédito.

3 Presentar este anuncio en la tienda.

4 Gastar cierta cantidad de dinero.

4. WRITING

a. NOTES

Write short notes in Spanish as directed below. Each note must consist of at least 12 words.

1. You're going out tonight and you want your Spanish-speaking friend to accompany you. Write your friend a short note saying where you are going and inviting him/her to go with you.

2. Your social studies class is going on a cultural trip. Write a note to your Spanish teacher explaining why you are not going to attend class.

3. You're at home waiting for your grandparents to arrive. You have to leave for a short while. Write a note telling them why you had to leave.

4 Your friend from Venezuela sent you some photographs. Write a note to thank your friend for the photographs.

5 You want to invite a classmate to a school dance, but can't get up the nerve to ask in person. Write a note inviting him/her to go with you.

b. LISTS

Write lists in Spanish as directed below. Each list must contain four items. No credit will be given for one-word items that are proper names.

1. You're telling a friend about the types of television programs you like to watch. Write a list of four types of programs you enjoy watching.

2. You're putting together a vegetable garden. Write a list of four vegetables you plan to grow.

3. You're going on a ski trip this weekend. Write a list of four articles of clothing you will need.

4. You and a friend are talking about the chores you have to do at home. Write a list of four chores you usually do.

5. You're attending a seminar during career day. Write a list of four careers that interest you.

Appendix

[1] REGULAR VERBS

INFINITIVE

cantar	beber	abrir

PRESENT

canto	bebo	abro
cantas	bebes	abres
canta	bebe	abre
cantamos	bebemos	abrimos
cantáis	bebéis	abrís
cantan	beben	abren

PRETERITE

canté	bebí	abrí
cantaste	bebiste	abriste
cantó	bebió	abrió
cantamos	bebimos	abrimos
cantasteis	bebisteis	abristeis
cantaron	bebieron	abrieron

IMPERFECT

cantaba	bebía	abría
cantabas	bebías	abrías
cantabas	bebía	abría
cantábamos	bebíamos	abríamos
cantabais	bebíais	abríais
cantaban	bebían	abríais

FUTURE

cantaré	beberé	abriré
cantarás	beberás	abrirás
cantará	beberá	abrirá
cantaremos	beberemos	abrire-
mos		
cantaréis	beberéis	abriréis
cantarán	beberán	abrirán

COMMANDS

canta no cant**es** } (tú)	beb**e** no beb**as** } (tú)	abre no abr**as** } (tú)
cant**e** (Ud.)	beb**a** (Ud.)	abr**a** (Ud.)
cant**emos** (nosotros)	beb**amos** (nosotros)	abr**amos** (nosotros)
cant**ad** no cant**éis** } (vosotros)	beb**ed** no beb**áis** } (vosotros)	abr**id** no abr**áis** } (vosotros)
cant**en** (Uds.)	beb**an** (Uds.)	abr**an** (Uds.)

[2] STEM-CHANGING VERBS

a. –ar Verbs

INFINITIVE	pens**ar** (**e** to **ie**)	mostr**ar** (**o** to **ue**)	jug**ar** (**u** to **ue**)
PRESENT	**pienso** **piensas** **piensa** pensamos pensáis **piensan**	**muestro** **muestras** **muestra** mostramos mostráis **muestran**	**juego** **juegas** **juega** jugamos jugáis **juegan**

b. –er Verbs

INFINITIVE	perd**er** (**e** to **ie**)	volv**er** (**o** to **ue**)	
PRESENT	**pierdo** **pierdes** **pierde** perdemos perdéis **pierden**	**vuelvo** **vuelves** **vuelve** volvemos volvéis **vuelven**	

c. –ir Verbs

INFINITIVE	ped**ir** (**e** to **i**, **i**)	sent**ir** (**e** to **ie**, **i**)	dorm**ir** (**o** to **ue**, **u**)
PRESENT	**pido** **pides** **pide** pedimos pedís **piden**	**siento** **sientes** **siente** sentimos sentís **sienten**	**duermo** **duermes** **duerme** dormimos dormís **duermen**

INFINITIVE	pedir (e to i, i)	sentir (e to ie, i)	dormir (o to ue, u)
PRETERITE	pedí pediste **pidió** pedimos pedisteis **pidieron**	sentí sentiste **sintió** sentimos sentisteis **sintieron**	dormí dormiste **durmió** dormimos dormisteis **durmieron**
COMMANDS	**pide** no **pidas** } (tú) **pida** (Ud.) **pidamos** (nosotros) pedid no **pidáis** } (vosotros) **pidan** (Uds.)	**siente** no **sientas** } (tú) **sienta** (Ud.) **sintamos** (nosotros) sentid no **sintáis** } (vosotros) **sientan** (Uds.)	**duerme** no **duermas** } (tú) **duerma** (Ud.) **durmamos** (nosotros) dormid } (vosotros) no **durmáis** **duerman** (Uds.)

[3] VERBS WITH SPELLING CHANGES

a. -cer and **-cir** Verbs

INFINITIVE	ofrecer (c to zc)	conducir (c to zc)
PRESENT	**ofrezco** ofreces ofrece ofrecemos ofrecéis ofrecen	**conduzco** conduces conduce conducimos conducís conducen
COMMANDS	ofrece no **ofrezcas** } (tú) **ofrezca** (Ud.) **ofrezcamos** (nosotros) ofreced no **ofrezcáis** } (vosotros) **ofrezcan** (Uds.)	conduce no **conduzcas** } (tú) **conduzca** (Ud.) **conduzcamos** (nosotros) conducid no **conduzcáis** } (vosotros) **conduzcan** (Uds.)

b. Verbs That Change **i** to **y** in the Preterite

INFINITIVE	le**er**	ca**er**	o**ír**	inclu**ir**
PRETERITE	leí	caí	oí	incluí
	leíste	caíste	oíste	incluíste
	leyó	**cayó**	**oyó**	**incluyó**
	leímos	caímos	oímos	incluímos
	leísteis	caísteis	oísteis	incluísteis
	leyeron	**cayeron**	**oyeron**	**incluyeron**

[4] VERBS WITH IRREGULAR FORMS

NOTE: Irregular forms are printed in bold type.

INFINITIVE	PRESENT	COMMAND		PRETERITE	IMPERFECT	FUTURE
caer *to fall*	**caigo**	cae / no **caigas** } (tú)		caí	caía	caeré
	caes			caíste	caías	caerás
	cae	**caiga** (Ud.)		**cayó**	caía	caerá
	caemos	**caigamos** (nosotros)		caímos	caíamos	caeremos
	caéis	caed / no **caigáis** } (vosotros)		caísteis	caíais	caeréis
	caen	**caigan** (Uds.)		**cayeron**	caían	caerán
dar *to give*	**doy**	da / no des } (tú)		**di**	daba	daré
	das			**diste**	dabas	darás
	da	**dé** (Ud.)		**dio**	daba	dará
	damos	demos (nosotros)		**dimos**	dábamos	daremos
	dais	dad / no deis } (vosotros)		**disteis**	dabais	daréis
	dan	**den** (Uds.)		**dieron**	daban	darán
decir *to say*	**digo**	**di** / no **digas** } (tú)		**dije**	decía	**diré**
	dices			**dijiste**	decías	**dirás**
	dice	**diga** (Ud.)		**dijo**	decía	**dirá**
	decimos	**digamos** (nosotros)		**dijimos**	decíamos	**diremos**
	decís	decid / no **digáis** } (vosotros)		**dijisteis**	decíais	**diréis**
	dicen	**digan** (Uds.)		**dijeron**	decían	**dirán**

INFINITIVE	PRESENT	COMMAND	PRETERITE	IMPERFECT	FUTURE
estar *to be*	estoy	**está** ⎫ (tú) no **estés** ⎭ **esté** (Ud.) estemos (nosotros) estad ⎫ (vosotros) no **estéis** ⎭ **estén** (Uds.)	**estuve**	estaba	estaré
	estás		**estuviste**	estabas	estarás
	está		**estuvo**	estaba	estará
	estamos		**estuvimos**	estábamos	estaremos
	estáis		**estuvisteis**	estabais	estaréis
	están		**estuvieron**	estaban	estarán
hacer *to do,* *to make*	**hago**	**haz** ⎫ (tú) no **hagas** ⎭ **haga** (Ud.) **hagamos** (nosotros) haced ⎫ (vosotros) no **hagáis** ⎭ **hagan** (Uds.)	**hice**	hacía	**haré**
	haces		**hiciste**	hacías	**harás**
	hace		**hizo**	hacía	**hará**
	hacemos		**hicimos**	hacíamos	**haremos**
	hacéis		**hicisteis**	hacíais	**haréis**
	hacen		**hicieron**	hacían	**harán**
ir *to go*	**voy**	**ve** ⎫ (tú) no **vayas** ⎭ **vaya** (Ud.) **vayamos** (nosotros) id ⎫ (vosotros) no **vayáis** ⎭ **vayan** (Uds.)	**fui**	**iba**	iré
	vas		**fuiste**	**ibas**	irás
	va		**fue**	**iba**	irá
	vamos		**fuimos**	**íbamos**	iremos
	vais		**fuisteis**	**ibais**	iréis
	van		**fueron**	**iban**	irán
oír *to hear*	**oigo**	**oye** ⎫ (tú) no **oigas** ⎭ **oiga** (Ud.) **oigamos** (nosotros) oid ⎫ (vosotros) no **oigáis** ⎭ **oigan** (Uds.)	**oí**	oía	oiré
	oyes		**oíste**	oías	oirás
	oye		**oyó**	oía	oirá
	oímos		**oímos**	oíamos	oiremos
	oís		**oísteis**	oíais	oiréis
	oyen		**oyeron**	oían	oirán
poner *to put*	**pongo**	**pon** ⎫ (tú) no **pongas** ⎭ **ponga** (Ud.) **pongamos** (nosotros) poned ⎫ (vosotros) no **pongáis** ⎭	**puse**	ponía	**pondré**
	pones		**pusiste**	ponías	**pondrás**
	pone		**puso**	ponía	**pondrá**
	ponemos		**pusimos**	poníamos	**pondremos**
	ponéis		**pusisteis**	poníais	**pondréis**
	ponen		**pusieron**	ponían	**pondrán**

INFINITIVE	PRESENT	COMMAND	PRETERITE	IMPERFECT	FUTURE
saber *to know*	**sé** sabes sabe sabemos sabéis saben	sabe (tu) **sepa** (Ud.) **sepamos** (nosotros) sabed (vosotros) **sepan** (Uds.)	**supe** **supiste** **supo** **supimos** **supisteis** **supieron**	sabía sabías sabía sabíamos sabíais sabían	**sabré** **sabrás** **sabrá** **sabremos** **sabréis** **sabrán**
salir *to go out*	**salgo** sales sale salimos salís salen	**sal** no **salgas** } (tú) **salga** (Ud.) **salgamos** (nosotros) salid no **salgáis** } (vosotros) **salgan** (Uds.)	salí saliste salió salimos salisteis salieron	salía salías salía salíamos salíais salían	**saldré** **saldrás** **saldrá** **saldremos** **saldréis** **saldrán**
ser *to be*	**soy** **eres** **es** **somos** **sois** **son**	**sé** no seas } (tú) sea (Ud.) seamos (nosotros) sed no seáis } (vosotros) sean (Uds.)	**fui** **fuiste** **fue** **fuimos** **fuisteis** **fueron**	**era** **eras** **era** **éramos** **erais** **eran**	seré serás será seremos seréis serán
tener *to know* *(how to)*	**tengo** **tienes** **tiene** tenemos tenéis tienen	**ten** no **tengas** } (tú) **tenga** (Ud.) **tengamos** (nosotros) tened no **tengáis** } (vosotros) **tengan** (Uds.)	**tuve** **tuviste** **tuvo** **tuvimos** **tuvisteis** **tuvieron**	tenía tenías tenía teníamos teníais tenían	**tendré** **tendrás** **tendrá** **tendremos** **tendréis** **tendrán**
traer *to bring*	**traigo** traes trae traemos traéis traen	trae no **traigas** } (tú) **traiga** (Ud.) **traigamos** (nosotros) traed no **traigáis** } (vosotros) **traigan** (Uds.)	**traje** **trajiste** **trajo** **trajimos** **trajisteis** **trajeron**	traía traías traía traíamos traíais traían	traeré traerás traerá traeremos traeréis traerán

INFINITIVE	PRESENT	COMMAND	PRETERITE	IMPERFECT	FUTURE
venir *to come*	**vengo**	**ven** no **vengas** } (tú)	**vine**	venía	**vendré**
	vienes		**viniste**	venías	**vendrás**
	vienes	**venga** (Ud.)	**vino**	venía	**vendrá**
	venimos	**vengamos** (nosotros)	**vinimos**	veníamos	**vendremos**
	venís	venid no **vengáis** } (vosotros)	**vinisteis**	veníais	**vendréis**
	vienen	**vengan** (Uds.)	**vinieron**	venían	**vendrán**
ver *to see*	**veo**	ve no veas } (tú)	**vi**	**veía**	veré
	ves		**viste**	**veías**	verás
	ve	**vea** (Ud.)	**vio**	**veía**	verá
	vemos	**veamos** (nosotros)	**vimos**	**veíamos**	veremos
	veis	ved no veáis } (vosotros)	**visteis**	**veíais**	veréis
	ven	**vean** (Uds.)	**vieron**	**veían**	verán

[5] PUNCTUATION

Spanish punctuation, though similar to English, has the following major differences:

(a) Questions are preceded by an additional question mark, in inverted form (¿).

¿Quién es?   *Who is it?*

(b) Exclamatory sentences are preceded by an additional exclamation point, in inverted form.

¡Qué día!   *What a day!*

(c) The comma is not used before a conjunction (**y, e, o, u,** or **ni**) in a series.

Hay clases el lunes, el martes   *There are classes on Monday,*
y el miércoles.   *Tuesday, and Wednesday.*

(d) Cardinal numbers are set off by periods, and decimal numbers by commas.

3,5 (tres coma cinco)   *3.5 (three point five)*
1.200 (mil doscientos)   *1,200 (twelve hundred* OR
                                one thousand two hundred)

(e) Final quotation marks precede commas and periods; however, if the quotation marks enclose a complete statement, they follow the period.

Cervantes escribió	*Cervantes wrote*
«Don Quijote».	*"Don Quijote."*
«Escribe pronto.» Con esas	*"Write to me soon." With those words*
palabras terminé mi carta.	*I ended my letter.*

[6] SYLLABICATION

Spanish words are divided at the end of a line according to units of sound or syllables.

(a) Syllables generally begin with a consonant and end with a vowel. The division is made before the consonant.

te-**ner**   di-**ne-ro**   a-**me-ri-ca-no**   re-**fe**-rir

(b) **Ch, ll,** and **rr** are never divided.

pe-**rr**o   ha-**ll**a-do   di-**ch**o

(c) If two or more consonants are combined, the division is made before the last consonant, except in the combinations **bl, br, cl, cr, dr, fl, fr, gl, gr, pl, pr,** and **tr**.

trans-**por**-te   des-**c**u-bier-to   con-**t**i-nuar   al-**b**er-ca

• BUT

ha-**bl**ar   a-**br**ir   des-**cr**i-bir   a-**pr**en-der

(d) Compound words, including words with prefixes and suffixes, may be divided by components or by syllables.

sur-a-me-ri-ca-no   OR   su-ra-me-ri-ca-no
mal-es-tar   OR   **ma**-les-tar

[7] STRESS

In Spanish, word stress follows three general rules.

(a) Words ending in a vowel, **n,** or **s** are stressed on the next-to-the-last syllable.

escu**e**la   de**sas**tre   **jo**ven   se**ño**res

(b) Words ending in a consonant that is not **n** or **s** are stressed on the last syllable.

compren**der**   ala**bar**   reci**bir**   se**ñor**

(c) All exceptions to the above rules have an accent mark on the stressed syllable.

sábado   **jó**venes   A**dán**   **Cé**sar   fran**cés**

Spanish-English Vocabulary

The Spanish-English Vocabulary is intended to be complete for the context of this book.

Nouns are listed in the singular. Regular feminine forms of nouns are indicated by **(-a)** or the ending that replaces the masculine ending: **abogado(-a)** or **alcalde (-esa)**. Irregular noun plurals are given in full: **voz** *f.* voice; (*pl.* **voces**). Regular feminine forms of adjectives are indicated by **-a**.

ABBREVIATIONS

adj.	adjective	*m.*	masculine
f.	feminine	*m./f.*	masculine or feminine
inf.	infinitive	*pl.*	plural
irr.	irregular	*sing.*	singular

abajo below, downstairs
abierto open
abogado(-a) lawyer
abrigo *m.* overcoat
abrir to open
abuela *f.* grandmother
abuelo *m.* grandfather
aburrido bored; boring
acá here
acabar to end; **acabar de** to have just
acompañar to accompany
acostarse (ue) to go to bed
actor *m.* actor
actriz *f.* actress
acuerdo *m.* agreement; **estar de acuerdo** to agree
además besides; in addition
adiós good-bye
admirar to admire
¿adónde? where to?
aeropuerto *m.* airport
afeitar: afeitarse to shave
aficionado(-a) fan, devotee
agrio, -a sour

agua *f.* water
ahí there
ahora now
ahorrar to save
aire *m.* air; **al aire libre** outdoors, in the open
ajedrez *m.* chess
alcalde(-esa) mayor
alcoba *f.* bedroom
alemán, (*f.* alemana) German
alfombra *f.* rug, carpet
algo something
algodón *m.* cotton
algún some
alguno someone
alimento *m.* food
almacén *m.* department store
almohada *f.* pillow
almorzar (ue) to have (eat) lunch
alquilar to rent
alto, -a tall; high
alumno(-a) student, pupil
amable nice
ancho, -a wide

andar *(irr.)* to walk, go
anillo *m.* ring
año *m.* year
anoche last night
ansioso, -a anxious
anteayer the day before yesterday
anteojos *m. pl.* eyeglasses
antes de before
antiguo old; ancient
antipático unpleasant, disagreeable
anuncio *m.* announcement
apagar: apagarse to extinguish, put out
aparecer (zc) to appear
apellido *m.* family name, last name
aplicado, -a diligent, studious
aprender to learn
aquel, -ella that; (*pl.* **aquellos, -ellas** those)
aquí here
árbitro *m.* referee, umpire
árbol *m.* tree
arena *f.* sand

arete *m.* tree
armario *m.* closet
arreglar to arrange; to fix
arriba above, upstairs
arroz *m.* rice
ascensor *m.* elevator
asiento *m.* seat; **tomar asiento** to sit down
asignatura *f.* class, subject
asistir (a) to attend
aspiradora *f.* vacuum cleaner; **pasar la aspadora** to vacuum
atracción *f.* (amusement) ride
aula *f.* (el aula) classroom
ausente absent
autobús *m.* bus
automóvil (auto) *m.* automobile, car
avión *m.* airplane; **en avión** by plane
ayer yesterday
ayudar to help
azúcar *m. / f.* sugar

bailar to dance
baile *m.* dance
bajar to go down; to descend; to lower
bajo, -a low; short
balcón *m.* balcony
banco *m.* bank; bench
bandera *f.* flag
bañar: bañarse to take a bath, bathe
barato, -a cheap, inexpensive
barbero(-a) barber
barco *m.* boat
barrio *m.* neighborhood
basura *f.* garbage
batido, -a shaken; **leche**

batida milkshake
baúl *m.* trunk
beber to drink
bebida *f.* drink; beverage
beca *f.* scholarship
biblioteca *f.* library
bien well
biftec *m.* beefsteak
billete *m.* ticket
billetera *f.* wallet
boca *f.* mouth
boda *f.* wedding
bodega *f.* grocery store
boleto *m.* ticket
boliche *m.* bowling
bolígrafo *m.* ballpoint pen
bolsa *f.* bag, purse
bombero *m.* fireman
bondad *f.* kindness; **tener la bondad de** please…
bonito, -a pretty
borrador *m.* (chalkboard) eraser
borrar to erase
bosque *m.* forest, woods
brazo *m.* arm
broma *f.* joke
bueno, -a good
bufanda *f.* scarf
buscar (qu) to look for
butaca *f.* armchair

¿cuál? (*pl.* **¿cuáles?**) which?, what?
¿cuánto, -a? how much?; *pl.* **¿cuántos, -as?** how many?
caballo *m.* horse
cabeza *f.* head
cacto *m.* cactus
cada each, every
cadena *f.* chain
caer (*irr.*) to fall; **caerse** to

fall down
caja *f.* box; cashier
calcetín *m.* sock
caliente hot
calle *f.* street
calor *m.* heat; **hace calor** it is hot
cama *f.* bed; **guardar cama** to stay in bed
cámara *f.* camera
camarero(-a) waiter
cambiar to change
caminar to walk
camino *m.* road, path
camión *m.* truck
camiseta *f.* t-shirt
campana *f.* bell
campeón (*f.* **campeona**) champion
campesino(-a) *m.* farmer
campo *m.* country, countryside
canción *f.* song
cansado, -a tired
cantante *m. / f.* singer
cantar to sing
cara *f.* face
cárcel *f.* prison
cariñoso, -a loving, affectionate
carne *f.* meat
carnicería *f.* butcher shop
carnicero(-a) butcher
caro, -a expensive; dear
carrera *f.* career; race
carro *m.* car
carrusel *m.* carrousel
carta *f.* letter
cartel *m.* poster
cartera *f.* wallet, purse
caso *m.* case; **hacer caso de** to pay attention to, to heed

castañuelas *f. pl.* castanets

catedral *f.* cathedral

celebrar to celebrate

celoso, -a jealous

cena *f.* dinner; supper

cenar to eat supper

centro *m.* center; downtown; **centro comercial** mall

cepillar to brush; **cepillarse** to brush oneself

cerca de near; close to

cerdo *m.* pork

cereza *f.* cherry

cerrado, -a closed

cerrar (ie) to close

cesar (de) to stop

chaqueta *f.* jacket

chofer (also **chófer**) *m. / f.* driver

chuleta *f.* chop; **chuleta de cerdo** pork chop

cielo *m.* sky

cien (ciento) one hundred

científico,(-a) scientist

cine *m.* movie theater, movies

cinta *f.* tape

cinturón *m.* belt

cita *f.* appointment, date

ciudad *f.* city

ciudadano(-a) *f.* citizen

claro, -a light (color)

clase *f.* class; kind, type

clavel *m.* carnation

clima *m.* climate

coche *m.* car

cocido, -a cooked; **bien cocido** well cooked (done)

cocina *f.* kitchen

cocinar to cook

cocinero(-a) cook

cola *f.* line; tail

colegio *m.* school

colocar to place, to put

comedor *m.* dining room

comenzar (ie) to begin; to start

comer to eat

comerciante *m. / f.* merchant, businessperson

cómico, -a comical, funny

comida *f.* food; meal

como as, like; **¿cómo?** how?, what?

cómoda *f.* bureau, dresser

cómodo, -a comfortable

compañero(-a) friend, pal

compartir to share

competencia *f.* competition

compra *f.* purchase; **ir de compras** to go shopping

comprar to buy

concurso *m.* contest

conducir (zc) to drive; to lead

confesar (ie) to confess

conocer (zc) to know (someone), to be familiar with (something)

consejero(-a) adviser

consentido, -a pampered, spoiled

construir (y) to build

contador(-ora) accountant

contar (ue) to count; to tell

contento, -a happy, content

contestar to answer

contra against

coro *m.* chorus

correo *m.* mail; post office

correr to run

correspondencia *f.* correspondence; **amigo por corres-pondencia** pen pal

cortar to cut

corte *f.* court, tribunal

cortés polite

cortina *f.* curtain

corto, -a short

cosa *f.* thing

coser to sew

costar (ue) to cost

creer (y) to believe; to think

criado(-a) servant

crudo, -a raw

cuaderno *m.* notebook

cuadro *m.* painting, picture

cuando when; **de vez en cuando** from time to time, sometimes; **¿cuándo?** when?

cuarto *m.* room; quarter, fourth; **una cuarta parte de** a quarter of, a fourth of

cubeta *f.* pail

cubrir to cover

cuchara *f.* spoon

cucharita *f.* teaspoon

dalia *f.* dahlia

dama *f.* lady; **jugar a las damas** to play checkers

dar (*irr.*) to give; **darse la mano** to shake hands

debajo de beneath, under

deber to owe; should, ought to

débil weak

decidir to decide
decir (*irr.*) to say; to tell
decorar to decorate
dedo *m.* finger, toe
defender (ie) to defend
dejar to leave; to allow;
  dejar de to fail to; to
  stop; to neglect to
delante de in front of
delgado thin, skinny
demasiado too much;
  excessively; too
dentro de within
dependiente(-a)
  salesperson
deporte *m.* sport
deportista *m. / f.* athlete
derecha *f.* right; **a la**
  derecha to the right
derretido, -a melted
desaparecer (zc) to
  disappear
desayunarse to have (eat)
  breakfast
descansar to rest
describir to describe
descubrir to discover
desear to wish; to want
desilusionado, -a
  disappointed
despacio slowly
despertador *m.* alarm
  clock
despertar (ie) to wake
  (someone) up;
  despertarse to wake up
después de after
desván *m.* attic
detrás de behind
devolver (ue) to return;
  to give back
día *m.* day
dibujar to draw

diccionario *m.* dictionary
dictado *m.* dictation
diente *m.* tooth
dificultad *f.* difficulty
dinero *m.* money
dirección f. address
disco *m.* record
disculpa *f.* excuse, apology;
  pedir disculpa to ask
  for forgiveness, apologize
diseño *m.* design
distancia *f.* distance; **larga**
  distancia long distance
distribuir (y) to distribute
diversión *f.* amusement
divertido, -a fun; funny,
  amusing
divertir (ie) to amuse;
  divertirse (ie) to enjoy
  oneself, have fun
dividir to divide
doler (ue) to be painful,
  to cause sorrow
dolor *m.* ache, pain
domingo *m.* Sunday
donde where; **¿dónde?**
  where?
dormir (ue) to sleep;
  dormirse to fall asleep
dormitorio *m.* bedroom
dueño(-a) owner, boss
dulce *m.* sweet, candy
durante during
durar to last, endure
duro, -a hard

echar to throw; to throw
  out, dismiss; **echar de**
  menos to miss
  (someone or something)
edad *f.* age
edificio *m.* building
egoísta *m. / f.* selfish per-

son; *adj.* selfish
emocionante exciting
empezar (ie) to begin,
  start
encantar to like a lot,
  love; **me encanta** I like
  it a lot, I love it
encontrar (ue) to find; to
  meet
enero January
enfermedad *f.* sickness,
  illness
enfermero(-a) nurse
enfermería *f.* infirmary
enfermo, -a sick, ill
enfrente opposite, facing
ensalada *f.* salad
enseñanza *f.* teaching
enseñar to teach
entender (ie) to understand
entonces then
entrada *f.* entrance; ticket
entrar (en) to enter
entre between, among
entrenador(-ora) *m.*
  coach, trainer
entrevista *f.* interview
equipaje *m.* baggage
equipo *m.* team
escalera *f.* staircase, stairs
esconder to hide
escribir to write
escritor(-ora) writer
escritorio *m.* desk
escuchar to listen (to)
escuela *f.* school
ese, -a that; *pl.* **esos, -as**
  those
espalda *f.* back (body)
esperar to wait for; to hope
esposa *f.* wife
esposo *m.* husband
esquiar to ski

esquina *f.* corner
estación *f.* season; (train) station
estadio *m.* stadium
estado *m.* state
estampilla *f.* stamp
estante *m.* shelf
estar to be
este *m.* east
este, -a this; (*pl.* **estos, -as** these)
esto this
estómago *m.* stomach
estrecho, -a narrow
estrella *f.* star
estreno *m.* opening (of a performance), show
etiqueta *f.* label, tag
excursión *f.* trip
explicar to explain
extranjero *m.* foreign; **al extranjero, en el extranjero** abroad

fábrica *f.* factory
falda *f.* skirt
falta *f.* mistake, error
faltar to lack, need
fanático(-a) fan
farmacéutico(-a) pharmacist
farmacia *f.* drugstore, pharmacy
fascinar to fascinate
favor *m.* favor; **por favor** please
fecha *f.* date *(month, day, and year)*
feliz happy
feroz ferocious
ferrocarril *m.* railroad
fiesta *f.* party; holiday
fijarse (en) to pay attention, to note
fila *f.* row
flan *m.* custard
flor *f.* flower
florería *f.* flowershop
fotografía *f.* photograph; **sacar fotografías** to take pictures
frecuencia *f.* frequency; **con frecuencia** frequently
fresa *f.* strawberry
frijol *m.* bean
frío *m.* cold; **frío, -a** *(adj.)* cold
frutería *f.* fruit store
fumar to smoke
función *f.* performance, show
funcionar to function; to work

galleta *f.* cracker
gallo *m.* rooster
gana *f.* desire, will; **tener ganas de (cantar).** to feel like (singing)
ganar to win, earn; **ganarse la vida** to earn a living
garaje *m.* garage
garganta *f.* throat
gaseosa *f.* soda pop
gastar to spend; **gastar dinero** to spend money
gasto *m.* expense
gato(-a) cat
gemelos *m. pl.* twins
geranio *m.* geranium
gerente *m. / f.* manager
globo *m.* balloon
goma *f.* (pencil or ink) eraser
gozar (de) to enjoy

grabadora *f.* recorder
gracias *f. pl.* thanks; thank you
grado *m.* degree, grade
graduarse (ú) to graduate
gran great
grande large, big
granja *f.* farm
gritar to shout
grueso, -a thick
guante *m.* glove
guapo handsome
guayaba *f.* guava
guerra *f.* war
guía *m.* guide
gustar to please
gusto *m.* pleasure; **mucho gusto** my pleasure

habitante *m. / f.* inhabitant
hablar to speak
hacer to do; to make
hacha *f.* (**el hacha**) ax
hacia toward
hallar to find
hambre *f.* hunger; **tener hambre** to be hungry
hasta until; as far as; up to
helado *m.* ice cream
hermana *f.* sister
hermano *m.* brother
hielo *m.* ice
hierba *f.* grass
hija *f.* daughter
hijo *m.* son
historia *f.* history; story
historietas *f. pl.* comics book, comic strip
hoja *f.* leaf
hombre *m.* man
hora *f.* hour; **¿a qué hora?** at what time?
horario *m.* schedule

horno *m.* oven
hoy today
huevo *m.* egg

ida y vuelta *f.* round trip
iglesia *f.* church
importar to matter
incluir (y) to include
independiente independent
ingeniero(-a) engineer
inglés English
insistir (en) to insist on
invierno *m.* winter
invitado(-a) guest
ir to go; **irse** to go away
isla *f.* island

jabón *m.* soap
jalea *f.* jelly
jamón *m.* ham
japonés (*f.* **japonesa**) Japanese
jardín *m.* garden
jaula *f.* cage
jefatura *f.* headquarters
jefe(-a) chief, boss
joven *m. / f.* young person
juego *m.* game
jueves *m.* Thursday
jugada *f.* play
jugador(-a) player
jugar (ue) to play
jugo *m.* juice
juguete *m.* toy
junto together
justo, -a fair, just
juventud *f.* youth

labio *m.* lip
ladrar to bark
ladrido *m.* bark
ladrillo *m.* brick

lago *m.* lake
lana *f.* wool
lápiz *m.* pencil; (*pl.* **lápices**)
largo, -a long
lavandería *f.* laundry
lavar to wash; **lavarse** to wash (oneself)
lección *f.* lesson
leche *f.* milk
lechuga *f.* lettuce
leer (y) to read
legumbre *f.* vegetable
lejos (de) far (from)
lengua *f.* tongue; language
lento, -a slow
levantar to lift; **levantarse** to get up
libra *f.* pound
librería *f.* bookstore
libro *m.* book
limón *m.* lemon
limpiar to clean
limpio, -a clean
listo, -a ready; **estar listo** to be ready; **ser listo** to be clever, smart
llamada *f.* call; hacer **una llamada** to make a call
llamar to call; **llamarse** to be named, be called
llave *f.* key
llegada *f.* arrival
llegar to arrive
lleno, -a full
llevar to carry; to take; to wear
llorar to cry
lluvia *f.* rain
locutor(-ora) announcer
luego then, next; afterwards; **hasta luego** until then, good-bye

lugar *m.* place
luna *f.* moon
lunes *m.* Monday

madrastra *f.* stepmother
madre *f.* mother
madrina *f.* godmother
maestro(-a) teacher
maleta *f.* suitcase
mal badly
malo, -a bad
maltratar to mistreat
manera f. way, manner; **de ninguna manera** no way
mano *f.* hand
mantequilla *f.* butter
manzana *f.* apple
mañana tomorrow
máquina *f.* machine
mar *m.* sea
marcador *m.* felt-top marker
marcar (un número) to dial (a number)
marco *m.* frame
martes *m.* Tuesday
más more; plus
máscara *f.* mask
materia *f.* subject
mayor older; oldest
medianoche *f.* midnight
medio, -a half
mediodía *m.* noon, midday
medir (i) to measure
mejor better
melancólico, -a sad
melocotón *m.* peach
memoria *f.* memory; **de memoria** by heart
menor younger; minor
menos less; except
menudo tiny, minute; **a**

menudo often, frequently
mercado *m.* market
mes *m.* month
mesa *f.* table
mesero(-era) waiter
miedo *m.* fear; **tener miedo** to be afraid, fear
miércoles *m.* Wednesday
mil one thousand
millón *m.* million
mirar to look
mismo same
mitad *f.* half
mochila *f.* knapsack
molestar to bother, to annoy
moneda *f.* coin
mono *m.* monkey
montaña *f.* mountain
montar to ride; **montar en bicicleta** to ride a bicycle
moreno, -a brunette; dark-skinned
morir (ue) to die
mostrar (ue) to show
mozo (-a) waiter
mucho, -a a lot
mueble *m.* piece of furniture; **muebles** *m. pl.* furniture
muela *f.* molar (tooth)
mujer *f.* woman
mundo *m.* world; todo **el mundo** everybody
muñeca *f.* doll

nada nothing; **de nada** you're welcome
nadar to swim
naranja *f.* orange
nariz *f.* nose; (*pl.* **narices**)
natación *f.* swimming

naturaleza *f.* nature
Navidad *f.* Christmas
negro, -a black
nevar (ie) to snow
ni neither; **ni... ni...** neither . . . nor . . ., either
nieta *f.* granddaughter
nieto *m.* grandson
nieve *f.* snow
ninguno none, not any
niña *f.* girl, child
niño *m.* boy, child
noche *f.* night; esta noche tonight
nombre *m.* name
norte *m.* north
nota *f.* grade; note
noticia *f.* news item; (*pl.* **noticias** news)
noticiero *m.* news broadcast
novia *f.* girlfriend; bride
novio *m.* boyfriend, groom
nube *f.* cloud
nuera *f.* daughter-in-law
nuevo, -a new; **de nuevo** again
nunca never

obedecer (zc) to obey
obra *f.* work, play
ocupado, -a busy
oeste *m.* west
oficio *m.* occupation
ofrecer (zc) to offer
oído *m.* ear
olmo *m.* elm tree
olvidar to forget
oración *f.* sentence
orden *f.* order
oreja *f.* ear
oro *m.* gold
orquídea *f.* orchid
oscuridad *f.* darkness

oso *m.* bear; **oso de peluche** teddy bear
otoño m. autumn, fall
otro other, another
oveja *f.* sheep

paciente *m. /f.* patient
padrastro *m.* stepfather
padre *m.* father
padrino *m.* godfather
pagar to pay (for)
página *f.* page
país *m.* country
pájaro *m.* bird
palabra *f.* word
palacio *m.* palace
pálido, -a pale
palomitas (de maíz) *f.* popcorn
pan *m.* bread
panadería *f.* bakery
panadero(-a) baker
pantalón *m.* pants, trouser
pantufla *f.* slipper
pañuelo *m.* handkerchief
papa *f.* potato; **papas fritas** French fries
papá *m.* father, dad
papel *m.* paper
para for, in order to
parada *f.* stop
paraguas *m. sing. & pl.* umbrella
parecer (zc) to seem
pared *f.* wall
pariente *m.* relative
parque *m.* park
párrafo *m.* paragraph
parte *f.* part; **en ninguna parte** nowhere
particular private
partido *m.* game, match
partir to leave; to depart

párvulo(-a) child;
escuela de párvulos
nursery school
pasado, -a past; **el año
pasado** last year; **la semana pasada** last week
pasar to pass; to spend (time)
pasatiempo *m.* hobby,
pastime
paseo *m.* stroll; outing
pasillo *m.* hall; aisle
pastel *m.* cake
pastelería *f.* pastry shop
patata *f.* potato
patín *m.* skate
patinar to skate
patio *m.* courtyard
pato *m.* duck
patria *f.* native land,
fatherland, motherland
pavo *m.* turkey; **pavo real**
peacock
pedazo *m.* piece
pedir (i) to ask for; to request; to order (food)
peinar to comb; **peinarse**
to comb one's hair
peine *m.* comb
pelear to fight
película *f.* film
pelirrojo, -a redheaded
pelo *m.* hair
pelota *f.* ball
peluquería *f.* hairdresser's,
barbershop
pensar (ie) to think; to
intend
pequeño, -a small
pera *f.* pear
perder (ie) to lose; to
waste; to miss (train, bus,
and so on)
perezoso, -a lazy

periódico *m.* newspaper
periodista *m. / f.* reporter
permiso *m.* permission;
con permiso excuse me
permitir to permit; to allow
perro *m.* dog
pesa *f.* weight; **levantar
pesas** to lift weights
pescado *m.* fish *(food)*
pescar to fish
pez *m.* fish
pie *m.* foot; **a pie** on foot;
de pie standing
piedra *f.* stone
pierna *f.* leg
pimienta *f.* pepper *(spice)*
pimiento *m.* pepper
(vegetable)
piña *f.* pineapple
pintura *f.* paint; painting
piscina *f.* swimming pool
piso *m.* floor, story (building)
pizarra *f.* chalkboard
plano *m.* map (city)
plátano *m.* plantain
plato *m.* plate; dish
playa *f.* beach
pluma *f.* pen
pobre poor
poco little
poder *(irr.)* to be able; can,
may
policía *m. / f.* police officer
pollo *m.* chicken
poner *(irr.)* to put; **poner
la mesa** to set the table;
ponerse to put on
(clothing)
porque because; **¿por
qué?** why?
por for, by, through; times;
dividido por divided by
poseer (y) to possess; own

postre *m.* dessert
practicar (qu) to practice
precio *m.* price
preferir (ie, i) to prefer
pregunta *f.* question
preguntar to ask
premio *m.* prize; award
prendedor *m.* pin
preocupado, -a worried
preparar to prepare
preparativo *m.* preparation
prestado, -a lent; **pedir
prestado** to borrow
prestar to lend; **prestar
atención** to pay attention
primavera *f.* spring
primero, a first
primo (-a) cousin
prisa *f.* hurry, haste; **de
prisa** quickly; **tener
prisa** to be in a hurry
producir (zc) to produce
programador(-ora)
programmer
prometer to promise
pronóstico *m.* forecast
pronto soon; **de pronto**
suddenly
propina *f.* tip
propio,-a own
próximo, -a next
proyecto *m.* project
prueba *f.* test, exam
pueblo *m.* town
puente *m.* bridge
puerta *f.* door, gate
pulsera *f.* bracelet
punto *m.* point; **en punto**
sharp (time)
pupitre *m.* (pupil's) desk

que who, whom, which,
that; than; **¿qué?** what?,

which?; **¡qué... !** what
a . . . !, how . . . !

quedar to be left;
quedarse to stay, remain

queja *f.* complaint

querer *(irr.)* to want; wish;
to love

querido, -a dear

queso *m.* cheese

quien who, whom;
¿quién? who?, whom?;
¿de quién? whose?

química *f.* chemistry

quitar to take away;
quitarse to take off
(clothing)

rama *f.* branch

rato *m.* while; (short)
time; **pasar un buen
rato** to have a good time

razón *f.* reason; **tener
razón** to be right

receta *f.* recipe; prescription

recibir to receive

reconocer (zc) to
recognize

recordar (ue) to remember

recreo *m.* recess

recuerdo *m.* remem-
brance; souvenir

referir (ie) to tell; to narrate

refresco *m.* refreshment;
soft drink, soda

regalo *m.* gift, present

regatear to bargain

regla *f.* ruler; rule

regresar to return

reloj *m.* watch; clock

remar to row

remedio *m.* remedy; **no
hay más remedio** it
can't be helped

reñir (i) to quarrel; to scold

reparar to repair, mend

reparto *m.* cast

repente *m.* sudden
movement; **de repente**
suddenly

repetir (i) to repeat

resfriado *m.* cold *(illness)*

resolver (ue) to solve; to
resolve

responder to answer

responsable responsible

respuesta *f.* answer

reunión *f.* meeting

revista *f.* magazine

rezar to pray

rico, -a rich

río *m.* river

rompecabezas *m. sing. &
pl.* puzzle

romper to break

ropa *f.* clothing

rosado, -a pink

rubio, -a blonde

ruido *m.* noise

sábado *m.* Saturday

saber *(irr.)* to know

sabroso, -a delicious

sacar to take out; **sacar
fotografías** to take
photos

sal *f.* salt

sala *f.* living room

salchicha *f.* sausage,
frankfurter

salida *f.* exit, departure

salir to go out; to leave;
salir bien (mal) to pass
(fail)

salón *m.* room, salon;
salón de belleza
beauty shop; **salón de**

clases classroom

salsa *f.* sauce

saltar to jump

salud *f.* health

saludar to greet

saludo *m.* greeting; regards

sandía *f.* watermelon

santo(-a) saint

sastre(-a) tailor

sed *f.* thirst; **tener sed** to
be thirsty

seda f. silk

segundo, -a second

semana *f.* week

señor *m.* mister, sir

señora *f.* madam, missus

señorita *f.* miss, young lady

sentado, -a seated

sentarse (ie) to sit down

sentir (ie) to regret; to be
sorry; **sentirse** to feel
sorry

ser *(irr.)* to be

serpiente *f.* snake

servilleta *f.* napkin

servir (i) to serve

siempre always

siguiente following; **al
día siguiente** on the
following day

silbar to whistle

sillón *m.* chair

simpático, -a nice

sin without

sobre on top of, over

sobrina *f.* niece

sobrino *m.* nephew

sol *m.* sun

solamente only

soldado *m. / f.* soldier

solo alone

sonar (ue) to sound; to ring

sopa *f.* soup

sorprendido, -a surprised
sorpresa f. surprise
sótano m. basement, cellar
subir to go up, climb; to raise
suburbio m. suburb
sucio, -a dirty
suelo m. ground; floor
sufrir to suffer
sur m. south

tacaño, -a stingy
talla f. (clothing) size
tamaño m. size
también also, too
tampoco neither, not either
tanto so much, as much; **no es para tanto** it is not a big deal
taquígrafo(-a) stenographer
taquilla f. box office
tardar to delay
tarde f. afternoon; evening; late
tarea f. assignment; chore
tarjeta f. card; **tarjeta postal** post card
teatro m. theater
tela f. cloth; fabric
telenovela f. soap opera
televisión f. television (industry); television (set)
televisor m. television set
temprano early
tenedor m. fork
tener (irr.) to have
tercero, -a third
tercio m. third (fraction)
terminal f. terminal; **terminal de autobuses** bus terminal
terminar to finish; to end
tía f. aunt

tiempo m. time; weather; **a tiempo** on time
tienda f. store
tierra f. earth, land
tigre(-esa) tiger
tintorería f. dry cleaner
tío m. uncle
tirar to throw
tiza f. chalk
tocadiscos m. record player
tocar (qu) to touch; to play (a musical instrument); **tocar (a uno)** to be one's turn
todavía still, yet
todo, -a all
tomar to take; to drink
tonto, -a dumb, foolish
trabajar to work
trabalenguas m. pl. tongue twister
traducir (zc) to translate
traer (irr.) to carry; to bring
traje m. suit; **traje de baño** bathing suit
tratar (de) to try to
travieso, -a naughty, mischievous
triste sad
tulipán m. tulip

uña f. nail (body)
unos, -as pl. some
usar to use; to wear
uva f. grape

vaca f. cow
vacío, -a empty
valer (irr.) to be worth
valor m. value
vapor m. steamship
vaso m. glass
vecino(-a) neighbor

vender to sell
venir (irr.) to come
venta f. sale; **en venta** on sale
ventana f. window
ver (irr.) to see; to watch
verano m. summer
verdad f. truth
verde green
vestido m. dress
vestir (i) to dress; **vestirse** to get dressed
veterinario(-a) veterinarian
vez f. time; **otra vez** again; **a veces** sometimes; **en vez de** instead of
viajar to travel
viaje m. trip; **hacer un viaje** to travel
vida f. life
viejo, -a old
viento m. wind; **hacer viento** to be windy
viernes m. Friday
visitar to visit
vista f. sight
vivir to live
vivo, -a vivid, bright (colors)
volar (ue) to fly
volver (ue) to return; to come (go) back
voz f. voice; pl. **voces**

ya already
yerno m. son-in-law

zapatería f. shoe store
zapatero m. shoemaker
zapato m. shoe
zoológico m. zoo

English-Spanish Vocabulary

The English-Spanish Vocabulary includes only those words that occur in the English-to-Spanish exercise.

able: to be able poder *(irr.)*; **to be able to** poder + *inf.*

about de, acerca de

absent ausente; **to be absent** estar ausente

acquaint: to become acquainted with conocer a

activity actividad *f.*

address dirección *f.*

after después de

afternoon tarde *f.*; **in the afternoon** por la tarde; PM de la tarde

again de nuevo; otra vez

age edad *f.* **your age** su edad *(irr.)*

agree: to agree with estar de acuerdo con

airplane avión *m.; by plane* en avión

airport aeropuerto *m.*

alone solo; **to be alone** estar a solas, estar solo

always siempre

amusing divertido

angry enojado

animal: stuffed animal animal de peluche *m.*

another otro

answer contestar, responder

any ninguno, ninguna

anyone alguien

appear aparecer (zc)

arrive llegar (gu)

art arte *f.* (el arte)

ask preguntar; **to ask a question** hacer una pregunta; **to ask for** pedir (i)

assignment tarea *f.*

attend: to attend school asistir / ir a la escuela

August agosto *m.*

avenue avenida *f.*

awake despierto; **to awaken (wake up)** despertarse *(ie)*

bank banco *m.*

bath baño m.; **to take a bath (bathe)** bañarse

beach playa *f.*

beautiful hermoso, bello

because porque

become llegar (gu) a ser; ponerse *(irr.)* + *adj.;* hacerse *(irr.)*

bed cama *f.*; **to go to bed** acostarse (ue)

before antes de

begin empezar (ie, c), comenzar (ie, c)

behind detrás de

better mejor

bicycle bicicleta *f.*

big grande

birthday cumpleaños *m.*

black negro

blue azul

boring aburrido

born: to be born nacer (zc)

box caja *f.*

boy niño, muchacho *m.*

boyfriend novio *m.*

breakfast desayuno *m.*; **to have (eat) breakfast** desayunarse

bring traer *(irr.)*

brother hermano *m.*

bus autobús *m.*

business negocio *m.*

but pero

by por; **by (bus, train)** en (autobús, tren)

call llamada *f.*; **to call** llamar

camp campamento *m.*

car auto *m.*, carro *m.*, coche *m.*

card tarjeta *f.*; **credit card** tarjeta de crédito

careful cuidadoso; **to be careful** tener cuidado

celebrate celebrar

chair silla *f.*

change cambio; **to change** cambiar

check cheque *m.*; **traveler's check** cheque de viajero *m.*

chicken pollo *m.*

childhood niñez *f.*

city ciudad *f.*

class clase *f.*

close cerrar (ie)

clothes ropa *f.*

coach entrenador *m.*

cold frío; **to be cold (weather)** hacer frío; **to be cold (person)** tener frío

comb peine *m.*; **to comb one's hair** peinarse

come venir *(irr.)*

company compañía *f.*

computer computadora *f.*

confess confesar (ie)

cook cocinar

cost costar (ue)

counselor consejero *m.*, consejera *f.*

count contar (ue)

country país *m.*; countryside campo *m.*

cry llorar

dance baile *m.*; **to dance** bailar

dark oscuro

day día *m.*

deal: a great deal mucho

decide decidir

defend defender (ie)

desk (pupil's) pupitre *m.*; escritorio *m.*

dictionary diccionario *m.*

difficult difícil

dinner cena *f.*

directly directamente

disagreeable desagradable

disappear desaparecer (zc)

discover descubrir

do: to do hacer

dog perro *m.*

doll muñeca *f.*

door puerta *f.*

downtown centro *m.*

dress vestido *m.*; **to get dressed** vestirse (i)

during durante

each cada

early temprano

earn ganar

eat comer; **to eat breakfast** desayunar; **to eat dinner** cenar; **to eat lunch** almorzar

electronic electrónico

employee empleado *m.*, empleada *f.*

end: to end terminar

English inglés *m.*

enjoy divertirse (ie, i)

evening noche *f.*

every cada, todos los, todas las

everyone todos; todo el mundo

everything todo, todas las cosas

exercise ejercicio *m.*

explain explicar (qu)

face cara *f.*

fall caer *(irr.)*; **to fall down** caerse

family familia *f.*

father padre *m.*

favorite favorito

feel sentir(se) (ie, i); **to feel like** tener ganas de

few unos

fifth quinto

film película *f.*

find encontrar (ue), hallar

fine fino; bien; *(weather)* hacer buen tiempo

first primero

flower flor *f.*

fly volar (ue)

follow seguir (i)

food comida *f.*

football fútbol *m.*

for para

forget olvidar

free libre

friend amigo *m.*, amiga *f.*

game partido *m.*; juego *m.*

get up levantarse

gift regalo *m.*

girlfriend novia *f.*

give dar *(irr.)*

go ir *(irr.)*; **to go away** irse *(irr.)*

gold oro *m.*

good bueno

grade nota *f.*, calificación *f.*

grandfather abuelo *m.*

grandmother abuela *f.*

great gran

green verde

greet saludar

ground suelo *m.*

guitar guitarra *f.*

gym gimnasio *m.*

gymnastics gimnasia *f.*

half mitad *f.*; **one-half** (un) medio

happily alegremente

happy contento, alegre

have tener *(irr.)*; **to have to** tener que + *inf.*

hear oír *(irr.)*

here aquí, acá

hide esconder(se)

home casa *f.*; **at home** en casa

hot caliente

hour hora *f.*

how ¿cómo?

hunger hambre *f.* (el hambre); **to be hungry** tener hambre

hurry prisa *f.*; **to be in a**

hurry tener prisa

ill enfermo
include incluir (y)
insist: to insist on insistir en
intend pensar (ie) + *inf.*
interesting interesante
island isla *f.*

just justo; **to have just** acabar de + *inf.*

key llave *f.*
kitchen cocina *f.*
know saber *(irr.)*; conocer (zc); **to know how** saber + *inf.*

last último; **last (month, year)** (el mes, el año) pasado
late tarde
learn aprender
leave irse *(irr.)*; dejar
library biblioteca *f.*
like gustarle (a uno)
line cola *f.*, fila *f.*
listen escuchar
little (quantity) poco; *(size)* pequeño
live: to live vivir
long largo
look: to look at mirar; **to look for** buscar (qu)
lose perder (ie)
lot: a lot mucho
loud en voz alta; **louder** en voz más alta
love querer *(irr.)*
luck suerte *f.*; **to be lucky** tener suerte
lunch almuerzo *m.*; **to**

have (eat) lunch almorzar (ue, c)

magazine revista *f.*
make hacer *(irr.)*
man hombre *m.*
many muchos, muchas; **how many?** ¿cuántos?, ¿cuántas?
matter asunto *m.*; **what's the matter?** ¿qué tiene?
meal comida *f.*
mean querer decir
meet conocer (zc), encontrar (ue)
member miembro *m.*,- socio *m.*
midnight medianoche *f.*; **at midnight** a medianoche
minute minuto *m.*
miss echar de menos
Monday lunes *m.*
money dinero *m.*
month mes *m.*
more más
morning mañana *f.*; **in the morning** por la mañana
most más
mother madre *f.*
mountain montaña *f.*
movies cine *m.*
much mucho; **too much** demasiado; **how much?** ¿cuánto?
music música *f.*

name nombre *m.*; **to be named** llamarse
near cerca (de)
need necesidad *f.*; **to need** necesitar, hacerle falta (a uno), faltarle (a uno)

nervous nervioso
never nunca
new nuevo
newspaper periódico *m.*
nice simpático
night noche *f.*; **at night** por la noche
no ninguno, ninguna, ningún; **no longer** ya no
no one nadie
noise ruido *m.*
noon mediodía; **at noon** al mediodía
north norte *m.*
now ahora
number número *m.*; **telephone number** número de teléfono

obey obedecer (zc)
October octubre
offer ofrecer (zc)
often a menudo
old viejo; **to be . . . years old** tener... años *(irr.)*
open abierto
or o, u; ni
other otro

parents padres *m. pl*
park parque *m.*
party fiesta *f.*
passport pasaporte *m.*
patience paciencia *f.*
pay pagar (gu); **to pay attention** prestar atención; **to pay attention to** hacerle caso a *(irr.)*
pen pluma *f.*; **ballpoint pen** bolígrafo *m.*
people gente *f.*; personas *f.*; **young people** jóvenes *m. pl.*

photograph fotografía *f.*; **to take pictures** sacar fotografías

phrase frase *f.*

pilot piloto *m.*

place lugar *m.*

plan: to plan pensar + *inf.*

play: to play (music) tocar (qu); **(game)** jugar (ue, gu)

pleasant agradable, simpático

please por favor; tener la bondad de, hacer el favor de

point punto *m.*

police policía *f.*

pool piscina *f.*

popcorn palomitas *f. pl.*

poster cartel *m.*

practice practicar (qu)

prefer preferir (ie, i)

pretty bonito

produce producir (zc)

program programa *m.*

purse bolsa *f.*

put poner *(irr.)*; **to put on** ponerse

quarter cuarto; **one quarter** un cuarto, una cuarta parte

rapid rápido; **rapidly** rápidamente

rare raro

rarely raramente

read leer (y)

recognize reconocer (zc)

record disco m.

red rojo

remember recordar (ue)

repeat repetir (i)

respond responder, contestar

rest descansar

return volver (ue), regresar; *(give back)* devolver (ue)

rice arroz *m.*

ride: to ride a bicycle montar en bicicleta

room cuarto *m.*, habitación; **roommate** compañero de cuarto

row fila *f.*; **to row** remar

rule regla *f.*

salary sueldo *m.*; salario *m.*

Saturday sábado m.

save ahorrar

school escuela *f.*, colegio *m.*; **high school** escuela secundaria

scold reñir (i)

sea mar *m.*

seat asiento *m.*; **seated** sentado

second segundo

see ver *(irr.)*

seem parecer (zc)

sell vender

serve servir (i)

several varios

sharp *(time)* en punto

shoe zapato *m.*

short corto

show mostrar (ue), enseñar

silly tonto

sing cantar

sister hermana *f.*

sit sentarse (ie)

skit escena *f.*

sky cielo *m.*

sleep dormir (ue, u); **to fall asleep** dormirse (ue, u); **to be sleepy** tener sueño

small pequeño

snow nieve *f.*; **to snow** nevar (ie)

soccer fútbol *m.*

soda refresco *m.*, gaseosa *f.*

some alguno, algún, unos, unas; **sometimes** a veces

song canción *f.*

soon pronto

soup sopa *f.*

Spanish español *m.*

spend (time) pasar; **(money)** gastar

spoiled consentido

star estrella *f.*

start empezar (ie, c), comenzar (ie, c)

station estación *f.*

stay quedarse; **to stay in bed** guardar cama

still todavía

stop dejar de + *inf.*

store tienda *f.*

street calle *f.*

strict estricto

student alumno *m.*, alumna *f.*, estudiante *m. / f.*

study estudiar

suitcase maleta *f.*

summer verano *m.*

sun sol *m.*; **to be sunny** hacer sol

Sunday domingo *m.*

sweater suéter *m.*

table mesa *f.*

take tomar; **to take**

pictures sacar fotografías
tall alto
teacher maestro *m.*, maestra *f.*, profesor *m.*, profesora *f.*
team equipo *m.*
tell decir *(irr.)*; **to tell about** referir (ie, i) de; **to tell the truth** decir la verdad
tennis tenis *m.*
test prueba *f.*, examen *m.*
that ese, esa; aquel, aquella
there ahí, allí, allá; **there is (there are)** hay
thing cosa *f.*
think pensar (ie)
thirst sed *f.*; **to be thirsty** tener sed
this este, esta
those esos, esas; quellos, aquellas
through por
Thursday jueves *m.*
ticket boleto *m.*, billete *m.*, entrada *f.*
time (hour) hora *f.*; **(in a series)** vez *f.* *(pl.* veces); tiempo; **on time** a tiempo; **to have a good time** divertirse (ie), pasar un buen rato
tired cansado; **to be tired** estar cansado
today hoy
together junto
tomorrow mañana

tonight esta noche
tooth muela *f.*, diente *m.*; **toothache** dolor de muela
train tren *m.*
translate traducir (zc)
travel viajar
tree árbol *m.*
trip viaje *m.*; **to make (take) a trip** hacer un viaje *(irr.)*
try tratar de
Tuesday martes *m.*
turn turno *m.*; **to be one's turn** tocarle (a uno)
typewriter máquinilla *f.*

understand comprender, entender (ie)
university universidad *f.*
use usar

vacation vacaciones *f. pl.*
very muy
visit visitar
voice voz *f.*; *(pl.* voces)

wait esperar
walk caminar, andar *(irr.)*; **to take a walk** dar un paseo
wallet cartera *f.*
want desear, querer *(irr.)*
wash lavar; **to wash oneself** lavarse
watch reloj *m.*; **to watch** mirar
wear llevar, usar; ponerse *(irr.)*

weather tiempo *m.*
Wednesday miércoles *m.*
week semana *f.*
well bien
what? ¿qué?
when cuando; **when?** ¿cuándo?
where donde; **where?** ¿dónde?; **(from) where?** ¿de dónde? **(to) where?** ¿adónde?
while mientras
white blanco
whom ¿a quién?
whose ¿de quién?
why ¿por qué?
wide ancho
win ganar
wind viento *m.*; **to be windy** hacer viento
with con; **with me** conmigo
without sin
woods bosque *m.*
word palabra *f.*
work trabajo *m.*; **to work** trabajar
worry preocupación *f.*; **to be worried** estar preocupado
write escribir
wrong: to be wrong no tener razón

year año *m.*
yesterday ayer
young joven; **younger** menor

Index